FLORIDA'S PAST

Volume 2

The horrendous Keys hurricane of 1935 (page 217)

FLORIDA'S

PAST

Volume 2

People and Events
That Shaped the State

Gene M. Burnett

Pineapple Press
Sarasota, Florida

Inquiries should be addressed to:

Pineapple Press, Inc.
P.O. Box 3889
Sarasota, Florida 34230

www.pineapplepress.com

Library of Congress Cataloging-in-Publication Data

Burnett, Gene M., 1928-1991
Florida's past.

Originally published in Florida Trend,
1972–1987
Bibliography: v. 1, p.
Includes indexes.
1. Florida—History. 2. Florida—Biography.
I. Title
F311.5.B87   1986   975.9   86-15048

First paperback edition
10 9 8 7 6 5 4 3 2

Printed in the United States of America

CONTENTS

ACKNOWLEDGMENTS

The efforts and assistance that devolved into this second volume of *Florida's Past* are so enmeshed with those producing the first volume that I would, but for space considerations, gladly reiterate the earlier acknowledgments. Suffice it to let them stand inclusive for those who may read both volumes. However, I have some additional acknowledgments to make, most of which might easily have been included in the first book, an omission due to some thoughtless distraction and not intent. As with the first volume, I remain grateful to the owners and publishers of *Trend*, the Times Publishing Company, for granting me exclusive permission to copyright the articles, all but two of which appeared in *Florida Trend* since 1973. I am also grateful to Clubhouse Publishers, Inc., of Sarasota, and to Pam Daniel, editor of *Sarasota* magazine, for permission to reprint the article, "Sarasota's Million-Dollar Belly Splash." I wish to give special thanks to *Florida Trend*'s able art director, Steve Duckett, for his patient assistance in the assembly of a substantial portion of the photographs and artwork that have appeared in both volumes of *Past*. I want to give special thanks to my young and able editor, Lisa Schoof, who with deft adroitness smoothly untangled the maze of scattered detail and put this volume all together. Finally, there are those whose aid has been of less specific nature but no less tangible during the years when both books were still in embryo. For their general support and encouragement I am thankfully indebted to Ed and Anita and Joan and Chuck and to members of the Agape fellowship. They greatly eased many of the stalled and frustrated moments that are often generic to the writer's lot.

INTRODUCTION

It is always gratifying to a writer to know that the fruit of his labor has met with some favorable reception among those who peruse the finished product.

So often as he lays fingers to keys—now haltingly, now in bursts, now in long, blank pauses—he wonders how anyone could possibly find interest in the marked up, scratched out, squeezed together tangle of words with which he has defaced so many nice clean sheets of paper. He is equally uncertain of his ability to pick through the labyrinth of notes and materials beside him and somehow distill it into a concise but readable narrative. And if he succeeds in doing so, he is at a loss to explain the process by which it occurred. I have found this to be as true with the second volume of these essays as it was with the first.

The historical alchemy that seeks to blend scholarly and literary elements with the base rock of historical facts (evidence) may sometimes be as elusive a quest as were the attempts by those chemists of the Middle Ages to turn zinc and lead into gold. Assigning credibility to sources can occasionally be strictly a judgment call as well. For example, in one story herein (on the old Portuguese ex-pirate John Gomez) I have taken a sort of pierhead leap by according to him some benefit of doubt. This is done on the theory that in much of what is essentially folkloristic there is now and then an element of truth lying at the core of otherwise embellished fancy. I agree with historians generally who assert that no such pirate as José Gaspar ever existed. At least there is not a whit of hard evidence to so indicate—this despite the propensity of certain bankers, insurance men, lawyers, and assorted pillars of Tampa to celebrate this mythical rogue as a role model once a year (at least we pray it is only once a year). But there is some oral evidence to indicate that Gomez himself may have indulged in a little maritime marauding in his early years. Thus in his case we have tempered historical discipline with a modicum of charity.

One of the more gratifying results of the first volume was the knowledge that I had reached the broad spectrum of readers that I had hoped to. They were young and old, male and female, academician and lay reader, and all from diverse backgrounds and occupations. This seemed to confirm my belief that history can never be abstracted from its human substance—from the broad cast of human beings who do in fact create it, whether noted and renowned or obscure and humble.

As with the first volume, I have furnished a selected bibliography, with one or two sources for each topic, for those who might wish to read further on a particular subject.

Gene M. Burnett

Florida's

Past

Volume 2

That which hath been is now;
and that which is to be
hath already been.
   Ecclesiastes 3:15 (KJV)

Achievers and Pioneers

1.
Tampa Bay's Great Flying Machine

Aviation history was made in 1914 with the nation's first commercial flight from St. Petersburg to Tampa.

The crowd of several thousand onlookers lining the downtown pier at the St. Petersburg yacht basin on New Year's Day morning, 1914, stared in fascination at a huge, boat-bottomed flying machine bobbing in the water. Its bulky, bi-winged shape seemed to resemble some oversized prehistoric pterodactyl. How, they wondered, could such a contraption float, much less rise up off the water? Only the day before, a shunted freight car had disgorged the big flying boat piece by piece after it arrived from manufacturer Tom Benoist of St. Louis. On hand to assemble the pieces were Benoist's head mechanic, Jay Dee ("Smitty") Smith, and chief pilot, 24-year-old Anthony Habersackt ("Tony") Jannus. Within an hour, the pair had the big machine in the water and taking off for a test flight. Everything checked out smoothly.

But the onlookers next morning, most of whom had never seen any kind of aircraft before, were perhaps too preoccupied in wondering whether the behemoth would actually fly to be able to grasp the significance of the occasion. Even so, they were about to witness aviation history over Tampa Bay: the world's first scheduled commercial air transportation flight, initiated by the St. Petersburg-Tampa Airboat Line.

Finally the young pilot arrived and climbed into the plane, and the crowd cheered loudly. Despite his youth, Tony Jannus was an early aviation veteran. He was the world's first licensed airline pilot, having learned to fly in 1910. In 1912, he had piloted the plane from which U.S. Army Captain Albert Berry made the first parachute jump, over Jefferson Barracks, Missouri, and he was chief test pilot for the Benoist Aircraft Company. Whatever the crowd's doubts about flying itself, this clean-cut, modest, intelligent young pilot had already captured the admiration and affection of that city's people. There was about him none of the barnstorming "daredevil" flair associated with so many of the early pioneer pilots. And yet his thoughts on flying conveyed a certain prescient ring, one that much later air pioneers would instantly recognize and share, such as: "To me, flying is not the successful defying of death but the indulgence in the poetry of mechan-

5

ical motion, a dustless, bumpless, fascinating speed, an abstraction from things material into infinite space. . . ."

Climbing in beside Jannus in the two-seater open cockpit was former St. Petersburg Mayor A. C. Pheil, who had just paid four hundred dollars at auction for the first passenger ticket. The two men seemed dwarfed beneath the 45-foot bi-wingspread fixed onto a 26-foot body, the odd "backward" propeller mounted at the rear of the cockpit. Colorful streamers and miniature flags fluttered from wing and fuselage. Then, at exactly 10:30 A.M., Jannus gunned the little 75-horsepower motor, and the big hydroplane roared down the basin. It slowly rose over the sun-dappled blue waters of Old Tampa Bay and headed for Tampa.

The idea for this historic flight had its genesis in the fancy of Percival E. Fansler, a St. Petersburg civic activist. Only the year before, this town of ten thousand souls had feistily shucked the yoke of Hillsborough County to create its own Pinellas County. Touting itself as "Health City," St. Petersburg was now enjoying a lively tourist business and a mild but prospering real estate boom. It had also built its first streetcar line and gas plant, and a new railroad (Seaboard) was about to come into town. Such an up-and-com-

Civic activist Percival Fansler (left), St. Petersburg Mayor A. C. Pheil, and pilot Tony Jannus pose near the Benoist plane. (Florida State Archives)

ing young city, Fansler decided, should have its own airline as well. Fansler aroused enough civic support to bring Benoist down from St. Louis and have him sign a contract with both the city and private merchants. Benoist received an operator's franchise, plus cash operating subsidies for the first three months. In return, the manufacturer would provide planes and crew to operate two scheduled flights daily between St. Petersburg and Tampa six days a week.

And now the big day had arrived and Jannus was already winging up to Hillsborough Bay, keeping a low, steady altitude of fifty feet at speeds between fifty and sixty miles per hour.

In Tampa, the crowd was no less enthusiastic: two thousand people flocked around the special landing dock downtown at the foot of Lee Street on the Hillsborough River, with fifteen hundred more on the opposite river bank and bridge. On spotting the distant plane, the crowd sent up a roar of cheering, waving hats and handkerchiefs wildly.

Before landing on the bay and taxiing up the river, Jannus brought the seaplane upward 150 feet as a greeting gesture; this drew even louder cheer-

Triumphant pilot Tony Jannus waves as he lands in Tampa on the first leg of the nation's first regularly scheduled commercial airline flight in 1914. (Florida State Archives)

ing. A *Tampa Times* headline that afternoon duly noted with awe that Jannus "can go even higher if he chooses."

City leaders flocked around Jannus as he stepped onto the landing, and veteran Tampa photographer W. C. Burgert captured the historic event on film. (A large mural painting in Peter O. Knight Airport's main building on Davis Island, Tampa, also commemorates the flight.) Exultant passenger Pheil assured reporters that he had no qualms on the flight. He then rushed off to telephone St. Petersburg to report his safe arrival. The next morning's *Tampa Tribune* heralded in trumpeting headlines the inauguration of the world's first commercial airline. Beneath the headline a subhead noted—somewhat incongruously—that passenger Pheil "Did Not Get Excited—He Declares." Newspapers around the country also hailed "this pioneer achievement down on Tampa Bay." The eighteen-mile trip had taken twenty-three minutes, compared to several hours on the 160-mile roundabout jaunt of the ACL railroad or the half-day or more by water.

Noel A. Mitchell had won second passenger honors for the return trip, paying only $175 for his ticket. (The regular daily one-way passenger fare would be only five dollars.) As he taxied down and rose off the river, Jannus drew more lusty cheering as he circled Hyde Park in a farewell salute, then sped over water to Ballast Point, crossed the peninsula, and followed the present Gandy Bridge route to the Pinellas coast and flew down to the yacht basin, where a jubilant crowd and a rousing band greeted him. Assisted by a good tail wind, the plane took only twenty minutes to complete the trip.

Scores of passengers had already booked flights for ensuing days. They included the first woman passenger, Miss Mae Peabody of Dubuque, Iowa. On January 12, the first air freight shipment was made. In St. Petersburg, L. C. Hefner, a local grocer, telegraphed an order for ham and bacon supplies to the Swift & Company warehouse in Tampa. Within an hour, by Benoist Air Boat, a forty-pound case of the porkstuffs was in Hefner's hands. A *Collier's* magazine story later headlined this as "the fastest delivery of merchandise on record." Swift depicted the episode thereafter in all of its national advertising.

The airline stuck to its twice-daily schedule without interruption, accident, or injury, eventually carrying more than twelve hundred passengers. Another plane and another pilot, Jannus's brother Roger, were brought in for an extended service to Sarasota, Bradenton, and Tarpon Springs.

Nevertheless, despite its functional success, the airline folded within three months. Equipment difficulties and limited mechanical resources, coupled with gathering war clouds abroad and money panics at home, caused a decrease in local subsidy support. As the novelty and publicity of the world's first commercial airline wore away, so apparently did the enthusiasm of local merchants.

In a curious and tragic intertwinement of fate, soon after the airline's demise, three of its principals would also meet untimely deaths. In Sandusky, Ohio, Tom Benoist leaned out of a streetcar window one day to wave to a friend; he failed to notice a telephone pole which he fatally struck. Jannus later joined the Russian army as a flight instructor after the outbreak of World War I. He was killed in 1916 when his plane crashed over the Black Sea at Sevastopol during a demonstration flight. His brother Roger, an air squadron captain in France, died when he was shot down.

Strangely enough, for four decades the city of St. Petersburg erased from mind its role as the birthplace of commercial aviation. Then, prompted by the golden anniversary in 1953 of the Wright brothers' flight, city fathers had old records checked and exclaimed, as it were, "That's right, we were once number one!" They rushed out and erected a monument and plaque to the historic occasion and placed it near the foot of the city pier.

2.
Governor Broward Moves a State

With a new century, he ushered in a new era with the battle for progress and reform.

Superficially he was a plain man, with even a touch of the mediocre about him, but perhaps it was this very trait—combined with unusual grit and single-mindedness—that enabled him to become governor during one of the most progressive eras of the state's history.

But the forces of liberalism and reform were sweeping the country at the turn of the century, even before Napoleon Bonaparte Broward became Florida's nineteenth governor (1905–1909). It was the era of William Jennings Bryan and his "cross of gold," greenbackers, muckrakers, labor reformers, farmers' movements, suffragettes, and a host of other progressive causes. It was the gilded age of the Vanderbilts, Morgans, and Goulds, along with Teddy Roosevelt's tirades against the "malefactors of great wealth."

In late nineteenth-century Florida, a groundswell of liberalism was repudiating the reactive status quo of Southern Bourbonism, and in the figure of Broward, the times had found the man who would give this surge direction, cohesion, and courageous leadership.

He fought uphill against the "predatory interests," especially corporate and railroad powers, charging that they had controlled—and corrupted—state executives and legislatures since 1876. Thus he incurred wrathful opposition from these interests, and his crusades often became embroiled in bitter controversy. Curiously, however, this former riverboat captain, sheriff, and popular gunrunner to Cuban insurgents would also reveal within himself a social temperament that seriously qualified his asserted desire to represent "all the people."

Even so, he would usher in a spirit of progress and reform that would later bear his name alone: the Broward Era.

Broward was born April 19, 1857, on a farm at Mayport, near Jacksonville. Orphaned at age 12 when his parents died soon after the Civil War, the boy worked at a variety of jobs, mainly on boats, until, in his twenties, he earned a pilot's license and saved enough money to become his boss's boat partner, modestly prospering as the steamboat tourist trade flourished on the St. Johns River in the 1880s. He also married the boss's daughter, but she

10

would die in childbirth that same year; the newborn son died six weeks later. The grief-stricken Broward mourned for a lengthy time but finally returned to captain his boat. Four years later, in 1887, he married the attractive Annie Douglass; they would eventually have eight children.

The tall, sun-browned, mustached figure, personable and good-natured, was a popular figure in Jacksonville and was not surprised when a citizens' group asked him to take the post of the Duval sheriff, recently removed for negligence. He accepted—in earnest. Broward was a Prohibitionist and personally observed strict standards of law and morality in other areas. His first act in office was to wipe out organized gambling in the county, convicting and jailing the vice's powerful proprietors. This won him state renown, and his reputation for political integrity and fair-mindedness was pruning him into a potential political force, both locally and statewide. Through some half-dozen years as sheriff, he demonstrated levelheaded calm in panic situations, nor did he fear an unpopular stand. In the great yellow fever epidemic of 1888, he prevented wholesale panic among Jacksonville's fleeing residents, even as he worked tirelessly to aid the victims and bury the dead. In 1892, when a white mob threatened to seize from jail a black man who had struck and killed a white man in a fight, some five hundred blacks, armed with rifles, knives, and revolvers, patrolled the streets and held off the disorderly throng while Broward placed the black man under special guard and summoned three companies of state militia. After three days, a potentially explosive racial conflict was defused as Broward gradually calmed the crowds. When a judge's order stopped Broward from halting the illegal heavyweight title fight between James Corbett and Charles Mitchell in 1894, Broward arrested the pair after the fight, charging them with assault and battery. (Corbett was acquitted; Mitchell's charge dropped.)

But through these years, political times were changing. The agrarian reform movement crested in 1890 with the mass meeting of the Farmers' Alliance in Ocala and the demand for radical reforms. Elsewhere, aggressive and liberal young Democrats were forcing a break with Bourbonism, and Broward was the flintpiece of their armory. He assailed the railroad moguls ("Chipley in the West . . . Plant in the South and . . . Flagler in the East") and pushed for a strong state railroad commission to regulate them. He lashed at freight rate discrimination, revealing how four railroads, with an interstate monopoly, manipulated rates to cause a state loss of over $400,000. He detailed how railroads dodged fair taxes by rigging their property assessments by several millions of dollars and accused the railroad-corporate bloc of making Florida a dynastic possession.

"I don't blame the railroads for taking all they can get," Broward plaintively fumed, "if the people will stand heedlessly by . . . and be treated this way. Nothing short of just and proper legislation will do us any good." In 1887, the reformists won their Railroad Commission Act, only to have their powerful antagonists cause its repeal in 1891. Finally, in 1897, the liberals triumphed with tough regulatory bills—and a commission.

They also won stringent primary election laws to prevent flagrant abuses at the polls. In one Jacksonville election, for example, conservative forces somehow won with enough votes to triple the town's voting population overnight. When Broward found it necessary in another crucial election to place lawmen inspectors at every polling place, a conservative Governor Henry Mitchell found a legal technicality enabling him to summarily remove Broward from office. (But Broward would defeat his replacement in the next election.)

In the interlude, Broward and two friends had built a powerful seagoing tugboat, *The Three Friends,* for a towing, wrecking, passenger, and freight business. But when a cigar manufacturer friend, J. A. Huau, contracted for use of the tug to run arms, supplies, and recruits to Cuban insurgents who were in open revolt against Spain, Broward, strongly sympathetic to the cause, dodged both Spanish and U.S. patrols to run eight exciting, hair-raising trips to the island. Spain priced his head at $25,000 "dead or alive" and he was federally indicted for violating neutrality laws, but Broward had become a national hero. When the Spanish-American War broke out in 1898, the indictment was dropped.

Through these years, Broward's liberal anti-corporate forces had gained such strength that they were able to elect as governor a moderate liberal, William S. Jennings (cousin to William Jennings Bryan), in 1901. Broward himself took a representative's seat in the legislature. But when Broward began his campaign for governor in 1903—drawing support mainly from farmers, small business, labor, and cattlemen—the state's mostly conservative press denounced him as a "demagogue, a visionary populist" and vilified him in countless editorials and cartoons. But the heated and bitter campaign ended with Broward's narrow victory over power-broker Robert W. Davis (22,979 to 22,265).

Despite the reform aura of the new administration, Broward's singular energies were focused in an area somewhat removed from social issues per se, namely, a bold and far-reaching program to drain vast portions of the Everglades around Lake Okeechobee and the lower east coast and reclaim millions of acres of rich fertile muckland for farming. It was hailed, even by his foes, as a "magnificent" project and area landowners especially endorsed it. But when the newly set up Board of Drainage Commissioners sought to levy a minimal special acreage tax to finance the mammoth undertaking, big area landholders such as The Southern States Land & Timber Company went to court to block the levy, and an injunction was issued preventing the tax's collection. But Broward managed to keep the project moving steadily and even caused some of the later land promoters and speculators to shoulder some of the cost of the project that would continue for many years, while it accelerated southeast Florida's sprawling development.

In another major accomplishment, Broward caused passage of the Buckman Act, which reorganized Florida's schools of higher learning, placing them under a central board of control with the eventual result of raising educational and scholastic standards at all the institutions. In a parallel effort, he pushed for longer regular school terms; a uniform textbook system; higher qualifications and salaries for schoolteachers; and strict state compliance with federal child-labor laws. He had a pure food and drug law enacted and fostered long-range conservation programs. He had less success in getting strict requirements to list election campaign expenses; in establishing severe penalties for vote miscounts at the polls and for bribery and intimidation of any voter or elected official; and with his proposed compulsory life insurance program for citizens, with the state operating as insurance company, which his perennial foes, the corporate interests, roundly defeated.

Nevertheless, in some areas critically crying for reform, Broward could maintain a curiously bland indifference, when not outrightly defensive. Florida's brutal and notorious convict lease system was the object of national attention, but Broward's tepid appeal to the legislature for "humane treatment" of convicts seemed cruelly inept, nor did he seek repeal of the infamous convict lease law. When a legislative report disclosed beatings, abuse, and neglect of patients at the state mental hospital, along with bad food and sanitation and drunkenness and immorality among nurses and attendants, Broward, out of concern for his administration's image before a hostile press, sought to squelch the report. But in the public outcry, the legislature was prompted to make drastic changes, shakeups, and reforms at the hospital.

After his term ended, Broward successfully sought election as a U.S. senator in 1910, but he died at his Jacksonville home before the term began.

Yet in spite of his occasional myopic narrowness toward critical areas of reform, Broward succeeded, as did no governor before him, in releasing a long-dormant spirit of reform and change while dramatically demonstrating that people can make republican government responsive to the needs of the many instead of the few. In fact, his dynamic refreshment of the sense of the democratic experience may have been the greatest single achievement of the Broward Era. The seeds of it bore fruit that he himself could not have envisioned even a generation later.

3.
Key West Gets a New Deal

The Depression-wracked island was transformed into a thriving resort by an enterprising New Dealer.

Throughout the 1920s, the people of the little tropical island of Key West shuffled along in a torpid daze of not-so-genteel poverty. Relatively untouched by Florida's boom, they were content to eke out a tenuous existence mainly from the meager coin of fishing and sporadic tourism, supplemented now and then with a little furtive rumrunning to Cuba.

Sailing into the town harbor in 1928 (for a twelve-year stay), writer Ernest Hemingway dubbed the island "the St. Tropez of the poor." Puzzled islanders figured, well, he got that second part right.

Thus, when the Great Depression rolled over the nation in the 1930s, no one was surprised to see the two-mile by four-mile island shattered to its coral rock bottom, laid low by an economic coma that officials called "more acute and oppressive" than any other in the country. By 1934, some eighty percent of Key West's 11,600 citizens were on relief, a bare relief at that. The city government, which already had defaulted on several millions in bonded debt, could no longer afford fire, police, or sanitation services. City employees were paid in script (merchants accepting the script used it to pay their city taxes). Instead of selling apples, men peddled coconuts on town streets or tried to catch sharks—$1.50 for a seven-footer. Children sold Spanish limes or dove off the Mallory docks for pennies tossed by occasional tourists.

Otherwise the men—native Bahamian-descended "Conchs," black and white, or Cuban sons of early cigar workers—sat at tables in Pepe's Cafe or Sloppy Joe's, munching penny "bollos" (cakes made from black-eyed peas) and bewailing the times.

The historic city had taken a long spiral down from its colorful shipwrecking days, barely a century ago, when it was the richest city per capita in the country. Much later, its thriving sponge industry would be pre-empted by the Greeks at Tarpon Springs, and its flourishing cigar factories, beset by labor rifts, would scurry to Tampa. Even its army and navy installations, its economic bedrock before and during three wars, were cut to skeletal status after World War I.

But the town's darkest days coincided with the arrival of President Franklin D. Roosevelt and the New Deal, and the little island was about to become an "experiment" that would capture national attention.

The experiment began dramatically enough. In an unprecedented act on July 2, 1934, the town sparked national headlines when desperate city fathers "surrendered" their powers of city government to the state. A sympathetic Governor David Sholtz, declaring a state of emergency, promptly authorized Julius F. Stone, Jr., Florida head of the Federal Emergency Relief Administration (FERA), to set up a local body, the Key West Administration, and implement a relief program.

An able, perceptive, and imaginative New Dealer, Stone faced three alternatives. He could pump in a $2.5 million relief program; he could simply dump the island and relocate its three thousand families; or he could give the town a job by which to create its own economy as an attractive tourist resort. With the island's native charm and tropical seclusion, plus the finest winter climate and fishing in the country, Stone envisioned a city that could more than rival Bermuda, a place where "there would be no blatant race tracks, no blaring night clubs attracting people who cannot appreciate the beauty, quiet and subtle charm of the city." Instead it would draw "the tired businessman, or woman, the convalescent and the artist in the broadest sense of the word."

Federal Emergency Relief Administration workers make repairs on Duval Street in Key West in 1935. (Florida State Archives)

Assisted by a bevy of bright, mostly young FERA men and women and armed with a $1 million allocation for the first eighteen months (much of this to provide direct aid to the needy), Stone plunged into the task. The infectious enthusiasm of the group fomented an intellectual excitement that soon enveloped the whole town.

Keenly aware of the need for national exposure for such a resort plan, Stone kept the momentum of the initial national publicity sustained with the aid of FERA publicist M. E. Golfond, who sent out a steady stream of news and feature stories to the national media. The project was highlighted with Stone's brainchild of calling for a "volunteer work force" to donate twenty-five hours a week to get the town in shape for the visitors.

The response was instant, and soon most of the town, including the mayor, was out cleaning up the streets and gathering the piles of uncollected garbage and rubbish to be burned. Eyesore shacks and scores of unsanitary outhouses were razed, and teams went in to beautify parks and build cabanas for beaches. Flowers, shrubs, and palm trees were planted everywhere while shabby gray houses were renovated and covered with new paint. A hospitality league and a band were formed to welcome visitors, and boat owners were given loans to repair their boats for charter fishing. Homeowners were urged to make over rooms and apartments into guest quarters, and the receivers were persuaded to reopen Flagler's plush Casa Marina Hotel. A guarantee given against losses proved unnecessary. For a resort, most rents were a steal at thirty-five to fifty dollars per month.

Federal artists and writers were brought in to paint historic murals on public and private buildings and to write descriptive guidebooks and attractive brochures. Teachers, also employed by the federal government, were sent down to instruct men and women in vocational skills using native materials and enabling them to operate handicraft shops. An out-patient medical and dental clinic was provided, with special health programs for children. And weekly shipments of fresh vegetables and surplus relief commodities were also distributed.

Cultural activities flourished. The town's distinctive architecture was repaired and restored, a little theater and a choral group were organized, and classes were held regularly in folk dancing and painting.

By the time the 1934-35 tourist season approached, the entire town had volunteered more than two million hours of labor. Governor Sholtz sent each volunteer an engraved certificate of recognition for his or her effort. More importantly, the town's spirits soared. As Stone later observed: "Last year, hopelessness and resignation ruled; now hope and confidence are on the throne."

The sweat and labor—and the publicity—paid off. As the season got under way, tourists began to pour in to the island by boat, plane, car ferry, and train. There were more than forty thousand of them, double that of previous years. FERA statistics cited the record increases: hotel guests up 86%; guest homes, 150%; restaurants, 84%. National luminaries also came down to see the phenomenon firsthand. They included Robert Frost, John Dewey, Wallace Stevens, Max Eastman, Hart Crane, S. J. Perlman, John Dos Passos, and Archibald MacLeish.

Journalist-newscaster Elmer Davis, a former visitor to "old" Key West, came to see the new one and returned to write an article, "New World Symphony," in *Harper's* magazine, reporting Key West as "the New Deal in miniature." He added: "The experiment . . . gave life there a fourth-dimensional flavor. Words are poor tools to convey the feeling created by the experiment and the atmosphere of continuous intellectual excitement and surcharged intensity. . . . Nothing quite like it will ever be seen again."

In mortal coma only months earlier, Key West was now on a vibrant road to recovery. Even the devastating hurricane that hit the upper Keys later that year and wiped out the Florida East Coast Railroad did not deter the recovery. The railroad's bridgework was used later, in 1938, to build the new overseas highway.

By 1936, when the Works Progress Administration (WPA) took over the second phase of the project (new sewerage, electrical, and water systems), unemployment was reduced by two-thirds. People were employed at essential jobs and local government resumed control.

Thus, where private initiative had failed, a group of intelligent, dedicated men and women, a renewed community spirit, and a benevolent government had restored a city to life. The long-range effects and benefits of that resurrection are still visible in Key West today.

4.
Florida's Forgotten "Chinese Burbank"

Lue Gim Gong won America's highest agricultural award for creating one of Florida's finest oranges.

Without a doubt, Florida's citrus growers and cultivators have turned out millions of fine oranges over the generations, but it took a meek, humble, and unassuming Chinese immigrant horticulturalist to show them how to produce what pomologists label the hardiest, juiciest, and sweetest orange ever grown in the country: the Lue Gim Gong orange.

In 1911, he was the first and only American up to that time to receive the highest national award ever given for creation of a new variety of orange. But Lue Gim Gong, of Deland, Florida, had to overcome formidable obstacles in the process. For the late nineteenth century was a period when living was precarious, if not outrightly dangerous, for a Chinese immigrant in America. At that time, the Chinese faced prejudice, beatings, "indentured" forced labor, and sometimes even death. It was the era of the virulent "yellow peril" fanaticism which culminated in passage by Congress of the notorious Exclusion Act that sought to bar any Oriental from entering the country.

Although Lue Gim Gong escaped the major effects of this aberrancy, he would not entirely avoid its toxic sting in later years. Citrus growers, for example, would fraudulently appropriate the unique budded stock he had created to their own profit, even as they were inducing citrus "experts" to cast doubt on the authenticity or the importance of Lue's achievement. As a result, the man once hailed nationally as a "Chinese Burbank" was often forced to live in poverty in his aging, ailing years, and once almost lost even his modest home to mortgage foreclosure.

Lue Gim Gong was born in a village near Canton, China, in 1860, the eldest son in a large farming family. A certain poetic fitness attaches to his later endeavors, since most authorities agree that all oranges originated in China and, specifically, the southernmost province in which Canton is situated. As a boy, Lue (pronounced Loo-ee) learned a variety of ancient farming skills, but a special and delicate one, taught him by his mother, was the art of cross-pollination.

His attention was engrossed as she gently took pollen with a soft brush from the stamens of one plant and carefully put it onto the pistil of another variety. If successful, she would obtain a superior variety to either of the two crossed. Lue learned this art as a very young boy but never dreamed that it would one day change his life. His only dream then was to go to America after hearing dazzling tales from his seafaring uncle about the riches and opportunities there—especially free schools for children, something unheard of in the China of that day.

His zealous persistence was so great that his parents finally consented to let him journey with five other adult men from another family; his uncle paid his ship fare. And so, on May 11, 1872, a very excited 12-year old Cantonese boy sailed into San Francisco Bay and disembarked for Chinatown.

The San Francisco of the 1870s was a wild, rough, and primitive settlement, especially for Chinese immigrants. Therefore, when a recruiter of Chinese workers for a shoe factory in North Adams, Massachusetts, appeared on the scene, Lue volunteered and headed east. It was a typical "wage slave" factory in the New England of those days, but to Chinese peasants who had known little more than a primitive poverty in their own semifeudal land, it seemed like modestly affluent living. Of even more value, however, was a school organized by the townspeople in which many individual citizens volunteered to teach the immigrants English, along with other "three-R" basics.

Lue, who had already chopped off his Manchu queue (pigtail) and swapped his flimsy pajamas for sturdy American winter clothes, plunged eagerly into his studies. Lue proved to be a bright and diligent student—so much so that he came to the attention of an intelligent and progressive lady of the town who semiformally adopted the boy and took him into the home she shared with her father, a prosperous hardware merchant.

Miss Frances Burlingame, known as "Miss Fanny" to townspeople, was a private school teacher and remarkably well educated for women of her time. Her interest in Lue's abilities was enhanced by the influence of her cousin, Anson Burlingame, a brilliant, likable, strongly Christian champion of civil liberties in that period. As U.S. minister to China, he forced through the signing of the Burlingame Treaty of 1868, guaranteeing fair trade relations and the equal respect of the rights of citizens of either country.

The Chinese, so long suspicious of the West and the greedy mercantile powers of Europe with their infamous "gunboat" diplomacy, came to like and respect Burlingame so much that when his term ended after six years, they asked him to serve as China's representative to the West!

Meanwhile, Lue himself eagerly embraced the Christian faith once he had discovered the momentous difference between Confucius and Jesus. His years growing up in the Burlingame household were happy ones.

He was encouraged in all of his studies, especially in the field of horticulture. Recalling the art he had learned at his mother's knee, he began experiments in the Burlingame fruit orchards. Historian S. W. Kung recalls that the youth was able to develop an apple that would ripen thirty days sooner than any other known variety and a peach that, with greenhouse care, would ripen in the coldest climate.

Lue was fascinated with the American form of government, and he and several Chinese youths drew up a similar constitution for China. They signed it, and Lue was elected "president" of the Chinese Republic. None of them dreamed then that an almost similar document would be drawn up for the first time in China in 1911 when the forces under Sun Yat-sen would overthrow the Manchu dynasty.

These good years were painfully interrupted for Lue when he contracted tuberculosis and, at the recommendation of doctors, returned to his warm, semitropical native home. Although glad to see his family again, Lue was homesick, for he had become fully adapted to his American upbringing. He wrote the Burlingames that he wanted to return, and they, having purchased a citrus grove and home in Deland, wired him a ticket and expense money and asked him to come straight to Florida. Here, aside from summer visits to North Adams where he was naturalized as a citizen in 1887, he would remain for the rest of his life.

Lue resumed his horticultural studies and became fascinated with the possibilities of citrus stock. When he was not packing and shipping fruit from the groves, he was experimenting with the varieties of plants and trees so similar to his native Canton. Already newspapers were running articles on the startling changes and improvements he was creating in the fruits of various plants. One day, he took two oranges that he preferred—Hart's Late orange and a Mediterranean Sweet—and carefully cross-pollinated the blossoms. When he had cultivated a dozen trees from the seed of the hybrid orange he had produced, he used a part of the tree with the best quality fruit to "bud" onto a rootstock. The result after several years was an amazingly delicious and sturdy orange, one like no one had ever tasted in Florida before. (He would do the same thing later on with a grapefruit, also named for him, but it lacked commercial appeal because it grew singly instead of in cluster form.)

But by the time Miss Fanny died in 1903, Lue's achievements were receiving national attention; he was being hailed as a "Chinese Burbank," a "plant wizard," and a "horticultural genius." After he had transformed his own grove, he produced budded stock of the Lue Gim Gong orange to sell to other growers who were only too eager to buy it.

The years were lonely after the death of his adopted mother and benefactress. Earlier, he had formed an attachment to the Burlingames' Swedish housekeeper, Liggate, but her father so furiously objected to their marriage that she was forced to return to Sweden.

But perhaps Lue's greatest day came in 1911 when he received in the mail an impressive-looking package, daubed with red sealing wax. The package contained the Wilder Silver Medal, the highest award ever made by the distinguished American Pomological Society, in honor of his creation of the Lue Gim Gong orange. Scientists and horticulturists, including Colonel G. C. Brackett of the U.S. Department of Agriculture, had already heartily endorsed the award, and Lue was stunned and overwhelmed by the honor. Aside from its luscious flavor, the fruit could be marketed over an unusually long period, even up to September; it could hang on a tree for two or more years and still be good to eat; it was highly frost-resistant; it bore consistently large and excellent crops; and it could be shipped long distances without spoiling (there were no refrigerated cars in those days).

But the simple, honest Chinese-American was victimized by unscrupulous growers who illegally appropriated the nursery-sold tree for budded stock at great financial loss to Lue. Later, they would even induce agricultural "experts" to downgrade the achievement itself. Friends urged him to take the miscreants to court, but Lue lived so deeply by his Christian beliefs that he instinctively shunned this form of retaliation.

His savings gradually melted away and he was reduced to the barest poverty. He could no longer meet the mortgage interest on his grove and home, and by 1922 he was threatened with foreclosure. But Edgar Wright, a friend and admirer of Lue and editor of a small horticultural magazine, *The Florida Grower,* learned of his plight and rallied his readers to buy bonds to prevent "such an injustice." They did. The mortgage was paid off, with enough left over for Lue to live on until his death in 1925.

As for the "experts," they were permanently refuted by Dr. H. Harold Hume, late dean emeritus of the College of Agriculture at the University of Florida, who pronounced the Lue Gim Gong orange as "the best" for rind, abundant juice, and rich flavor, adding that the fruit was probably "the hardiest of all sweet orange varieties" ever grown in America.

Lue was held in great affection by the people of Deland, and at his death, an artist was commissioned by them to create a face-mask of him which still remains in the library at Stetson University. A bust of him was also created for honorary exhibit by Florida at the World Fairs of 1933 and 1939.

But Lue's role in Florida history might have been forgotten except for a simple but moving and well-informed biography written by a Floridian, Marian Murray. And, of course, except for his townspeople, one of whom— a close friend—called him "the finest character Florida ever knew."

5.
Moore Haven's Benevolent Duchess

Marian O'Brien put a Lake Okeechobee town on the map, but stormy weather and unruly citizens defaced its future.

In the *Literary Digest* of September 15, 1917, she was hailed as the "Duchess of Moore Haven," and even before that, a *Saturday Evening Post* column extolled her in "Who's Who—and Why."

She was Marian Newhall Horowitz O'Brien, wealthy Philadelphia socialite who, in early 1916, swapped her salon slippers for sturdy riding boots and left the Main Line for the mucklands of Florida's Lake Okeechobee–Everglades country. Thirtyish, lithe, and handsome, the daughter of a major Pennsylvania Railroad official and sister of a J. P. Morgan partner, Marian had talents, energy, and executive acumen to spare, and she brought it all to bear on the toddling, barely year-old settlement of Moore Haven on Okeechobee's southwest lakeshore. Moore Haven *Times* publisher Will Stevens was certain the hamlet was destined to be the "Chicago of the South." And for seven flourishing years, it looked as if Marian was going to make it happen. Unfortunately, man's passions and nature's caprice would abort the dream before it was fulfilled.

Moore Haven was named for founder James A. Moore, a Seattle developer who visited the lake country in 1914 and envisioned a cornucopian farm belt in the vast, dark, richly fertile mucklands. He bought some 100,000 newly drained acres of it and laid out streets for a town along the canal linking the lake to the Caloosahatchie River and Fort Myers. He formed the South Florida Land Company, put up several buildings and a hotel, and sent salesmen out over the Midwest promoting his "farmland paradise." He even persuaded two ex-presidential candidates, Judge Alton B. Parker and William Jennings Bryan, to buy modest chunks of the muck. By 1915, the town had drawn 397 men and three women.

But Moore had overspent himself, and in 1916, he sold his interests to New Jersey developer Clarence Busch. Two other interest holders, John J. O'Brien, a former Philadelphia city editor, and an attorney friend, George Horowitz, fell out with Busch for "overpricing" the acreage ($75 to $100 an acre for land costing $5.75 an acre) and formed their own DeSoto Stock

Farms Company. Then Horowitz died suddenly. Enter his widow, the "Duchess."

Marian plunged into the farm venture with enthusiasm; she and the gruff Irishman became smooth working partners. They opened a general store, formed a vegetable exchange, organized the First Bank of Moore Haven, planted large farm tracts, and promoted various civic and cultural projects for the town. The partnership blossomed personally as well. When O'Brien was inducted for World War I service (becoming a captain), the two were married. In his absence, Marian worked from daybreak to dusk, horseback riding over her farms, securing the most modern farm machinery, managing their many interests, and once even leading a fight to protect farmers' rights against Busch's rival company (he had disputed some settlers' land claims).

Well before the Nineteenth Amendment, Marian made certain that local women enjoyed equal suffrage. When Moore Haven was incorporated in 1917, she was elected its first mayor, one of the first woman mayors in the United States. The town, too, took shape, with new families and new houses, paved streets, trees and shrubs, and long rows of royal poinciana

Philadelphia socialite Marian O'Brien worked hard to make Moore Haven the "Chicago of the South," but this dream was not to be. (Florida State Archives)

along the main street. A steamer scheduled daily trips to Fort Myers, and two new theaters featured musicals and cultural events. A new power and ice plant enabled the town to capture a large share of the lake's flourishing catfish industry.

Above all, the rich muckland farms infused a flush prosperity with record yields of beans, potatoes, tomatoes, onions, lettuce, and other truck produce. More acreage was drained and the land business boomed. Bargeloads of fresh produce were piled house-high on the city docks. Marian's farms shipped 100,000 bushels of potatoes alone in 1918; these wartime foodstuffs commanded premium prices, too. To cap this commercial achievement, the Duchess persuaded Atlantic Coast Line (ACL) to push its railroad line from Haines City to Moore Haven.

Nevertheless, embers of grudge and discord smouldered beneath this halcyon facade of harmony. Many of the area's hard-nosed Crackers, "cow hunters," and assorted mavericks resented the O'Briens' "high-toned" Northern mannerisms and even their fancy riding breeches. They also resented a colony of retired British officers' families whom Marian had persuaded to settle north of town—"furriners" they were, who took tea and smoked cigarettes in long holders. O'Brien himself, a staunch Catholic in a time of anti-Catholicism, was often a target of hostile sentiment. But the harshest prejudice surfaced when the O'Briens brought in badly needed black laborers to harvest crops and work on railroad construction. Malcontents would hide in the underbrush and take pot shots at the workers. Finally the mayor rounded up and jailed the more violent of these "vigilantes," and the harassment ceased.

A drive by Moore Haven citizens to carve their own county out of huge DeSoto County succeeded in 1921. In fact, key lawmakers, encouraged by the surreptitious receipt of some $20,000 from county sources, gratefully sliced the sprawling DeSoto into not only Glades (with Moore Haven the county seat), but also Highlands, Hardee, and Charlotte counties.

But this event only intensified a larger political factionalism that roughly aligned Busch's interests against those of the O'Briens. Earlier, publisher Stevens sold his *Times* to Andrew Carter, a Busch ally, while Stevens' son, Wallace, began the rival *Glades County Democrat*. Later, in an attempt to harmonize the town's fractious feuding, young Stevens arranged to buy Carter's paper, ignoring violent opposition threats against the move. Then, the night before Stevens was to take over the sheet, its entire plant was destroyed by unknown arsonists, who had also sabotaged the fire truck and hose.

But larger calamities loomed. That same year, a woman's gasoline iron exploded and the resultant fire wiped out twenty-two businesses. Then came the floods in 1922. Farmers were unaware that they had enjoyed an unseasonable freak of nature with the seven-year dry spell. But with heavy rains came lake overflow, inundating entire fields on the eve of the harvest. One typical loss was seven hundred acres of tomatoes, which were underwater and unpickable.

These occurrences all together had by now so discouraged the Duchess that the couple decided to start a new town twenty miles southeast of Moore Haven. Once again, the ACL extended a line to the new town, named Clewiston for the Tampa banker A. C. Clewis who had an interest in the venture. A store and hotel were built on the lake wharf, and Boston city planner John Nolen was called in to lay out the city.

But the old enmity had followed the O'Briens. A specially virulent prejudice was aimed at O'Brien's arrangement to have a Tampa priest say Mass in the O'Brien's home every six weeks. The service drew many, including farmers in the area. Then one night, a shot was fired into their home. O'Brien was absent, but Marian sustained a severe scalp wound. The final crisis came when, in their absence one night, their home was burned to the ground.

It was the final straw for Marian. If seemingly a lofty "Duchess," she had surely been a gracious and benevolent one to the people of the area; this response appeared to her grossly inequitable, even mortally hazardous. The O'Briens packed up and went north to Detroit where, after a serious illness, Marian died in 1931.

Clewiston would remain relatively undeveloped until its later accession as the capital of Florida's sugar industry. As for Moore Haven, it was virtually destroyed when the great hurricane of 1926 smashed down the flimsy muck lake levees and flattened the town with torrents of water, killing over two hundred people.

6.
Pioneer Pilgrims on the
St. Johns River

*French Huguenots fleeing religious oppression came close to
making Florida the first Plymouth Rock.*

Not many are aware today that Florida, not Massachusetts, almost became
the site of the first pilgrim colony in America, settled by those legions who
once fled religious persecution in Europe.

The St. Johns River Bluff came close to replacing Plymouth Rock in
history when the French Huguenots sailed up the St. Johns River and set up
Fort Caroline in 1562 (over half a century ahead of their spiritual brethren,
the Puritans).

Had it not been for a fateful misjudgment and a bad turn of Florida
weather, it seems this first permanent European colony in America would
have been safe. Moreover, there would have been no St. Augustine today,
because it originally was only a random supply dump for Pedro Menendez
de Aviles, whom King Philip II of Spain sent to wipe out the new French
colony.

But the Huguenots were zealous and determined because they were
fleeing from persecution more severe than that endured by their later Puritan
counterparts. Both groups were born of the Protestant Reformation and the
teachings of Martin Luther and John Calvin, and thus they incurred the savage wrath of the Church of Rome and Philip II. It was the time of the Inqui-
sition, when the possession or reading of a Bible was punishable by death.
For this, during the sixteenth century and later, the Huguenot "heretics"
would suffer torture on the rack and death at the stake or the gallows. Then,
too, France was dominated by an entrenched feudal system and an armed
aristocracy. At the same time, Rome's ecclesiastical power brought oppression to the illiterate, impoverished, and brutalized peasantry. Against such
a backdrop, the Huguenots seemed threatening. They were an emerging middle class—self-reliant burghers, businessmen, artisans, and skilled crafts-
men. They were mostly educated, prosperous, and zealous in their new
Protestant faith. And so it seemed inevitable that the hatred of their tormen-
tors would ultimately culminate in a horrible early-day version of the "final
solution": the St. Bartholomew's Day massacre in 1572, the blackest day in

French history, when thousands of Huguenot men, women, and children were slaughtered throughout France.

In 1561, the Huguenot leader, a nobleman named Admiral Gaspard de Coligny, persuaded Queen Catherine de Medici to let the renowned Huguenot navigator, Jean Ribault, and the equally able sea captain, René de Laudonnière, search for a site for Huguenots to colonize in America. On May 1, 1562, this expedition entered the mouth of "a majestic river," the St. Johns, and named it then the River of May. Arriving at a seventy-foot river bluff (today's St. Johns Bluff ten miles east of Jacksonville), Ribault pronounced the land "the fairest, frutefullest and pleasantest of all the worlde." The Frenchmen then held a solemn thanksgiving service and met with local Indian tribes and chiefs, notably Timuquan Chief Saturiba. By presenting the Indians with small gifts and treating them with great cordiality, the émigrés sealed a lasting friendship with them.

Erecting a column at the site, the expedition returned to France to gather Huguenot colonists and adequate provisions. They also left thirty men at another site, Charlesfort (Parris Island, South Carolina), but, decimated by hunger, many died and the site was later abandoned.

But hitches developed in Laudonnière's plan. France was in a religious civil war, Ribault was temporarily imprisoned on a trip to England, and not until a peace was signed was he again authorized to embark with a colony of settlers—three hundred of them in three ships, in April 1564.

They arrived at the river bluff that June. After being greeted by friendly Indians, they began erecting Fort Caroline. Before long, the small colony boasted a number of homes, a flour mill, a bakery, and a blacksmith. Among the Huguenots, the artist Jacques Le Moyne would leave a valuable collection of drawings of the Indians and of Florida's flora and fauna.

Laudonnière had sped two of his ships back to France for more colonists and supplies, but political intrigue at home delayed their return. Near-famine soon threatened, and Laudonnière had to impose a tight discipline, especially on some "infidel" Moors and French seamen, some of whom revolted and stole a vessel to use in piracy against the Spanish. They were later tried by the colonists and several were executed. Laudonnière's colonists declined an offer from the English privateer John Hawkins to carry them home. Hawkins had traded the settlers food and a ship for a cannon. Not long after the settlers decided to stay, Ribault arrived with seven ships, six hundred colonists, and abundant provisions.

But by now Menendez, sent by Spain to attack the Huguenots, had arrived at the river's mouth. At first Ribault outsailed and eluded him. Menendez returned to the small inlet he called St. Augustine where he had left supplies. And then came a fateful decision for history.

Ribault decided on a bold attack before Menendez and the Spanish could settle in, but Laudonnière strongly objected for two reasons: The hurricane season was well under way, and the Huguenot fort would be left virtually unmanned. But Ribault overruled him and set sail. He almost succeeded in his surprise attack, and Menendez barely escaped being captured. Unable to cross the harbor sandbar, Ribault waited for high tide, but brisk winds had turned into a full hurricane and the Huguenots' ships were swept down the coast and wrecked.

Menendez seized this chance to march overland and take the nearly undefended French fort. He slaughtered many of the occupants and held some women and children for sale in the slave market. He also hanged 143 men. An ailing Laudonnière, who had stayed to protect the fort, fought almost alone before finally escaping to the woods with a band of some fifty-five Huguenots who managed to reach unharmed two ships still at anchor. They returned to France where, much later, Laudonnière would write the story of the Huguenot colony.

Several days after Laudonnière's escape to the woods, Menendez hunted down the unarmed and near-starving shipwreck survivors and mas-

bault and the last remnants of his force capitulated
to death. Each body was tacked with an
t stated that the victims of S

Spanish soldiers, led by Pedro Menendez de Aviles, killed 350 French Huguenots on the beaches near Jacksonville. (Florida State Archives)

sacred them on the beach. Ribault and 350 men perished; 150 others had fled the scene. All of France was outraged at the massacre, and ironically, it would be a Catholic, Dominique de Gourgues, who two years later would avenge the dead. With 180 men and many of Saturiba's Indians, he surprised the fort, which had passed to Spain and was now named Fort San Mateo. Some four hundred Spaniards were killed, forty-five of them by hanging. Spain's Philip II shrilly demanded that de Gourgues be hanged, but Catherine feigned ignorance of the expedition and de Gourgues returned a hero—at least a hero to the Huguenots.

In the next century, thousands of Huguenots would join the Puritan pilgrims in America. Two of the first pilgrims, Priscilla Mullins and John Alden, their names anglicized from Moline and Jean Alden, were Huguenots. So was Philippe de la Noye, whose anglicized name, Delano, would grace a famous descendant, Franklin Delano Roosevelt.

But, perhaps fittingly, it would be the descendants of Chief Saturiba's tribe who would most poignantly memorialize these first pilgrims in America. Later settlers in Florida were often astonished to hear these Indians singing hymns from the Book of Psalms—in French.

7.
Florida's Scottish-Indian Statesman

Alexander McGillivray guided his Creek nation through the diplomatic intrigues of three world powers.

Alexander McGillivray, sketched by frontier artist John Trumbull.

Alexander McGillivray was a true statesman among the Creek Indians. Widely regarded as the "Talleyrand" of the red men, he forced negotiated peace more than once and managed to gain the respect of the world's most important leaders.

When he died at age 34 in Pensacola in 1793, his burial was attended by honors from three powerful nations: Spain, Britain, and the United States.

As an adult, McGillivray was deferred to by kings and feted by George Washington. He shunned the tomahawk for the more subtle art of statesmanship and thereby successfully juggled the most turbulent international forces of the time. Even one hundred years after his death, President Theodore Roosevelt wrote that McGillivray's "consummate craft" and "cool masterly diplomacy" enabled the Creek Indian nation for a generation "to hold their own better than any other native race" against the white man's encroachment.

Born in 1759 to a wealthy Scottish trader, Lachlan McGillivray, who, as a loyalist, fled to Scotland during the American Revolution, and Sehoy Marchand, an Indian princess whose father was a French army captain, Alexander was sent to his father's cousin, Rev. Farquhar McGillivray, a Charleston Presbyterian minister, to begin a classic education at age 14. Well-grounded for his future tasks, he returned to his Indian nation and, due to his mother's "royal" line in the Wind clan, became a chieftain and began his apprenticeship in statecraft.

With the Floridas under British rule, Pensacola was then the bustling center of a soaring Indian trade, one which would make a millionaire of another Scottish trader—and loyalist—William Panton, of the trader company Panton & Leslie.

McGillivray willingly became Panton's "silent partner." Personally, Alexander was bitter toward the American colonists for confiscating his loyalist father's properties near Savannah. But, more importantly, knowing Panton could do little trading without him, he sought British protection for the Creek nation, especially from the Georgia colonists who were attempting to grab the hunting land comprising the Creek nation's eastern border. Coveting not only a stable West Florida government but the vast trading commerce as well, the British eagerly consented to provide the Creeks with arms and assistance to resist white border speculators. They also made Alexander an honorary British colonel, at full pay.

But McGillivray's uppermost ambition was to promote the welfare and security of his beloved Creek nation, and to do so, he firmly believed, he had to survive the "plotting whites" by being as cunning as they had proved to be.

Tall, with piercing black eyes and an inscrutable, reserved expression, Alexander looked every inch a diplomat. His skills in directing men in council and at the negotiating table, and especially his intimate knowledge of the white man's words and ways, won him the admiration of other Creek chieftains, and he soon became the unofficial spokesman for all the Creeks. Yet he was plagued with poor health—stomach gout, respiratory ailments, and other infirmities—that would eventually cause his death.

The Creeks were prospering and, under McGillivray, organized when rebel-weary Britain ceded the Floridas back to Spain in 1783. McGillivray convinced a panicky Panton to remain in Pensacola, noting that he and Panton held the vital key to open the gate to a trading empire. True enough. The Spaniards, still suspicious of both Britain and the new America, even waived the requirement of an oath of allegiance from Panton. McGillivray was made a full Spanish colonel, again with pay. But the astute Alexander shrewdly persuaded the Spanish to put "in writing" any necessities they felt they had for aid, arms, or assistance to the Creek nation.

To prove his own loyalty, McGillvray spurned the first treaty overtures from the Americans, observing that the Washington delegates sent to his nation talked down to his people, citing how one of them apparently came "to play the fool which he performed with considerable insolence." He told the Americans he could not discuss treaty relations until Georgia colonists withdrew from the Oconee Riverlands "on which 1,500 Creek families depended for a living." The Georgians, meanwhile, were even attempting to push further into Creek territory with the infamous Yazoo land grants, which invited speculators to overrun major Creek hunting lands. The Creek tribes fiercely resisted and contained the would-be encroachers.

Finally, President Washington sent his own personal envoy, Marinus Willett, a fair-minded, genial delegate who found the Indian chief to be "a man of open, generous mind, with good judgment, and a very tenacious memory." He told McGillivray that Washington was furious over the "illegal" Yazoo land grants and that the U.S. was prepared to guarantee Creek boundaries and respect all their proper claims.

This persuaded McGillivray and the chieftain council to journey to New York where they were festively greeted, McGillivray staying as guest at the home of War Secretary Henry Knox. With much give and take, a treaty was finally hammered out in August 1790. The U.S. government agreed to protect the Creek with the help of Spain. The Creeks in turn gave up some land already settled by Georgia colonists, but Georgia would be forced to stay put. In loyalty to Panton, McGillivray held out on a request for Creek trade but permitted a secret treaty clause allowing renegotiations on trade in two years. Another secret clause made McGillivray a U.S. brigadier general, at $1,200 annual salary.

The Georgians raged against a treaty "loaded with favors . . . for a savage." The treaty also alarmed and rankled both Spain and Panton, and the former began a "whispering campaign" among the Creeks, implying that the Indians had lost much land and trade in secret agreement. McGillivray calmly exposed the false rumors, noting that he had given up neither Panton's trade nor Spain's protection and had quelled the "rebellious vagabonds [Georgians]." In exasperation, he concluded: "I signed the death sentence of the [Georgian] Company of the Yazoo, and if our allies and western protectors do not help us greatly, I shall have to accept the title of Emperor of the West, which was offered me [at New York] and which I then refused. On the contrary, I want some rest after so long drawn out a dispute."

Although over the next eighteen months McGillivray's influence and power had risen to their zenith in the southeastern United States, especially among western Indians, he was not to enjoy the full fruits of his masterly diplomacy, nor his rest. With severe and lingering complications of his illnesses, he died at Panton's home on February 17, 1793. McGillivray was honored by both America and Spain at his Pensacola burial and as far away as London, in an obituary in the *Gentleman's Magazine* in a column usually reserved for royalty and nobility. The obituary hailed him for his unique statesmanship and "the vigour of his mind which overcame the disadvantages of an education had in the wilds of America."

The mourning Creek nation might have called this "typical British understatement."

8.
Palm Beach Gets an Architectural Facelift

Architect Addison Mizner revamped the wealthy colony with lavish "designer" mansions.

Weary, dispirited, and in ill health, the amazing architect Addison Mizner came to Palm Beach in 1918 to die. This bleak thought soon bored him, so he decided to change the face of Palm Beach. And he did.

Within less than a dozen years—most of them in the golden, manic boom-time twenties—this brilliant mixture of artist-artisan-supersalesman-speculator-grand designer brought an Old World renaissance to this American Monaco with the most ornate, lavish, and artistic homes and estates in the country.

The nation's gas, oil, steel, railroad, food, straight-rye, and patent medicine magnates were literally lined up to get one of his creations, with price no object. Heiresses and matrons with silos of cash vied for his talents; Whitneys, Wanamakers, and Vanderbilts alike wielded pen and checkbook lavishly for the sake of art, romantic splendor, and ostentation. The shrewd Mizner soon became a multimillionaire. It was simple.

The typical Mizner client, after all, wanted grandeur as an index to his wealth and social position. He also wanted a combined amusement park and country club for his house parties and other festivities. Mizner's massive, formidable, and ornate but gay edifices met this need.

Working much as at an oil canvas, he would often rip, tear out, and rebuild a mansion as he went along, prompting the lament as from one contractor, "This is going to cost a lot of money, Mr. Mizner" and the rejoinder: "Listen, these people can't stand the sight of anything that doesn't cost a lot of money."

But Mizner's distinctive adaptation of Old World Spanish architecture created a unique American style of its own. Criticized by some for "a bastard style" (often less from artistic sensibilities than envy), his work was praised by men as diverse as Frank Lloyd Wright; Harvey Corbett, a Rockefeller Center designer; or the sculptor Jo Davidson, who called him an "architectural genius."

His Playa Rienta, for example, built for the Joshua Cosdens, has been termed "one of the great American houses."

Prior to Mizner's grand structures, architecture for the well-off of the area had been little more than bland clapboard, a style closer to Early New England Outhouse than art. If imitation is the sincerest flattery, then Mizner's influence was indelibile, from Merrick's Coral Gables to a huge Jacksonville Baptist Church, as well as in nearly every coastal resort city.

When the Florida boom busted, Mizner was caught at the very top of the golden bubble and he sank with it, but not before he had lent one of the most colorful chapters to that time of gaudy lunacy, land delirium, and conspicuous splendor.

He was colorful himself. Mizner was born to a family of pioneer stock near San Francisco, one of six boys. The beauty of sixteenth-century Spanish architecture first fired his senses in Guatemala, where his father served as U.S. minister plenipotentiary. Later, he studied in Salamanca, Spain, but he was a poor formal student, and he spent a few years just knocking about the world—living on paintings and sketches in Hawaii and Samoa, boxing in Australia, selling doorknobs in Tokyo, traveling with a brother to the Klondike gold rush, hobnobbing with New York City's bluebook set—until restiveness, illness, and an old injury brought him, in his forties, to Palm Beach as the guest of Paris Singer, the sewing machine heir.

Singer recalled Mizner, a six-foot-two, fat but brawny 260 pounds, as a man of cheerful aspect, a combined expression of joviality, authority, innocence, and worldly wisdom, with a touch of the bawdy Elizabethan.

"His mastery of Tavern English is a joy to everybody within hearing," and it fell on the ears of grande dame and autocrat alike. He would not hesitate to give a big name a crude putdown. Or indulge in comedy. He had a tiff once with Major Barclay Warburton, John Wanamaker's son-in-law, for whom he had just built a fine house, and he formally ran Johnny Brown, his pet monkey, against the Major for mayor of Palm Beach.

A veteran wit and courtier, he was also a wizard at proving it was an economy to spend $200,000 instead of $100,000 and at comforting a client when the final bill was $400,000.

It was Singer, Palm Beach's social potentate and all-round art dilettante, who inspired—and financed—Mizner's career with his first creation, the famous Everglades Club, first intended as a rest home for World War I officers.

But the project was "different," and some blueblooded arteries were hardened to it. Labeling it a "monstrosity" that would "ruin the town," they opposed it and hinted strongly of injunctions.

Built in the style of an early Spanish monastery, a stucco building with red tile roof, medieval turrets, and wrought iron grillwork, its like certainly had not been seen since railroad tycoon Henry Flagler had cleared and developed this barren, elongated sandbar in 1894.

But it finally opened to public verdict. And Mizner sweated unnecessarily, for the most gushing superlatives issued from none other than the Queen Emeritus of Palm Beach, Mrs. E. T. Stotesbury; she promptly commissioned a villa and other buildings on her forty-two-acre estate, El Mirasol.

This royal wandstroke made Mizner. The commissions poured in and architectural history began.

Mizner's genius lay in seeing how suitable the Spanish adaptation was to Florida's climate and landscape. His houses were built with courtyards and gardens on various terraced levels to break the land's flat monotony. They were replete with arcades and lofty galleries, exposed rafters and vaulted ceilings, tiled pools and mosaic murals.

As a landscape expert he had a special feeling for the exotic botany of Florida and knew how to mount his showplaces with intriguing backdrops, and as artist, he used color with bold and attractive effect.

Singer classed him with the Middle Age architect, "a master of all the crafts that served his profession. He paints, carves wood, works in metal,

El Mirasol, residence of Edward Stotesbury, designed by Addison Mizner. (Florida State Archives)

knows all about making glazed pottery and his wrought iron is second to none in Old Spain."

He also furnished his houses.

"I have looted cathedrals," Mizner remarked, "churches and palaces, and brought a shipload or two of everything from stone doorways to fine laces from both Central America and Europe."

He imported the finest grades of Italian walnut logs for carving to make durable, handmade antique pieces of furniture. He set up his own terra cotta factory and had roof tiles made by hand. His iron forge made hand-wrought lamps, candlesticks, railings, balconies, grills, door latches, and hinges in Spanish patterns. He would cast doorways, window frames, and fountains and then machine-tool over them for hand-cut effect. He used sandblasters, stains, and colorings to give the effect of age, and made his own stained and leaded glass windows.

One critic notes that Mizner "is never satisfied in building unless he can give a hint of tradition, of romance, an impression of the centuries it has taken to create the great houses, the great cathedrals of the world."

Mizner himself added, "Most modern architects have spent their lives carrying out a period to the last letter and producing a characterless copy-book effect. My ambition has been to take the reverse stand—to make a building look traditional and as though it had fought its way from a small unimportant structure to a great rambling house that took centuries of different needs and ups and downs of wealth to accomplish."

It is not surprising, then, that owning the biggest Addison Mizner house had become the touchstone of Palm Beach social supremacy. The railroad car set would almost beg for a house, and Mizner might do no more than breezily sketch something on an envelope or, as he did for one imploring matron, in the soft wet sand of the beach, to have a draftsman later actually copy it. He was considered one of the four pillars of Palm Beach's Golden Hordes in the twenties, the others being Flagler, Singer, and Colonel E. R. Bradley, roulette king and civic leader.

Thus, at the height of his vogue with a billion-dollar clientele, Mizner contracted the most fateful disease of the day—land-boom fever, then at its frenzied peak. Hoping to bring both Venice and the Riviera to Florida, he began what was to be the most exclusive and wealthy of cities, Boca Raton.

He started with one of his finest buildings, the medieval-styled Cloister (later to be a hotel). To its entrance was laid out the broadest highway in the world—twenty lanes—with a Grand Canal down the center bearing traffic of electric gondolas.

The entire master plan called for oceanfront estates with flowing parks and gardens; millionaires were soon flocking to the endeavor. An estimated

$11 million in lots were sold in one day. The promoter Harry Reichenbach, dubbed the most gifted ballyhoo artist since P. T. Barnum, was brought in.

The enterprise was studded with big celebrity backers: General T. Coleman duPont, Harold Vanderbilt, Elizabeth Arden, Irving Berlin, George Whitney, Marie Dressler, James M. Cox. In the fashion of the day, royalty and nobility were also sprinkled about, including Countess Salm, Lord Ivor, Charles S. Churchill, the Rumanian Princess of Ghika. (The Princess did not seem to find lot-peddling déclassé, but her bearing did seem somewhat less than regal when she burst into Mizner's office one day shouting: "Where's my money? If you think I'm in this goddam plebian swamp for my health, you're crazy as hell!")

But the boom was a paper nightmare—paper cities on paper oceans and lakes, with paper coliseums and casinos—and it only had one direction to go. The bust was signaled when General duPont, the former president of E. E. duPont de Nemours and Company, withdrew his Boca Raton backing— some say over false ads that slipped by or through Reichenbach. Others report duPont wished to clear himself of lawsuits. Regardless, his dropout caused a panic, and Mizner woke up one morning to find himself alone in a sea of paper—this time, lawsuits.

Mizner assumed all responsibilities for Boca Raton debts, but he had lost his own wealth in the process. In another misfortune, he found his architectural style declining in favor as new groups, tiring of an old trend, wanted anything but Spanish.

"I can't bring myself to do this Colonial and Georgian stuff," he confided once to a friend. So in his last years, he lived mainly on loans from his wealthy cronies. When he died in February 1933, his estate was insolvent.

But the legacy of his pioneer architecture will always be around to remind people of the era when Old World style and splendor were translated to the shores of Florida by a unique Renaissance man.

9.
Lake Monroe's Baron deBary

Champagne was the fuel for his elegant backcountry oasis and a pack of steamboats.

Despite his titled, old-European hauteur, the Belgian baron learned quickly how to blend continental mystique with Yankee enterprise.

After amassing an early fortune by refining the crude nineteenth-century American palate with a sparkling new beverage called champagne, Baron Frederick deBary journeyed into the heart of Florida's wilderness to build one of the first winter playground resorts for America's gilded set, long before Miami and Palm Beach were anything more than sand pits and mangrove jungle.

The baron's colonial mansion, DeBary Hall, sits on a high plateau overlooking the north shore of Lake Monroe at the head of the St. Johns River. Today it is a state historic memorial; but in another time, it stood like an elegant oasis, secluded in the wild natural beauty of the St. Johns River country—a champagne watering hole where presidents, royalty, the wealthy, and the celebrated gathered to frolic and revel, dine at gourmet banquets, or hunt and fish in a sportsman's paradise.

Samuel Frederick deBary was born in Germany on January 12, 1815, to a Belgian noble family which later moved to Rheims in northeast France, an area famous for its wines. Young deBary became a close friend of the G. H. Mumm family, which was renowned for its excellent champagne. Viewing a virgin market in the growing United States, Mumm saw in young Fred the right mix of intelligence, geniality, and ambition to exploit that opportunity.

In 1840, when Fred was 25, Mumm sent him to New York to be the sole import distributor and salesman of Mumm's champagne and other European wines.

A fast-rising new class of wealthy merchants, such as the Astors and Vanderbilts, was then emerging. And in those days, the social prestige of the new rich was often measured by their consumption of European luxuries. With his cultural credentials and business acumen, the young baron soon developed a flourishing import empire that would prosper well into the next century. In 1844 Frederick deBary went to Germany to bring his 24-year-old bride, Julie Scherpenhauser, back to New York. They would have a son, Adolphe, and a daughter, Eugenie, before Julie died in 1868.

By 1870 the baron was a millionaire and, at age 55, still young enough to enjoy the fruits of his industry. He traveled to Florida and rode a St. Johns River steamboat to Enterprise, on Lake Monroe. An avid huntsman, deBary was enchanted by the natural beauty of the region and the unlimited wild game.

He bought a large tract of land on a high point of Lake Monroe's north shore, two miles from Enterprise, where he erected his mansion and established a game preserve. The large, colonial-style two-story structure was built of cypress, a wood that becomes granite-like with age (the building today is as sturdy as ever). The mansion's large iron cookstove, its huge ice boxes which once held imported northern ice, and its unique, manually operated elevator are still in perfect condition today.

The estate was also self-sufficient, for on its grounds were a vegetable farm, cows, a thriving orange grove, and a freshwater spring. The amenities included flower gardens and a large swimming pool. Each winter the baron arrived from New York with many notables, including the Vanderbilts, Presidents Grant and Cleveland, and celebrities like the Prince of Wales and Fred Hope, owner of the famous Hope diamond. Hunting trips with hound and horse were a daily activity, and in 1875 the baron bought a luxury steamboat, the *George M. Bird,* for scenic party cruises.

Then, almost by accident, he turned his pleasure steamboat into a commercial fleet that would sharply spur east Florida's economic development in the post–Civil War era. Central Florida was burgeoning in those decades: General Sanford had settled his growing town nearby; wealthy hatmaker John B. Stetson had arrived in Deland; central Florida citrus groves were flourishing; and by the mid-1880s Jacksonville was packed with sixty thousand Northern visitors. With limited water transport and no railways as yet, deBary found the need to put his own boat into commercial service to get his orange shipments to market. This action revealed to him the critical transport needs of the area, so he began to acquire steamboats (thirteen in all) to form the DeBary Steamship Line. The line proved enormously successful until it was displaced by railroads at the end of the century.

DeBary died in December 1898, but his numerous descendants lived in his mansion until 1941. During World War II, the DeBary estate was tied up in complex probate and would pass through several hands until the late 1940s, when a development firm acquired the mansion and sixteen hundred acres and built the community subdivision now called DeBary. In 1959 the town deeded the house to the Florida Federation of Art, which today uses it as its state headquarters. Then, in 1967, at federal instigation, DeBary Hall was designated a state historic memorial, and funds were made available to restore the great house.

Thus, a noble immigrant peddler of wine, oranges, and steamboat travel was able to leave to his adopted state an enduring symbol of a grand era in Florida's early development, an era that would not have been the same without him.

10.
Trailblazers of the Great Swamp

It took blood and sweat and tons of dynamite to build the Tamiami Trail across the Everglades.

It was literally "hell and high water" for the men who built the highway—many drowned, died of snake bites, or were blasted away by dynamite.

In fact, the death and injury toll in building the Tamiami Trail (U.S. 41) through the pristine and impenetrable Everglades in the 1920s was unprecedented. The feat itself was unprecedented: cutting, hacking, blasting some seventy-five miles through muck, water, sawgrass, and cypress, all of it resting on a thick submerged floor of flint-hard limestone (it would take forty thousand pounds of dynamite per mile to clear a roadbed). The Trail would be the first highway link from Gulf to Atlantic in south Florida.

The Trail's builders had hoped to cash in on the great land boom just getting under way, siphon off some of the tourist hordes pouring into the Gold Coast and Miami, and spur development in southwest Florida. But the land boom had busted by the time the road was finished, and the Depression was just ahead. The Trail became an anachronism, even an ecological calamity of sorts. "Progress" had never seemed so backward.

Former Dade County Tax Assessor J. F. Jaudon first promoted the idea for the Trail in 1915. He hoped to develop large land holdings in the western Everglades and around Chevalier Bay in north Monroe County. Skeptics jeered at the notion of a road over an ocean of grass and jungle, inhabited only by 'gators, snakes, and Seminole Indians.

But Jaudon and a road promotion group were able to convince Lee, Dade, and Monroe counties of the Trail's value and feasibility. So in 1916, the three counties, plus Jaudon's Chevalier Corporation, entered an agreement to sell bonds to begin construction. Dade raised $125,000 and managed to grade a rough road from the eastern part of the county up to the edge of the Glades. Lee (then the largest county in the eastern United States) nibbled away at the jungle with dredges to a point four miles from Everglades City. World War I halted both projects, but they resumed after the war. By 1921, however, Lee's funds were exhausted, and the Trail project went into limbo. Initially, the counties did not realize the huge costs such an undertaking would require; they learned quickly.

Meanwhile, Jaudon had surveyed and staked out the most feasible route for the Trail. In April 1923, a Lee civic group called the "Trail Blazers" widely publicized a motorcade of eight Model T Fords and two other vehicles that would travel this route to Dade to prove that it was traversable. After a rough and exhausting twenty-three days of sweating, hacking, and heaving through muck and cypress, travelers in seven of the Model Ts made it into Miami. The resultant publicity made the Trail the most talked-about road project in the state.

Just as the Trail was getting known around Florida, a benefactor arrived on the scene who would alter its course in a big way. His name was Barron G. Collier, a millionaire streetcar-advertising tycoon. Between 1921 and 1923, Collier had purchased more than a million acres in south Lee County for development. Collier, naturally, was all for the Trail, even to the point of guaranteeing its completion. But he set two conditions. First, Collier (whose home was in Everglades City) suggested that Lee County was just too big to meet properly the needs of residents in the southern part of the county. Why not just have our own county? he asked. Residents eagerly agreed. So did the

The builders of the Tamiami Trail, underway above, had to brave chest-high water, mosquitoes and snakes, and dynamite blasts. Many did not survive. (Florida State Archives)

legislature, and in 1923 a new county was carved away, over the vociferous protests of residents in northern Lee. Lawmakers also thought it fit to call it Collier County since the man did own ninety percent of it.

A second furor arose when Collier insisted on rerouting the Trail across his county, bypassing Monroe and Jaudon's Chevalier Bay tract. Protesters argued that the counties had an unbreachable legal agreement and that the Jaudon route was the best one, lying through more open country. Then one weekend, Collier invited two guests to his home—Governor John W. Martin and State Road Board Chairman Fons Hathaway. A few days later, Martin announced that the Trail would be routed through Collier.

The Seminole Indians resented this intrusion into their ancestral territory, but they did not quite feel up to starting a Fourth Seminole War over it. They were given a bridge over their canoe trail.

Collier had picked his county commission by now, and with his underwriting, it issued $350,000 in bonds for the Trail. Work began again in October 1923.

For the horde of laborers on the project, both before and after the war, working conditions were primitive at best. First, crews would wade through

The first barrier ever erected against the natural flow southward of the Glades, the Trail was found to be the cause of erratic flooding in south Florida. (Florida State Archives)

often chest-high water with axes and machetes to cut a swath through the tangle of mangrove, cypress, and sawgrass. Other crews then followed, binding large cypress log "rails" over which to drag the heavy drilling machines. Then, through water and up to four feet of muck, holes would be drilled through a couple of limestone strata into harder rock stratum that was usually three feet thick. Wagons, each drawn by six oxen, floundered through the mud and water to bring up the dynamite for insertion into the holes. The rock would then be blasted out.

Dredges came next. They varied from the crawler dredge to the floating steam dredge, but the largest one ever used was the twenty-ton Monegan "walking dredge." This dredge moved along steel rails set twenty-nine feet apart, enabling it to dig a twenty-four foot-wide canal with a dipper arm as it moved along. It threw up the rock debris onto the roadbed beside the canal. Men had to move ahead of the dredge stacking brush mats four feet high to keep the monster machine from sinking into the mud. Often the heavy machines and wagons would sink deeply into the mud, requiring days of backbreaking labor to pull them out. Inching along up to two miles a month, the road builders used three million pounds of dynamite to blast out some seventy-five miles of solid rock.

But this was the easy part. A broiling tropic sun, mosquitoes, and giant horse flies inflicted fever and death on a few men. Snakes, water, and dynamite caused the most casualties. Even though armed men stood guard against moccasin swarms, coral snakes, rattlers, and alligators, more than a few men died from encounters with these creatures, and others were crippled by them. Other workers drowned when they would suddenly sink in the water and muck, unable to surface with their feet mired in the quicksand-like ooze. Even in sleep, around open campfires, the men were prey for mosquitoes and snakes. (Later in the project, portable bunkhouses would ease this problem.)

Dynamite-blasting signals often went unheard over the roar of machines, and many men were either killed or seriously injured by concussion. A full-time doctor and nurse team often worked around the clock in a hastily set up hospital at Everglades City for casualty treatment. Understandably, the labor turnover was high. Crews recruited mainly out of the Tampa Bay area were rarely told the full extent of working conditions or hazards. Only a few of the first recruits were around for the end of the job.

In August 1926, the state road department officially took over the final twelve miles of the Glades section to link up with the Dade side and then went on to finish the whole Trail project. This was also the year of the land boom's bust, and consequently, when the 109-mile Glades section officially opened to traffic on April 25, 1928, there was very little traffic to bear. Even fewer people traveled the Trail during the Depression. It had taken thirteen years, thirteen million dollars, and an unusual toll of human life to complete. Later, the Trail—the first barrier ever erected against the natural flow southward of the Glades—was found to be the cause of erratic flooding in south Florida. This condition was compounded later by the South Florida Flood Control District and Everglades Parkway (Alligator Alley).

Collier would never see his development plans unfold; he died, broke, in 1939 at age 66 but with his vast estate intact. And so, the Tamiami Trail never did catalyze the golden promise so fervently extolled by its promoters. Today it remains the relatively quiet two-lane lonesome stretch it has always been.

Nevertheless, on reflection, it seems that there might be one way to view the road in a more laudable perspective: as a memorial to the scores of men who gave their health or lives to open up south Florida.

11.
Florida's
Outstanding
Black
Achiever

*Josiah Walls rose from
slavery to the halls of
Congress in the turbulent
era of Reconstruction.*

*Josiah T. Walls, U.S. congressman and successful lawyer, mayor, newspaper publisher,
and farmer.* (Florida State Archives)

He rose from slavery to become Florida's first black politician of national
prominence at a time when it was risky business for any man, especially a
black man, to be in politics at all.

Yet, against the stormy and often violent backdrop of post–Civil War
Reconstruction, Josiah T. Walls tenaciously held his own. Elected three
times as U.S. congressman (and unseated twice because of contested
results), he also found time to become an attorney, mayor, county commissioner, newspaper publisher and editor, and successful farmer. It would be a
remarkable career in any era, much less for an ex-slave in the chaotic, war-
torn Florida of the late 1860s. But then Walls was a singular man.

Born to slave parents in Virginia on December 30, 1842, Walls was
later pressed into Confederate service. Captured and freed by Union forces
in 1863, he joined the first black U.S. infantry regiment, serving through the
war until his discharge as a sergeant major at Jacksonville in 1865. Moving
to the fertile farmland area of Alachua County near Gainesville, he met and
married Helen Fergueson. Some early schooling, plus an intense self-tutoring program in the war years, enabled him to get a job teaching in nearby
Archer.

With the beginning of military Reconstruction in March 1867, the
newly enfranchised free men flocked to the Florida Republican party (Lincoln's party). In some counties, like Alachua, black voters far outnumbered
white voters. Many conservative whites, resenting the dominance of the mil-

itary-civilian Northerners whom they dubbed "carpetbaggers," refused to sponsor candidates or to vote. The conservative Gainesville *New Era* briefly endorsed as a delegate to the 1868 state constitutional convention Garth James (younger brother of the renowned William and Henry James) until learning that James considered U.S. Reconstruction measures to be "eminently wise and just."

Walls was elected a delegate to the convention, and although he aligned himself with the radical Republican "mule team" faction, he voted for the somewhat moderate state constitution which was finally adopted. Walls foresaw only negative results from a rigid radical stance. He felt it more important to keep a continuous black presence within the mainly white political structure as well as to seek future alliances with moderate whites such as Ossian B. Hart and Marcellus Stearns (both of whom were governors later).

Returning home, he discovered he had a solid political base in Alachua among whites and blacks, and he easily won election as a legislator in the lower state assembly (the House) in 1868. Later that year, he won a state senate seat, but he and other blacks found it increasingly frustrating to secure civil rights measures, such as the right to use public hotels "without distinction," or, more critically, protection against terrorist activities by the Ku Klux Klan and fanatics in the Young Men's Democratic Clubs. These groups were conducting a campaign of terror against blacks and white Republicans across the state with intimidation, beatings, burnouts, murders, vote frauds, and armed blockades of roads leading to voting precincts. (In Alachua County alone, in the period 1867–71 there were nineteen murders and numerous less-serious frays, all instigated by these two groups. Some Southern historians have presented a contrived portrayal of the state as being "ravaged" by radical "carpetbaggers" and "illiterate" blacks. To a great extent, a reverse "ravaging" actually prevailed.)

Bound and limited at the state level, Walls decided to run for higher office. In 1870, he squared off against Conservative candidate Silas L. Niblack, a Confederate veteran and former slave owner, in a race for Congress. Niblack made an issue of Walls's self-educated, ex-slave background.

In an election marked by fraud, ballot-stuffing, and sporadic fighting (in a racial disturbance at one rally, a bullet missed Walls "by inches"), Walls won by a 627-vote margin. Walls took his seat in the House of Representatives on March 4, 1871, but earlier that year, Niblack contested the election. The U.S. House Committee on Elections held lengthy witness hearings on the matter—so lengthy that when they finally decided in Niblack's favor in January 1873 by accepting three Duval County precinct returns that the state canvassing board had first thrown out as fraudulent, there were only two months left in the contested term. Worse for Niblack, Walls ran against him for a second term and won by 1,662 votes. The Conservatives did not contest this outcome. Ossian B. Hart, the moderate white Republican, also won the governorship.

During these years, Walls was also busy in other pursuits. He had studied, passed exams, and was admitted to the Florida bar. With two other blacks, he formed a law firm. He had also served brief terms as Gainesville mayor and as a county commissioner and was named a brigadier general in the Florida State Militia. Most of his savings he invested in a large, 1,175-acre farm, and he became one of the state's most successful truck farmers. He also parceled out small plots to poor black families who, if able to pay, were charged only a token rental. Another venture was his purchase of the Gainesville-based *New Era* with basic aims of promoting harmonious race relations—he said, "we have nothing to gain by an issue with the white race"—and development of the county's resources through "education, temperance, thrift, economy and industry." To this end, after he appointed Thomas Gibbs, son of distinguished black Florida Secretary of State Jonathan Gibbs, to West Point, he named Acton Walker, son of the the strict Conservative and former Governor David Walker, to the U.S. Naval Academy.

In 1874 Walls won his third congressional term against former Confederate General Jesse Finley by a margin of 371 votes. Finley contested the outcome. The House committee found "irregularities" in one black precinct sufficient to void its returns (including 588 votes given Walls), and Walls was unseated in March 1876.

While he was in the legislature, Walls sought to be responsive to all the state's needs. He boosted Florida's appeal to new settlers and investors; secured railroad, waterway, and other internal improvements; improved the state's mail system; and, above all, fought for educational opportunities for his people. In one of the few times he alluded to the race question, he argued that Southern lawmakers used "states' rights" as a subterfuge to deny both blacks and poor whites education. Arguing for the first federal education aid bill, he declared—prophetically—that if education were left solely to the states, blacks would suffer. He successfully secured ninety thousand acres of public land at Tallahassee for Florida Normal College (now Florida A&M). As a public servant, Walls was termed in one Tallahassee newspaper as "able, clearheaded, honest"; as far away as St. Louis, he was called by the *Globe* "an effective, tireless worker; tactful, foresighted and practical."

With the return to power of the Democrats in the 1880s, Walls gradually withdrew from "ineffective" political activity. The death of his wife, his own failing health, and financial ruin after his citrus groves were wiped out in the disastrous 1895 freeze prompted Walls to move to Tallahassee where he became director of the Florida Normal College farm until his death there in May 1905.

12.
The Pioneers of Opportunity

*The Webbs were a prototype family among those who wrested
life and substance from the Florida wilderness.*

We often wonder at, and even admire, the rugged, primitive living conditions of Florida's wilderness pioneers. But as we switch on the air condi-
tioner, forage the fridge, and settle on the sofa to watch TV, we may shudder
at the thought of living that way today.

Pioneer living certainly could be ascetic and strenuous. Wresting one's
subsistence from a wild and pristine habitat usually demanded rigorous
labor and the keenest ingenuity. Nevertheless, the pioneer lifestyle often gar-
nered blessings that the modern-day suburbanite might well envy. A micro
look at one such family may offer a fairly representative picture.

Most Florida pioneers came from other states, as did John and Eliza
Webb, an educated farm family from Utica, New York. Their doctor had
advised a Southern climate because of Eliza's severe asthma. They were
drawn to Florida by the offer of free land to settlers under the recent Homestead Act. So they sold everything and headed south with their children—
Anna, 21; Will, 18; Lizzie, 12; Jack, 9; and Ginnie, 7—and also Eliza's
father, Samual Graves, and her sister, Emily, plus furniture, farm imple-
ments, and a penful of chickens.

In the spring of 1867 they made their way to the little "one-store" settlement of Manatee on the Manatee River. They stayed with the Edmund Lee
family until they could search out "a high and beautiful" point of land that
an old Spanish trader in Key West had told them of. Using a small sloop to
scout the area, they finally found a plot of land just right for them that July.

Their new bayfront homestead was situated high atop three huge adjoin-
ing Indian middens and was surrounded by densely overgrown, fertile hammock lowland through which a small spring flowed. Webb first called it
Spanish Point but later changed it to Osprey, for the gorgeous brown fish
hawk then in the area; the name remains today. Exulted daughter Anna: "It
is one of the most lovely spots I was ever in."

Building first a crude "kitchen" shack for temporary quarters, the
Webbs plunged at once into the backbreaking toil of clearing the hammock's
thick scrub and jungly overgrowth until, a month later, they had cleared the
first acre for a "garden." They planted tomatoes, beans, potatoes, and other
vegetables, plus fifty banana trees and a stand of sugar cane. But they had

to sleep with rifles at bedside to keep the wild turkeys, panthers, deer, wild cats, raccoons, and other wildlife from munching the tender plantings or snaring a chicken. And, to Eliza's horror, now and then a rattlesnake was drawn to her aromatic kitchen.

With lumber they acquired in Manatee, some forty miles and about two days sailing away, they slowly built a home. Its partitioned sides were filled in with mortar that Webb made by burning oyster shells and reducing them to lime. Coquina rock was quarried from the offshore keys for fireplaces and chimneys, and the roof was "contemporary frontier" with its thatched palmetto fronds. Rooms consisted of a large parlor, dining room, three main and three split-level bedrooms, and windows opening at floor level for access to the three bayfront porches. A large cistern was built to store rainwater.

Meanwhile, their health thrived in the salubrious climate; Eliza's asthma gradually disappeared, as did her father's rheumatism. The vegetables yielded early and copiously in the fertile hammock, and with steady supplies of fresh turkey and venison and a bay teeming with fish and oyster beds, the Webb homestead was virtually self-sufficient in its first year.

In season, the huge loggerhead turtles came to the beaches, providing turtle steaks and plentiful eggs for cooking and baking. Gelatin was extracted from seaweed, and a fabric dye for their simple homemade clothes came from boiled oak bark.

Webb sent up North for calfskin, thread, awls, and sole leather to make the family's shoes. A bright parlor lamp was devised by Will, who carved a high stool atop which iron spikes held a plate in which resinous lighter-pine knots were burned.

Their first natural calamity came on Christmas Day 1868, when an unusual and sudden freeze kept the men working twenty-four hours to salvage the first cane harvest, their cash crop. The oaken cogs on the crude pine log roller mill broke as fast as Will could carve new ones, trying to press the frozen stalks. Most vegetable crops were lost, but they managed to produce a barrel and a half of "fine syrup."

Yet, despite the incessant labors, isolation, and privations, Eliza could write a Northern sister: "I am much happier here than I have been in years past. We have seen hard times since we came, but who does not on going into a new country." And she would always quote her favorite scriptural passage: "Sufficient unto the day is the will thereof." She delighted in writing friends of the plentiful game in her back yard and seafood in the front yard. "I wish you were here to eat oyster pie with us this noon," she wrote one of them.

The laborious land clearing continued, and by 1869 Webb had two full acres of "splendid" cane. "The stand is excellent and the growth is full, one month ahead of last year," he wrote to a relative. "I can tell you, Brother

Adams, there is money and health here for such thin-chested men as you and I." By now Webb had located in Manatee and purchased on credit an old half-ton iron mill. Within a few years he would be operating Sarasota County's first manufacturing plant, contracting to mill the harvests of other area cane growers. The garden steadily expanded to include oranges, watermelons, pineapple, and castor oil beans; all of Webb's surplus produce found a premium market at Key West.

To relieve the lonely isolation, the Webbs visited their neighbors, making such occasions festive holidays of sorts. The Webbs' nearest neighbors were the Bill Whitaker family, fifteen miles northward. Whitaker was the first settler of present-day Sarasota. Later, the Jesse Knights and their fifteen children settled fifteen miles southward. The families gathered at Spanish Point as often as they could and had "some lively times together," Eliza noted.

By the mid-1870s, the Webb homestead was thriving with sixteen acres of crops, six of them in sugar cane. This was also the period when winter visitors were discovering Florida in increasing numbers. One such visitor, an old friend of Webb's and a noted Smithsonian Institute naturalist, Ezekial Jewett, found the Webb place to be "a little corner of paradise." He urged Webb to open a resort hotel. Jewett drew other Smithsonian people to the Webb home, one of whom enthused: "The whole country [here] is in as wild a state as when Columbus discovered America." The group was able to make valuable studies of marine and animal life, fossils, and Indian burial relics in the area.

After he built additions to his home, Webb began a resort hotel, the first on the west coast, and he was the first to advertise in Northern newspapers, offering hunting, fishing, and a "reasonable good table of seafood, venison, game and vegetables in abundance" for thirty-five dollars a month. He was soon hosting up to twenty visitors a year, enabling him to purchase a small schooner, both for carrying passengers from Tampa and freighting products to Key West.

As the years passed and more people moved into the area, a county government was formed and Webb was elected a county commissioner; he later served as a county judge. Anna and Lizzie both married local men, Robert S. Griffith and Frank Guptill, respectively, and the Webb family expanded in numbers. (The founder of Osprey and most of his family are buried there today.)

The rugged years and sacrifices of wilderness pioneering had never dismayed the Webbs; they viewed it all simply as opportunity, a view that proved both enduring and fruitful. And that is probably why Eliza often concluded her letters north with the entreaty: "Pack up the children in a trunk and come first chance."

13.
Silvia Sunshine Rescues Florida's Past

Abbie Brooks disinterred some three hundred years of the state's history but remains a mystery herself.

She was—and remains—the mystery woman of Florida history; anonymity enshrouds her life like mists from a Florida swamp.

The elusive persona of Miss Abbie M. Brooks seems even more incredulous since she lived and traveled in the state for a number of years and authored two prodigious historical works on Florida. Of course, the lady herself had a penchant for anonymity. For one of these works—a classic of its kind—the unusual travel guide *Petals Plucked From Sunny Clime,* she employed the whimsical pseudonym "Silvia Sunshine."

But to this day, the most persistent scholars have been unable to trace even elemental facts about her: her birthplace, background, education, personal facets of her life, or when and where she died. Even custodians of her original works at the Library of Congress knew her only as "the remarkable Miss Brooks."

And so she was. Her travel book, *Petals,* a delightful, colorful, and graphic "ramble" over Florida of the 1870s and earlier, seems in retrospect to have been a lighthearted dalliance that blossomed into serious romance, one that would consume most of her later years and culminate in her most formidable scholarly achievement: five volumes of translations of original Spanish records covering more than three centuries of Florida's past and a book, *The Unwritten History of Old St. Augustine.*

Petals, of course, remains her most popular work, perhaps because it is so unlike the reams of travel books written about Florida during its first great tourist boom after the Civil War. The book covers the period 1876–78, and there is little that eludes the sharp and graphic pen of Silvia Sunshine, whether traditional or offbeat. *Petals* is more like a pulsing, rambling narrative, ranging from sober appraisal to critical satire, droll irony to an airy Victorian-style lyricism. Woven throughout are vignettes of legend, lore, and early history.

She briefly encapsulates Jacksonville's tourist-thronged, cosmopolitan, free-style atmosphere. Here, in a mix of celebrities, millionaires, and natives, "no costume, however peculiar, appears out of style, or the wear-

ers, as in some other places, obliged to seek protection from the police. Mar-
ket-women don the Bloomer costume without attracting any more attention
than the lazy loungers around the markethouse. The citizens are so accus-
tomed to sightseeing that nothing would astonish them but an honest politician." Later she gives us a humorous glimpse of Harriet Beecher Stowe in a
Jacksonville church where her husband is preaching. Stowe, being "so confident that her husband's sermon can be conveyed without her watchful eye,"
promptly nods off to sleep.

Silvia steamboats down the St. Johns River, thence into the forest-dark,
narrow twisting Oklawaha River, the haunt of "the genuine cracker." She
roundly rebukes "some scribblers" on Florida travel for their denigration of
this "specimen of humanity." She is aware that they are not fastidious about
their habitations ("crude dirt-floor cabins"), but "the cracker has a hearty
welcome for the stranger, which puts the blush of contempt upon those
claiming a much higher degree of civilization. All in his home is free to visitors and while the fare is not gourmet, it is bountiful . . . plates piled high"
with chicken, sweet potatoes, cornbread, and strong coffee.

A Cracker figures as the quixotic hero in one of her most amusing tales.
The account of Matt Driggers and the great mastodon hunt is almost vintage
Mark Twain.

But Silvia Sunshine does not always shine on her fellow tourists. She
castigates them for "vandalizing" pieces of St. Augustine's ancient city
gates (the city whose antiquity would come to haunt her). She classifies
three types of Florida visitor: the defiant, who assails "with vehement
irony" everything in sight; the enthusiast, whose fertile imagination gives
"exaggerated . . . highly colored" accounts of the real Florida; and the
indifferent, "an anomaly . . . why he ever thought of leaving home to travel
. . . is an unsolved problem," considering his "undemonstrative nature and
unbroken reticence" at the scenes and sights before him. "His general
appearance evinces the same amount of refinement as a polar bear, his perceptive powers the acuteness of an oyster, his stupidity greater than
Balaam's saddle-animal."

At Key West, Silvia finds a "temperate, frugal, industrious" citizenry,
busily engaged in fishing, wrecking, sponging, and cigar making. In one
cigar factory she observes "80 females," mother and daughter side by side
stripping tobacco leaf. "The daughter puffs a delicate cigarette, while the
mother smokes a huge cigar, it [the cigar] being considered a disgrace for the
young ladies to use."

She finds no such bustle on viewing "the remains" of slumbering
Tampa. She remarks on the town's "deep, sandy sidewalks . . . decaying
structures and dilapidated fences" and concludes: "The place looks discouraged from sheer weariness in trying to be a town."

The foregoing examples give an idea of the range, style, and informality of this absorbing and atypical travel guide. But it tells us nothing of Miss Brooks except that she was a professional writer of modestly independent means and suffered periodically from an unnamed illness. Extensive research later in Nashville, where *Petals* was published in 1880 by the Southern Methodist Publishing House, also proved fruitless.

But it was in St. Augustine that Miss Brooks fell under the spell of what one historian calls her "almost mystical empathy" for Florida's antiquity and its unique blend of Old and New World. And the mystery of almost 150 years of a forgotten past, "shrouded in awful obscurity," aroused in her the challenge to dig out that past. This led her to Seville, Spain, and the Archives of the Indies where she began the laborious task of transcribing in longhand, as an Archives clerk translated from the Old Spanish, more than three hundred years of records and events in Florida history, from 1500 to 1810. Returning home, probably in the latter 1880s, she would take up residence in St. Augustine where she would complete her most important and formidable achievement: five volumes of her translations, divided into periods, covering 310 years. The work was sold to the Library of Congress for three hundred dollars in April 1901. From this monumental work, one of the few of its kind ever done prior to then, she wrote *The Unwritten History of Old St. Augustine*. This was probably completed in the early 1900s, but the book carries neither the imprint of the printer nor the place and date of publication, once more precluding research about the author herself.

Judging from a copy of a typewritten note appended to this book, written to a Charles H. Coe in Washington on February 23, 1907, she may have published the book herself, and apparently her finances by then were becoming strained. She recalls the "fearful price" she had to pay to the Archives translator, but her "ambition" was such that she would publish this work "if I bankrupt myself." A copy of the book was presented to the Library on February 20, 1909.

Nevertheless, aside from the record of a street address number where she had resided in St. Augustine, Abbie Brooks, at this point, vanished from sight. She remains as much unknown as the forgotten Florida past she had labored so long—and so successfully—to uncover. One can only hope that one day some diligent and dedicated scholar will rescue from obscurity "the remarkable Miss Brooks" herself.

14.
When Mail Carriers Were Trailblazers

Whether barefooted or "acre-footed," those delivering mail in the early Florida wilderness faced a lonely and rugged task.

Today, the typical local mailman usually has a short, clear-cut, eight-to-five suburban route that he can walk, cycle, or drive at a reasonable pace without fear of wild animals or natural hazards.

But in the late nineteenth century, on both coasts of southern Florida, mailmen were almost the stuff of legend as they traipsed wilderness routes that today might span a score of cities.

On the east coast walked the barefoot mailmen, celebrated in murals, plaques, and even a novel and a movie, and one of whom became a postal martyr. On the southwest coast there was only one: a physical giant known as "Acrefoot" Johnson who walked an incredible sixty-five miles a day and quit only when the postal service refused to let him carry a back-passenger to earn a few extra dollars.

The barefoot mailman was so called because he found it much easier to walk barefooted on the hard-packed surf's edge on his sixty-six-mile jaunt from Palm Beach to the trading post village of Miami. In the early 1880s, a letter from Miami going less than eighty miles up the coast to Jupiter had to travel first to Key West, then to Cuba and up to New York, and then back by train and boat, taking six to eight weeks. But finally settlers in the Lake Worth area secured a post office—and barefoot was born.

The route was a lonely wilderness along that still sparsely settled coast where the only likely encounters were with snakes, an occasional bear or panther, and either shark or alligator at the inlets. Small skiffs were concealed in overgrowth at each inlet to provide crossing, and the one-way route was walked in three days—a six-day work week for six hundred dollars a year. The mailman usually stayed overnight in one of the small houses of refuge scattered by the government along the coast to provide shelter for shipwreck victims. The carrier walked under broiling sun, in cold rain, storms, and even hurricanes, and he traveled light. Aside from mail, his small pack usually carried matches, salt pork, potatoes or grits, and a small fry pan. But this meager fare was supplemented with the abundant supplies of fish, clams, and oysters or an occasional huge turtle egg to be procured along the way.

Despite the rugged conditions, the mail was always on time—except once. In 1886, the shipwreck of a Spanish barkentine strewed some fifty miles of beach with hundreds of 100-gallon casks of Spanish Claret, plus many smaller kegs of Malaga and Double Superior. In his pause that refreshes, the mailman paused a little too long over a keg and lost track of a full day. But many settlers along the route had also recovered kegs, and likewise, they were blissfully unaware of the delay. Sometimes the carrier would carry "foot-passengers" at five dollars per head, but few could maintain the mailman's rugged pace and the practice was soon dropped. One carrier, H. J. Burkhardt, who doffed not only his shoes but his clothes, was known as the "naked mailman." He was a sun enthusiast but was always careful to dress again when approaching settlements or wayfarers.

The most famous carrier was a strapping young Kentuckian, Ed Hamilton, age 32, who presumably met a terrible martyrdom. On October 11, 1887, Hamilton arrived on his route at Hillsborough Inlet (Pompano Beach) and found that his skiff had been taken by someone and rowed to the other side. An excellent swimmer, he decided to swim across the two-hundred-foot inlet and retrieve the skiff, after hanging his mail pouch and clothing on a sea-grape tree (where a searching party discovered them days later). He never made it back.

Many shocked coastal settlers theorized that a shark had attacked him or that a strong current had swept him out to sea. But after the main search, pioneer settler Charles W. Pierce decided to investigate the scene on his own. He knew that days before Hamilton was lost, there had been strong flood tides resulting from heavy rainstorms. He theorized that the tides probably swept the huge lairs of alligators further inland downstream to the beaches. Journeying down the inlet banks, he discovered swarms of alligators "in unusual numbers" as well as countless 'gator tracks in the shore mud. The animals were apparently trying to return to their inland lairs. The sudden, terrible conclusion seemed foregone to Pierce. Strong as he was, the young carrier would have been no match for a pack of alligators. Years later, Pierce's theory seemed almost confirmed when an inlet cruising party discovered on the bank a man's partial jawbone containing a gold-filled tooth. None of Hamilton's friends could recall if he had such a filling, but Pierce's grim theory now seemed almost certain.

The barefoot route continued, however—without another fatality—up to the early 1890s when Flagler finally brought his train as far as Miami.

In southwest Florida, 24-year-old James Mitchell "Acrefoot" Johnson (his huge feet prompting the nickname) received the contract for the first overland mail route in the area, a route running from his home area of Fort

Ogden in present-day DeSoto County to Fort Meade and Bartow sixty-five miles northward and back again. Acrefoot was a physical giant—6 feet 7½ inches and over 250 pounds—and literally strong as an ox. With his bare hands, he could grub out palmettos—a grueling task then—faster than a man could stack them, and once did so to win a bet. Too poor to buy a horse, Acrefoot chose to walk the route, a hazardous one in those days with snakes, wild animals, and alligators in abundance and few trails except those he cleared himself. But he astounded Peace River Valley settlers by walking the sixty-five miles in a day, making a twice-weekly round trip. (The unusual feat is still on postal service records.)

And he was fast. Once a settler in a horse and buggy turned to see Acrefoot suddenly walking abreast of him. He offered the mailman a ride. "No thanks," drawled the plodding carrier. "I'm in a sort of hurry."

But the super carrier was finding it difficult to get by on his monthly salary of $26—he now had a wife and eventually eight children. One day a neighbor came by to see him testing out a squat, sturdy homemade chair which he secured to his back with wide rawhide straps. At the neighbor's puzzled query, Acrefoot replied: "Well, you see, the babies are coming along now and I need to make a little more money. I'm going to take a passenger along with the mail." In response to the neighbor's retort of "That's impossible," Acrefoot had him "hop in" and then took off "at a dog trot" for a mile and then returned. Later, the astonished neighbor related: "He wasn't even winded."

But Acrefoot's novel sideline plan, which could have made his the first overland Star Mail route to carry passengers, was turned down by the post office. When an appeal was again refused, Acrefoot resigned permanently. Moving his family to Nocatee, near Arcadia, he went into business cutting crossties and cordwood for the Florida Southern Railroad then being built from Punta Gorda to Bartow. He was modestly successful and his growing family prospered. (The genetic source of Acrefoot's giant physique turned up in a grandson, J. G. Brogden, of Tampa, who at 6 feet, 10½ inches, was reported in 1957 to be the state's tallest man.)

It is not known whether Acrefoot ever offered to race the new mail train. But chances are that the "world's greatest walking mailman" would have given the sluggish woodburner a run for the money—that is, if his back passenger didn't get "foot-sick."

Villains and
Characters

15.
"Water Boy" Rules the Poshest Resort

Utilities magnate Clarence "Water Boy" Geist, snubbed by a Palm Beach club, builds his own at Boca Raton.

Clarence H. Geist was crude, profane, eccentric, overbearing (and often unbearable), but in 1928, he created at Boca Raton on Florida's Gold Coast one of the most luxurious and opulent private clubs for millionaires in the world.

Going from poor farm boy to canny horse trader to multimillionaire utilities magnate, Geist had never really shed his barnyard mannerisms or ethics, and he ruled the Boca Raton Hotel & Club like a hybrid version of Citizen Kane and Huey "Kingfish" Long—dictatorial, pompous, egocentric, and, at times, loudly boorish. He could make the most illustrious titans of steel, oil, soap, or pills feel somehow that they were there merely at his sufferance, even though they had just plunked down $5,000 in annual dues and would spend thousands more per week through the season.

Hotel historian Andrew Hepburn termed Geist a man of "arrogant pomposity" derived from "an overwhelming inferiority complex." True or not, it was said that a major motive for creating the lavish Boca Raton Club was due to a snubbing for membership in the exclusive Everglades Club of Palm Beach because of his "bizarre and uncouth" behavior. If so, then he scored a major coup in one-upmanship, for the Boca Raton Club's original building was considered to be the finest creation by the flamboyant architect Addison Mizner; the Everglades Club was Mizner's first effort.

In spite of his tyrannical bluster, the big, barrel-bodied magnate had a phobic fear of being kidnapped, and he took extreme precautions against his phantom pursuers (who, of course, never materialized). In this respect, he was almost a prototype for the late Howard Hughes. To foil his would-be nappers, he never permitted a picture to be made of himself, and there is none known of today.

Born in La Porte, Indiana, of a poor farming family, Geist had little schooling before heading out west to become a young horse trader. He later returned to Chicago to work as a railway brakeman while dabbling in developing cheap subdivisions for immigrant families. He then began investing in public utilities, and with those horse-trading skills so adaptable to juggling companies at the highest level—mainly water utilities—he soon controlled huge water companies in Philadelphia, Indianapolis, and numerous cities in between. He was nicknamed "The Water Boy" and his fortune grew until, by 1928, when he came down to Palm Beach and bought a small mansion, he had amassed $54 million.

Two years earlier, the Florida bust had busted Addison Mizner's grandiose creation, the Cloister Inn at Boca Raton, and the architect sold it for debts to Charles Dawes, a vice president of the United States, and his financier brother, Rufus. The Dawes, who had once had utility dealings with Geist, persuaded the latter of the hotel's potential, and Geist, shrewd as ever, picked up the club and its large land holdings for a song, $200,000.

Geist was never blackballed from the Everglades Club, says writer Nixon Smiley, because no one would have dared sponsor him. At any rate, he now had his very own club and he intended to make it the world's most exclusive: it would make the Everglades look like merely a fancier Howard Johnson's.

He first called in the architects Schultze and Weaver to add an additional 300 rooms (elaborate suites) while maintaining Mizner's distinctive style. The structure then totaled 450 rooms, rising six stories. The vast spacious lawns, studded with exotic flower gardens beneath towering royal palm trees, the four tennis courts and Olympic-sized swimming pool, and the rambling 18-hole golf course sprawled over some one thousand acres. There was also a marina for yachts and fishing boats ten minutes away from the ocean. One entered the Camino Real's guarded gates and rode up the winding double road around sculptured fountains to the city-block-length lobby, which contained a dazzling tropic setting of flowers, plants, shrubs, and towering kapok trees. By the time he was finished, he had spent $10 million for an edifice larger than most European castles.

Geist soon had a healthy cross-section of America's wealthiest eagerly shelling out the fat $5,000 annual club dues. (He had planned to double the dues, but the Depression intervened.) On any festive eve in the elaborate dining room, one might easily view several millions of dollars in jewels and furs on display; finicky patrons often furnished and decorated their own suites as well as the smaller cottages of their staffs. Guests could also acquire one of two hundred cabanas on the beach a mile away, to which they were bussed back and forth and where the most lavish steak cookouts were often staged.

Aside from the pink towers visible from Route One, outsiders knew little of Geist's golden "playhouse"; reporters were lepers to "The Water Boy" and forbidden entrance. The fabulously rich sought, and received, total anonymity.

But the sultan sometimes treated his glittering nabobs like trespassers. Often he would walk up to one, tap him with his cane, and half-shout, "I'm the owner of this club, who are you?" and then utter some coarse remark and guffaw on his way to another member. After a golf game, he might decline a change of clothes and stride into the lobby in only a bathrobe. Once in the elevator, he would command, "Sixth floor!" while other occupants hurriedly looked away. He was carried straight up; the others got off on the way down.

Evening movies in the auditorium didn't begin until Geist got there, no matter how long the delay. He would walk down to the front row, turn around and gaze over the assemblage, sit down, rap the floor with his cane, and loudly announce, "I'm here!" and the movie began. On the golf course, his chauffeured limousine followed him over the fairways (no electric carts then). If he didn't like a $20,000 carpet, he would simply spit on it.

He also overlorded the little town of Boca Raton (population six hundred) like some country squire, strolling about with his bodyguard and poking with his cane any nearby citizen with, "Do you know who I am?" They usually did since most of them depended for a living, directly or indirectly, on Geist.

A somewhat comic-opera scene began each season, when club employees and relatives were herded together to greet Geist when he arrived in his private railroad car. Like a grand duke, he would alight to the strains of band music and move down a receiving line shaking hands with each of his "subjects," the deity-turned-democrat; each spring, there was a reverse of the same performance. He also ran the town politically and officials were generally obeisant. He had the town charter rewritten to have elections held in February instead of November so his club staff could vote (no matter whether or not they were citizens, or spoke English).

Once, however, Geist smarted from an unexpected comeuppance when he snarled at a young golf caddy who had just lit a cigarette. "Put it out!" snapped Geist. The caddy, first startled, then angry, refused. "You can't order me around like you do everybody else." "What?" roared Geist. "Why, you old s.o.b.," the caddy retorted, "I'm going to tell you just what people really think of you," and he hotly proceeded to do just that, then threw down the golf bag and stalked away.

A stunned Geist simply stared after him while others present strained to keep a straight face. Later, Geist ordered, "Bring that kid to me. Anybody with nerve enough to tell me things like that, I want working for me." The caddy, finally located, refused Geist's offer, making perhaps a second "first" in a day.

But the mighty magnate was haunted by thoughts of death—specifically his own—and the obsessive fear of being kidnapped. He kept two burly guards on twenty-four-hour watch outside his suite and a killer police dog in his sitting room. He also began to change suites now and then, so that no one could guess his real one. But this was not enough. He finally had a private elevator built to his suite and kept the key to it under guard. At the club entrance, shotguns and pistols were always within easy reach of the guards. He once had all members of the club staff fingerprinted to see if any had a criminal record. He refused to let any picture of him be taken, and he kept one of the largest checking accounts in the world, with at least a million dollars in ready cash for any sudden ransom need.

This paranoid jousting with invisible foes amused a number of his cronies, such as one of them who wryly observed: "Nobody who knew him would want to kidnap him; if they did, they would have regretted it."

By 1938, Geist felt at least secure enough to relax his vigil somewhat. But unfortunately, he died that same year, at age 71.

In its day, the Boca Raton was probably the most exclusive millionaire's club in the world, but it never paid for itself. Geist left it $100,000 a year for five years for upkeep, but the army took it over in 1942 for a radar training school. It later passed successively through the hands of such tycoons as J. Myer Schine and Arthur Vining Davis. Today it is a popular resort hotel— popular in the sense that middle-class folk register there.

But never before and never since has there been so lavish and opulent a monument to ultra-exclusive privilege as in the decade when "Water Boy" Geist built a playhouse for millionaires but ruled it, as often as not, like a barnyard.

16.
A Murder Born of Blind Ambition

*The disappearance of a Palm Beach County judge and his wife
exploded into the state's most celebrated murder trial.*

Political corruption sometimes takes on such bizarre and baffling forms that the very term "corruption" seems to redefine itself.

Such was the case more than thirty years ago in Palm Beach County when a distinguished circuit judge, Curtis E. Chillingworth, 58, and his wife, Marjorie, 57, disappeared from their beach home at Manalapan, just south of Palm Beach, on June 15, 1955. There were no solid clues, witnesses, or corpus delicti; the couple was never found. For more than five years the case would baffle authorities—and then it would explode into the most celebrated murder trial in Florida's history.

Joseph Alexander Peel, Jr., the only municipal judge of West Palm Beach, was a popular political figure in his home town. In 1955, at 31, he had been re-elected to his second term on the bench. After graduation from Stetson Law School in 1949, he also had served as a city prosecutor and once was picked "man of the year" by the Junior Chamber of Commerce. Lean, wavy-haired, and handsome, with a sharp intelligence and much personal charm, Peel had a political firmament that seemed to glitter with promise. He had an attractive wife, Imogene, and two children. He exuded a "Southern gentleman" style, often dressing in white linen suits, and he drove an air-conditioned Cadillac; Imogene drove a Lincoln Continental. But while his lifestyle mirrored the elegance of an ad in the *New Yorker,* his salary (roughly three thousand dollars a year) suggested something closer to Sears, Roebuck. The opulent image seemed awry. It was.

Judge Peel had a highly lucrative partnership with two kingpins in the country's thriving bolita and moonshine liquor rackets; they were Floyd "Lucky" Holzapfel, a local mechanic and ex-con, and George "Bobby" Lincoln, a poolroom and taxicab owner. Warrants for police raids on moonshine and bolita nests had to come from Peel; he demanded payment from all of them for "tip-off" protection. From this lush enterprise, the trio often took in three thousand dollars a week.

Cupidity infected Peel's private practice, too. Once already, in 1953, he had stood before the stern Judge Chillingworth on a charge of representing both parties in a divorce action. Peel was relieved at getting off with a sharp public reprimand. But he faced the judge again in 1955 after falsely telling a woman her divorce was final and she later, unwittingly, committed bigamy.

Word reached Peel that the incensed senior judge would "break" him this time. This meant only one thing: disbarment. A panic-stricken Peel hastily obtained a hearing continuance until June 15. His golden sideline, his whole future, was about to collapse. His partners, too, saw the writing on the wall. So when the threesome huddled together one night and Peel bluntly told them, "We'll have to get rid of the judge," they readily agreed.

During the five years after the Chillingworths' disappearance, Peel's moves were erratic. After getting off with a ninety-day bar suspension, he inexplicably resigned his judgeship. In May 1959, he quit law, sold his practice, and organized an investment firm, Investment Capital Corp. (ICC). He still met occasionally with his ex-partners, who remained in the rackets, along with two other fringe underworld figures, bail bondsman P. O. "Jim" Wilbur, an ex-cop, and James Yenzer, an insurance agent.

Yenzer and Holzapfel often drank together, and one night, the loquacious, boastful Holzapfel vaguely suggested that he, Holzapfel, had something to do with the Chillingworth case. This disturbed Yenzer but he said nothing and just listened. In this same period, Lincoln slipped and drew five years at a Tallahassee federal center for moonshining, while Holzapfel drew fifteen years for an aborted arms hijacking. But Holzapfel appealed and Wilbur got him free on bail.

The Chillingworth case seemed all but closed when, in November 1958, the body of moonshiner Lew Harvey of Jacksonville was found floating in a canal near West Palm Beach. (His slayers, Holzapfel and Lincoln, mistook him for an informer.) Since two counties were involved, the Florida Sheriff's Bureau sent an agent, Henry Lovern, to work on the murder.

Lovern resembled a citified Li'l Abner—shy, slow-talking, easygoing, constantly chewing gum. The air was deceptive. The former army intelligence agent and political science graduate of Florida State University was bright and stubborn.

Drifting about the edges of Palm Beach County's underworld, he met Yenzer one day, and they began chatting about the Harvey case. When Yenzer mentioned knowing something about the Chillingworth case, Lovern almost stopped chewing. But he covered his surprise by feigning indifference. Yenzer, somewhat piqued, persisted, adding that Peel was connected also. Lovern, chewing casually now, said he doubted the bureau would be interested in anything but the Harvey case. The two men parted amiably. Lovern then raced excitedly downtown to check out some of Yenzer's statements. They clicked. He called his supervisor, Ross Anderson, who told him to keep on it while continuing to work on the Harvey case.

But Lovern was in no hurry with his fishing; he sensed a whopper on the other end and he reeled his line with care. During the rest of 1959 and 1960, he persuaded first Yenzer, then Wilbur, to become undercover agents for the bureau. Meanwhile, Holzapfel, fearful for his appeal, jumped bail and fled to Brazil. Peel, who wanted to kill Holzapfel for talking to Yenzer about the Chillingworths, nevertheless made Holzapfel a partner in ICC and then encouraged his flight to Brazil, providing the funds for it.

Then Lovern got Wilbur to lure Holzapfel back to Florida. The fugitive arrived at a Melbourne motel in September 1960. Joined at once by Yenzer and Wilbur, the three went on a four-day drinking spree during which Holzapfel gushed the whole Chillingworth affair. In a room next door, Lovern and Anderson quietly recorded him on tape.

Events moved swiftly. Holzapfel was jailed without bond; Lincoln, in jail, gave the critically needed confession after promise of immunity; then Holzapfel confessed, and Lovern traced Peel to Chattanooga, where he arrested him in November 1960. Peel pleaded not guilty.

In March 1961, in a Fort Pierce courtroom, Peel's three-week trial began. The room was packed daily for the most publicized trial in Florida history. Peel, defended by ex-Stetson classmate Carlton Welch, kept his confident, smiling mien throughout the trial, wife Imogene always nearby. But the grim-faced prosecutor, Phil O'Connell, who once gave young law graduate Peel free office space to get him started, now pounded relentlessly for the death penalty as the horrid details of a brutal and heinous crime unfolded.

At 1 A.M. that June 15, Holzapfel and Lincoln gained entrance to the beach home on a ruse, bound both judge and wife, and led them to their waiting boat. Holzapfel struck the wife when she screamed once and struggled on the beach staircase. Far offshore, Holzapfel fitted weights around the diminutive woman's waist and lifted her, while the judge shouted to her, "Remember, I love you," and she answered, "I love you, too." Then a loud splash. The judge twisted and forced himself overboard and, still bound, began swimming away but was caught by the pair and drowned with a crude concrete anchor.

The pair returned to shore before daylight and called Peel with a pre-arranged message: "The motor's fixed."

On March 30, Peel was convicted as an accessory before the fact of first-degree murder and sentenced to life. In April 1962, he also drew eighteen years for mail fraud with his ICC firm. Thus, after parole from Raiford in August 1980, he went straight to a federal prison hospital after developing cancer of the colon, liver, and lung. Given only weeks to live, he won a federal parole on June 24, 1982, and went to live in Jacksonville. Then, on July 1, 1982, in a newspaper interview given just four days before his death, the fallen political star confessed for the first time to his guilt in the murders of Judge and Mrs. Chillingworth.

17.
Pogy Bill: Outlaw to Lawman

Pogy changed from a brawling rowdy into a peace-keeping sheriff, but his view of law became too flexible.

He could be as volatile and tempestuous as the frothy, roiling waters of the great Lake Okeechobee in a wild storm, or as ornery-tough as the catfish he wrestled from that vast inland sea to earn his daily bread.

Of all the colorful souls who were nurtured in the muck and mud of that raw frontier of lake and sawgrass country in its earliest settling days, one William E. ("Pogy Bill") Collins rivaled any in memory. When he wasn't hauling his nets from the lake, he was indulging his favorite pastimes: drinking, gambling, and fighting, especially the latter.

With his long, lean frame and powerful arms, his brawling prowess quickly earned him the undisputed kingship over even the toughest of his rowdy fishermen brethren. He might have to fling one crashing through a hard cypress wall or even dispatch a half-dozen of them unceremoniously out a barroom door in order to assert his right to reign. But no one ever challenged him—successfully.

And when these boisterous fisherfolk were not battering each other, after the bulging net hauls were traded for bulging rolls of cash which in turn were swapped for gallons of liquid lightning, they were good-naturedly indulging another shoreside recreation: literally tearing the town apart.

Town merchants and citizens in Okeechobee City and surrounding settlements came to dread the arrival of the fishing boats; it could herald (and usually did) a night of smashed windows, splintered store fronts, or one or more innocent heads bonked. Area authorities seemed almost helpless in efforts to prevent these revelling rampages. Pogy Bill, after all, took his sovereignty seriously.

And thereby hangs the story of how the legendary lawless ruler of the great lake country early in this century became an equally legendary law enforcer on the same primitive frontier—the metamorphosis from town ruffian to town marshal to Sheriff Pogy Bill, stalwart citizen. Of course, it wasn't easy.

Pogy Bill's early origins are sketchy. He was born to American parents on an American vessel in the harbor of Sydney, Australia, and spent his early teens working on cargo ships until, tiring of the rough and strenuous existence, he jumped a ship at Buenos Aires and made his way across the Andes to Chile's Pacific coast and, from there, to Tampa where he took a job as a boilermaker. While there, he dabbled in Tampa's rough politics so successfully that rival factions imported a pugilist to ease him out of the game. Instead, Pogy laid the pugilist out, thereby fixing his fisticuff renown early on.

In 1910, Pogy became a fisherman on Lake Okeechobee. The wild, rough, exciting calling plus the frontier spirit and the excellent pay were a natural attraction to a man with similar spirits. Within a short time, he had his own fish camp. He derived his nickname, it is recorded, when he once tried to market some bony, inedible fish called "pogies," which were commonly used only for bait. But for the rest of his life, he assumed the name, and no one ever thought of referring to him by any other.

Pogy's undaunted pugilistic prowess, after many scars and battles, soon earned him the tacit leadership of the rugged lake fishermen. Once, a rival camp owner, Buck Tillman, invited Pogy and his crew to celebrate his building of a new cypress wood camp and kitchen (most camps had only tarpaper shanties). But as the voluble quantities of food and whiskey diminished, the cordiality did likewise, and the party got contentious. So much so that Pogy threw a haymaker that sent one brawny rival clear through a sturdy cypress wall. As others intervened, he similarly hurled them, one by one, through any aperture he could find—or make. When the dust had settled, only the roof of the new structure remained, and it hung precariously. No one had ever been known to best Pogy in a fight, although one tenacious combatant won at least a technical point by refusing to separate his teeth from Pogy's finger until that member was crunchingly separated from the rest of Pogy.

But Bill had a code of fairness, too, especially for innocent victims in unequal struggles. The town baker, Albert Berka, a Viennese immigrant, was awakened one night by ten very drunk and very hungry fishermen who demanded food. He consented to serve them but became fearful for his safety when, over the drunken yells, he heard pistol shots and ran to see his rows of canned fruit punctured and spurting juice like so many fountains. Fortunately, Pogy suddenly appeared on the scene and, with judicial sternness, asked the baker, "Will $25 apiece pay for this mess?" It was less a query than an order, and soon the grateful baker had in hand exactly $250.

But the "roughest, toughest catfisherman who ever tore up Tantie [Okeechobee City]" was becoming too much for the law-abiding folk—and for the justice of the peace, Judge H. H. Hancock. Once, when several miscreant cronies were brought to court (Dr. Darrow's drugstore) for disposition, Pogy had friends disarm the marshall and then delayed the judge somehow while Pogy himself presided on the bench. Bill then solemnly found all guilty, fined them a quart of liquor each, payable at once, and then adjourned court to Mr. Bryant's Rough House saloon on Taylor's Creek.

A fuming Judge Hancock vowed to capture Pogy. The judge became even more irritated when Pogy sent word that he would gladly dump His Honor into the lake. Finally, with the aid of some sturdy local cowhands, Pogy was arrested, slapped into a makeshift "boxcar" jail, then brought into court. A crowd of armed and angry fishermen looked on as a glowering Pogy watched the judge leaf through what looked like a store catalog (statute book). Pogy suddenly blurted, "I ain't gonna be sentenced with no damned Sears, Roebuck catalog," whereupon he turned the table over, spilling a water pitcher into the judge's lap. His waterlogged Honor promptly slapped on Pogy a ninety-day term in the Fort Pierce jail.

But the pressure to commute Pogy's sentence became so great that Judge Hancock decided to go personally and talk to the offender. They had a long talk, and the end result left everyone nonplussed. Pogy agreed not only to use his considerable talents in law-abiding pursuits but, upon his immediate release, also sought and was given appointment as town marshal, a job hitherto void of applicants.

Few brought more firsthand knowledge of the ways of lawbreakers to a job, and within a short time, Pogy was fighting, jailing, and generally subduing many of his former cronies. He was then elected sheriff of Okeechobee County, a post he would hold for fourteen years.

But Pogy's regeneration was not merely confined to cleaning up fighting, gambling, and other nefarious activities. He saw the need for healthy energy outlets and was soon organizing sports activities, especially a town baseball team which he gently but firmly "coaxed" both natives and newcomers to join.

It was a personal "new" Pogy, too. He had already given up drinking and smoking and was soon married to a nice local girl and settled into a new home. He collected a small library to begin a process of self-education, and once even took a fling at the theater in a local amateur production of the "Men's Flapper Chorus" which, for the benefit of the Eastern Star, local ads urged readers to be sure to see "Pogy Bill's $1,000,000 legs." In the great 1928 hurricane-flood, in which more than two thousand perished, his services were invaluable since he knew everyone on the lake and could quickly identify all victims.

His special concerns were children and the needy. It was said he never had a dime because he gave it all away. Having no children of his own, he was the unofficial father of every orphan in the county. "Every widow or family in distress was likely to find some groceries, clothes or shoes on the doorstep," a contemporary noted, and they also knew the unknown party it came from—Pogy. He organized a Boy Scout troop and raised the funds to keep it going.

By 1928, the *Okeechobee News,* noting Pogy's growing statewide reputation, opined that since his "wild fighting career," he had become one of the country's "best citizens" and "one of the best officers in the state." All true enough—but it was not to last. Prohibition, that "impossible burden" of all law enforcement, would end the saga of Pogy Bill.

No drinker himself, Pogy was still against Prohibition. "It's the bunk," he declared. But on the other hand, he was not going to let "bootleggers set up and run wild" in Okeechobee. He proved this by flushing out any number of stills over the county. When Scarface Al Capone sent some hoods prospecting into Okeechobee as an "ideal site" for a liquor depot, Pogy let them know that they would have a very uncomfortable time of it. They looked elsewhere.

In that vast lake country of undergrowth, scrub, and hammock, so ideally adapted for concealing what has been estimated at hundreds of "stump lightning" stills, the enforcement task was not unlike draining the lake with a spoon. "I'm spending all my time just trying to keep those fellows from selling the stuff in the post office," Pogy once complained.

But Pogy had his own code for supervising the bootleggers, views not quite in line with the federal regulators. Moreover, hard times and much grim poverty had hit the lake country in the late twenties, and this was a sensitive sore for the large-hearted lawman. In 1929, Pogy and his deputy were caught guarding the road while some hootch was being loaded in barrels in some hollowed-out lumber railroad cars, unbeknownst to the lumber company.

Pogy was tried twice in Miami in 1931; the first jury hung, the second convicted. He received a six-year sentence, reduced after appeal to probation. He resigned his post but only, he said, to save Governor Doyle Carlton embarrassment since ninety percent of Okeechobeeans petitioned the latter not to accept the resignation. In 1932, he once again ran for his old post but lost—by three votes. Later, he took a job as police chief in Frostproof, to which the city fathers were "delighted" to appoint him. Then, in 1934, enroute to a fire, the fire truck overturned, pinning him beneath it. He died several days later of injuries complicated by pneumonia.

Pogy's death was mourned throughout the lake country and in much of the state. The region of the big lake would never seem quite the same, people felt. And so they remembered. They remembered so well that, more than a generation later, a candidate for sheriff of Okeechobee felt obliged to promise that, if elected, "I'll try to run this county the way that Pogy Bill would want it to be run." That epitaph alone would doubtless have more than pleased the late high sheriff himself.

18.
Sir Gregor MacGregor: Would-be Conqueror

The Scottish adventurer sought to seize Florida from Spain and sell it to the highest bidder.

Of all the early maverick idealists, adventurers, plunderers, and would-be conquerors who haunted Spanish Florida's turbulent frontier in the early nineteenth century—Nicholls, Panton, McGillivray, Bowles, McIntosh, McGirth—none compared in grandiose ambition or audacity with a wily British soldier of fortune called Sir General Gregor MacGregor.

The title of knighthood may have been less the king's idea than MacGregor's, but the Scotsman's bold design to seize the Floridas, East and West, from Spain and deliver them to the United States was as authentic as it was quixotic. And for a brief moment in history, this grand project came near succeeding when MacGregor hoisted his Green Flag of Florida over a valuable chunk of the Spanish crown's real estate near Jacksonville, the fourth flag to fly over the territory since the American Revolution. Plans for a second invasion into Tampa Bay to sew up the entire peninsula were later frustrated, but for one glorious moment, even Secretary of State John Quincy Adams eyed the venture with keen interest since Florida was considered a natural if not official appendage of the new republic.

However, piracy, lawlessness, raids, and renegades proved an unsavory mixture with the heady brew of colonial liberation, and this toxic potion would undo the best-laid plans.

Nevertheless, in a cavalier style worthy of Walter Scott, preceded by a preposterous bluff that left Spanish authorities red-faced, the youthful MacGregor's grand expedition assumed, at times, an aspect of pure opera bouffe while dramatically marking Spain's declining power in the New World.

The two most important ports in the Floridas then were Pensacola westward and Amelia Island on the east; the latter, guarded by Fort San Carlos, was the general's target.

Gregor MacGregor had served as a British officer under the Duke of Wellington, hero of Waterloo, in the Napoleonic Wars when his imagination was fired by the spirit of rebellion in Spain's New World colonies. At age 25, he went to Caracas in Venezuela, married, and joined the army of Simón

Bolívar, patron liberator of Venezuela, in 1816. He was lauded by Bolívar for his distinguished service as a general.

But his calculating eye was turned mainly to the Floridas where, with shrewd Scottish prescience, he perceived both the shaky grasp in which Spain held them and the future territorial imperatives of a burgeoning U.S. frontier. Explaining his goals to Baltimore postmaster J. Skinner, he aimed to "wrest Florida from Spain" and encourage "the existing disposition of the people in that section to confederate with the United States, leaving it to the will and policy of the government . . . to indicate the most favorable time for their admission into the Union." MacGregor, of course, was not solely motivated by altruism. True to his Scottish blood, he hoped to secure a bonnie price for the Florida lands. In fact, Secretary Adams noted at the time that if the price were not "bonnie" enough, "there is some reason to suppose that he [MacGregor] had made indirect overtures of similar nature to the British government."

But his exuberant confidence and distinguished military record, not to mention official Washington's discreetly covetous views of the territory, served him well in his travels up and down the U.S. coast seeking support. A group of merchants in Savannah, for example, contributed generously after agreeing with MacGregor to buy thirty thousand Florida acres at one dollar each after the conquest. Young men of good family in Charleston, along with some War of 1812 veterans, volunteered to serve, but many of the "recruits" were of rougher and more mercenary inclinations.

MacGregor shrewdly estimated that he would need artillery to soften up the enemies' ranks; indeed, his strategy might easily rank him as a pioneer in psychological warfare. Sending a disguised agent ahead to mingle among the soldiers and residents, the agent spoke in awed tones of the formidable might of this "army of 1,000 men," their ruthless skill and daring, and the likely helplessness of any small garrison (i.e., Fort San Carlos) to withstand them. So effective was this propaganda that half the residents fled their homes almost at once. (Actually, MacGregor had only 150, not 1,000, men, and used only 55 musketeers for the initial attack.) On the day of invasion, June 29, 1817, the Scotsman parked five modest-sized vessels in the harbor for show. He then approached the fort under cover of the woods and creeks and ingeniously deployed his men to converge toward the fort in groups of two or three from several sides, thus giving the impression that each group was merely the advance guard of a much larger force.

Meanwhile, within the fort, a frightened commandant, Colonel Francisco Morales, shrugged and queried to no one in particular: "What can I do?" He then surrendered the garrison without a shot fired and dutifully signed MacGregor's articles of capitulation.

A fort resident, Mrs. Susan L'Engle, recalled the scene. "A splendid army!" she wrote. "Every man with a long green plume in his hat—*muy hermoso*. [The plumes were really only stalks of the profuse dog-fennel plant.]

"They marched quietly into the city, took possession of the abandoned houses [where the inhabitants had fled], and made themselves comfortable. Their chief, Sir Gregor, who was a splendid-looking man . . . established himself in the largest and finest house in town. He assumed great style; sentinels paced before his door, and formalities had to be observed to gain approach to him."

MacGregor promised to protect the settlers remaining, let others return, and give them time to sell their property if they did not care to "join the standard of independence." He then hoisted the Green Cross of Florida over the fort.

At St. Augustine, Spanish Governor Jose Coppinger was so enraged by this defeat that he slapped Colonel Morales in irons, court-martialed him, and had him sentenced to die, although the execution was later commuted.

But the general's funds had been already extravagantly depleted, and the Green Cross Republic quickly turned to more dubious sources of revenue. Thus, MacGregor fatefully permitted Fernandina to be a port of entry for pirates and even commissioned several of his own privateers to prey on Spanish ships. After failing in efforts to get area settlers to join forces with him against St. Augustine, he quietly ignored the depredations of his more renegade followers who began plundering plantations up and down the St. Johns River, taking property and slaves to be sold for the Green Cross treasury. But with no steady payroll for his troops, operations, and other supplies, and with his forces steadily dwindling from desertions, MacGregor began to despair of his grand scheme. At the same time, a militia of settlers joined the Spanish in a plan to drive MacGregor out. On learning of it, the general sought outside aid, unsuccessfully; his American backers saw only dim prospects for a quick return of their investments and pointedly rebuffed him. When the militia-Spanish attack came on September 10, MacGregor had already delegated command to two assistants and betook himself to his brig in the harbor, ready for a hasty departure to "regroup" himself in the event of defeat. In this first round, MacGregor's men were thrown back into the fort, and had they pressed this route, the attackers might easily have taken the garrison since their force numbered three hundred strong to about eighty somewhat demoralized men inside.

But while the victors tarried, an event straight out of some slapstick comedy occurred. The men inside, certain now of defeat, haphazardly expressed this mood by firing aimlessly over the parapets and sending a few heavier shells into the air at random. A few of the stray missiles landed in the midst of the opposing forces and threw them into complete panic. The

Spanish major in charge ordered full-scale retreat while the bedraggled men within stared in exultant disbelief. (The major was soon after relieved of his command and jailed.) The Green Crossers had won by freak accident.

But MacGregor saw the handwriting on the wall. The few remaining men were a wild, unstable lot, made even more so by scanty rations and no pay for long weeks, plus a debt-ridden treasury. It is not surprising, therefore, that when the notorious French privateer (legal pirate) Luis Aury sailed into Amelia Harbor a few days later, MacGregor sold him the fort and all its arms and properties for $50,000—enough to pay his men, plus the "Republic's" debts, plus a modest profit for the general. The island soon became a hotbed of piratical and criminal activity, especially slave-smuggling, the latter finally prompting the United States to land two hundred men on the island. Aury screamed his protests, all the while packing his bags for a quick exit. Secretary Adams answered Governor Coppinger's diatribes by sarcastically observing that "if Spain could have protected her own territory the U.S. would not have had to do it for her."

Meanwhile, MacGregor had sailed for Nassau, where the British Captain George Woodbine persuaded him that Tampa Bay could be successfully invaded with some recently disbanded veterans, some freed black slaves, and over one thousand Indians who would join them at the bay for a sweep up the entire state. In early 1818, a skeptical but still hopeful MacGregor ordered R. C. Ambrister plus some blacks and Indians to hit Tampa Bay and move up the coast while he sailed to England to raise funds, arms, and supplies. But the Ambrister force accidentally stumbled into a camp set up that April by General Andrew Jackson near the Suwannee River and were promptly arrested. Ambrister and Alexander Arbuthnot, a British merchant, were shortly thereafter executed by Jackson for inciting the Indians. It marked the end of MacGregor's dream of Florida conquest.

The next few years found MacGregor privateering among the West Indies, seizing an island here and there, and later capturing the then Porto Bello in Nicaragua, where he wangled a concession of several million acres from the Indians and promptly entitled himself "His Highness Gregor, Cacique of Poyas." He was last heard of some twenty years later, still alive but inactive and living quietly on his retirement pay as a general in Bolívar's army, but doubtless recalling now and then how close he came to his "impossible dream."

19.
The Boat Captain Who Was a Spy

Miami's Hermann Schroetter was part of one of the most elusive Nazi espionage rings in America—until he got caught.

The spate of U.S. spy stories in recent years calls to mind the case almost fifty years ago of the first and only Floridian ever convicted of espionage.

The story's characters were diverse, from the crafty Nazi spy leader, a protege of Heinrich Himmler, to his attractive teen-age "Mata Hari," but it had only a tragic denouement for the Floridian.

The late 1930s were halcyon years for German espionage in America. In terms of security, the country was wide open. Data on defense plants, armaments, industrial production, army and navy installations, shipping and cargo movements, and much else was exposed to almost casual scrutiny by a host of Nazi agents fanned across the country. They operated with deadly efficiency. Details of the United States' top-secret Norden bomb sight were in Nazi hands as early as 1937. Data on U.S. aviation technology enabled Hitler to have his Luftwaffe combat-ready by 1939 and hence able to go to war long before he otherwise might have. Monitored shipping, especially any bound for Great Britain, gave Nazi U-boats a heyday. Not until 1941 was the FBI, with assistance from British intelligence, able to smash most of the major spy rings. And one such ring led them to Miami.

Along Miami's waterfront in the early 1930s, John Charles Post was familiarly known as "Captain Jack," operator of a fishing and sightseeing charter boat called *Echoes of the Past*. Post enjoyed his work, but business was slow. So in late 1935 he sold the boat and opened a parking lot near the West Flagler Kennel Club. In this same period, he also worked as a cook at the Greyhound Club, a popular hangout for servicemen from the Opa-Locka naval air station.

Fortyish, heavyset, with close-cropped blond hair and a conspicuous scar on his cheek, Post lived a quiet, retiring life with his wife in their home on Thirty-third Avenue. They were considered solid citizens. Once, Post was the first to be called upon to serve as a voter registration clerk in the local precinct, a job he performed with "polite efficiency," the city clerk recalled. The couple seldom socialized, but Post corresponded often with a friend in New York, a man about his own age. One day in July 1941, the friend, accompanied by a pretty young woman he called his secretary, made a surprise visit to Post. The two men huddled for a lengthy talk, and then the man and the woman went on to Key West. But the visit had left Captain Jack visibly disturbed.

Then, weeks later, on September 3, Miami breakfasters studied an anxious gaze peering out from a large photograph alongside the lead front-page story of the *Miami Herald*. The photo was Post's, but the caption bore another name, Carl Hermann Schroetter, and the story told of his arrest by the FBI as a "stationary agent" for a major Nazi spy ring. An angry Schroetter, held under $25,000 bond, protested his innocence, claiming he was a "victim of circumstances." He later learned his arrest was triggered by the July visit of his New York friend. His friend was Karl Frederick Ludwig, one of the most elusive Nazi spy masters in America. He had been arrested days earlier, along with his 18-year-old secretary, Lucy Rita Boehmler, and six other members of a New York-based ring.

Schroetter, Swiss-born and German-educated, came to America in 1913 and later became a citizen. He assumed the alias of Post when he settled in Miami in 1930 and gave his birthplace as Marshall, Texas. (The FBI confirmed that his U.S.-born wife had no knowledge of her husband's espionage activities.) Since 1920, Schroetter had made five trips to Germany to visit his sister living there. His last trip coincided with Hitler's 1939 invasion of Poland, and before his return home, a Nazi official contacted him and suggested he get in touch with Ludwig. Schroetter then began a frequent correspondence with Ludwig during 1940 and 1941. Schroetter later insisted that the prime inducement for his association with Ludwig was the welfare of Schroetter's sister.

Ludwig, 48, born in Fremont, Ohio, but raised in Germany from age 2, was a successful Munich businessman who wanted to "do something" for the Reich. His friend, Heinrich Himmler, encouraged him to go to New York and recruit a spy ring, primarily from members of the pro-Nazi German-American Bund. Ludwig did so and soon had a small, tightly knit group that was supplying the Abwehr (the Nazi CIA) with vital defense data and ship and convoy schedules. In Lucy, the attractive blonde born in Stuttgart, Germany, and raised in New York, Ludwig found a cool and efficient companion. Together they toured by auto from New York to Key West, visiting and photographing defense plants and army and navy bases, with Lucy providing the perfect foil and lure on these travels. They often picked up hitchhiking servicemen; lonely soldiers and sailors were flattered by Lucy's attentions and talked freely about their units. At the spy trial later, a juror described Lucy as a "Teutonic image of uncommon beauty" but with some "essential coldbloodedness." Lucy would tell the jurors that she joined the ring simply because "it sounded like a lot of fun." She had pleaded guilty and was a major prosecution witness.

But by 1941, the FBI, aided by British agents and an ingenious double agent, William Sebold, began picking up the spies one by one. In June 1941, U.S. officials arrested thirty-three New York-based agents. The crafty Ludwig remained at large until an alert British female censor in Bermuda became suspicious of one of his many typewritten letters to Europe and, after much chemical testing, discovered invisible ink messages on the back of each letter. Slowly the FBI traced the writer's code name, "Joe K.," to Ludwig, and G-men kept him under twenty-four-hour watch.

Ludwig, sensing the closing net, made his hasty visit to Schroetter that July, hoping to flee by boat to Cuba. Schroetter informed Ludwig he had long since sold his charter boat and would be unable to come by another boat anytime soon. Later, after returning to New York to retrieve his vital papers, Ludwig headed to Seattle—with FBI agents in hot pursuit. The spy master hoped to get a ship to Japan and was arrested just before reaching his port.

Schroetter, who apparently had furnished some data to Ludwig on the Opa-Locka naval air station, the Richmond air base, and foreign shipping, had pleaded guilty but with such faltering equivocation that the prosecutor offered to let him withdraw the plea and stand trial. Schroetter declined. At the trial in March 1942, he drew ten years in prison. Lucy, who pleaded guilty and testified against her cohorts, was sentenced to five years. Ludwig and most of the nine-member ring drew the maximum twenty years. (Had their espionage occurred in wartime, they would have been executed.)

But Schroetter protested the "severity" of his sentence. "I was more or less pushed into the case," he told the court. "What I have done is to protect somebody's life. I agreed to do something, but when I was contacted, I refused to go through with it," referring to Ludwig's boat request. He added that he was "coerced" into working for Ludwig because of his sister in Germany. (The court possibly considered such mitigation on giving the Miamian the lesser sentence.)

As he entered his cell at the Atlanta federal prison, the former boat captain must have wistfully, and ruefully, recalled his former vessel, *Echoes of the Past,* echoes of a simpler, peaceful time. Ten days later, on March 30, the Justice Department issued a brief statement noting that the prisoner Carl Hermann Schroetter had slashed his wrists with the diaphragm of a radio headset and then hung himself with a bed sheet tied to a utility pipe in his cell.

20.
Demagoguery Wins the Governorship

Sidney Catts rode a tide of bigotry and prejudice right into the governor's mansion.

Like a dark political cloud, he rose out of the Florida panhandle, gathering thunderous volume and drenching the state in its stormiest and most ignominious election in history.

Sidney J. Catts, a self-styled preacher and insurance salesman, was a political nonentity even up to the start of the 1916 Florida gubernatorial race. But he had shrewdly assessed the latent political power of the state's apathetic Cracker electorate, voters long ignored by the primarily urban-based political parties of the early twentieth century. He listened to their grievances and frustrations, but he took special note of their fears and prejudices. It was those biases he shamelessly exploited while he rode a tide of religious and class bigotry right into the governor's mansion. In the process, he would fracture the state's Democratic party structure, defeat four of its native stalwarts, and plunge Florida into bitter religious turmoil, mired in an irrational, almost psychotic, anti-Catholic sentiment.

Catts was very much a part of the genre of Deep South demagogues of that era: the Watsons, Tillmans, Vardemans, and Heflins. Two of them, in fact, would be his mentors of a sort.

Born July 31, 1863, at Pleasant Hill, Alabama, Catts had no sooner acquired a law degree from Cumberland University in 1882 when he felt "a call" to be a Baptist minister. After marrying Alice May Campbell, he was pastor of several Alabama churches until 1903, at which time politics proved to be a stronger, though less divine, calling. He ran against the demagogic J. Tom Heflin for an Alabama congressional seat. This proved an indelible lesson; he would not forget the tactics Heflin used to defeat him and four others.

In 1911, Catts moved his family to DeFuniak Springs, Florida. Here he was pastor of a church for a brief time before he resigned to sell life insurance. As he traversed the panhandle's isolated small towns and hamlets, listening to the grievances and woes of what he termed "the little people"— farmers, fishermen, and laborers—he sensed before him a vast political pool, hitherto untapped, and he began quietly making plans to enter the 1916 governor's race. He confided his plans to, and enlisted the aid of, another salesman, a sympathetic and affable native Cracker named Jerry Carter. (Carter, witty and even-tempered, the one man capable of balancing Catts's excesses, would prove the more durable of the two in future state political elections.)

But Catts needed an issue, a "battle cry." Taking a cue from Heflin, he found one ready-made. A rising tide of nationalism in the United States prior to World War I had somehow fostered a virulent strain of anti-Catholicism, especially in the South, where the notorious white supremacist, Tom Watson of Georgia, had begun organizing a secret society, the Guardians of Liberty, with two major aims: to oppose foreign immigration and Roman Catholicism. Clubs of Guardians began proliferating in north Florida, and by 1916, they posed a powerful bloc with an estimated forty thousand members. These clubs, led by firebrand Pennsylvanian Bill Parker, were already fanning the flames of religious bigotry when Catts entered the scene; he quickly embraced the Guardians' political support.

At this time, most of Florida's 921,618 citizens lived in rural areas, almost half of them in west and north Florida. The state's 24,658 Catholics made up less than three percent of this population. But as 1916 approached,

Governor Sidney J. Catts was sworn into office in 1917. (Florida State Archives)

Catts was already inciting an intense emotionalism among rural crowds as he warned of a "sinister Romish conspiracy" that controlled most of the state's political machines, the press, and corporate special interests.

A man of irascible temper, Catts nevertheless cast an imposing presence on the stump—six feet, two hundred pounds, with a wild shock of red hair, he had a compelling Cracker rhetoric, a droll and biting humor interlaced with solemn scriptural allusions (often suggesting he somehow had a corner on divine favor), punctuated now and then with the dramatic. Speaking solemnly and vaguely of a shadowy "Jesuit menace," he would lower his voice to confide the latest report of a Catholic plot to assassinate him. Pausing with due effect, his voice would then rise shrilly as he thrust both hands into coat pockets, grasping two pistols that were "loaded in every chamber" to take care of such exigencies. Or he would titillate his listeners with dark hints of "the goings-on" in convents and how he would have them opened up to public inspection.

But Catts's candidacy was not even suspected by the State Democratic Executive Committee when it met January 6, 1916, to adopt a resolution intended to head off the injection of religious or racist issues into the campaign in the wake of strident Guardians' activities. The committee declared that voters should not be influenced by religious considerations or by secret groups promoting such hostile activities. Ineptly drawn, the resolution with its undemocratic nuances provoked a storm of protest statewide. It was rescinded February 24, but not before Catts, almost ready to drop out of the race, turned it into a cause célèbre by persuading crowds that the resolution was directed solely against him and was a plot to "Romanize" Florida by denying anti-Catholics the ballot.

The furor catapulted his candidacy from obscurity to major status, but it inflamed an already seething religious turmoil. Said the Jacksonville *Times-Union:* "We may now look for the nastiest, most abusive campaign that Florida has ever known." And state historian W. T. Cash contends that, without the Democrats' resolution, Catts could never have been elected governor.

Of the other candidates running for governor, William V. Knott, an able and genial Tallahasseean who was then state comptroller, was clearly the front-runner and supported by most of the press. But he too would hand Catts a bonus made to order. When Catts emerged the clear victor in the June 6 primary, with 30,092 to Knott's 24,765 votes, Knott asked the Supreme Court to order a vote recanvass due to the confusion over second-choice balloting. A crescendo of protest followed. Even the major newspapers, while lamenting the outcome, conceded the fairness of Catts's win. On September 21, when the court declared Knott the winner by 21 votes, many newspapers switched their support to Catts in a form of symbolic protest.

Now removed from the Democratic ticket, the ever-resourceful Catts merely switched over as the Prohibition party candidate, and riding the theme of "the stolen nomination," he handily defeated Knott on November 5 by 39,546 to 30,343 votes.

Nevertheless, aside from some lavish ladling at the public trough for family, relatives, and cronies eagerly munching the plums of some eighteen hundred state jobs, the Catts administration was remarkably uneventful, neither worse nor better than many before or after it. Almost in spite of himself, two of his appointments proved distinctive: J. S. Blitch, Raiford prison reformer, and Jerry Carter, hotel commissioner. As for the "little people," upon whose expectations he rode to victory, the memory of them seemed gradually to fade amid the plush amenities of power. But they never forgot the Catts of 1916. Catts's try for the U.S. Senate in 1920 and twice more for the governorship in 1924 and 1928 were soundly defeated.

21.
Rumrunners Dealt in Booze and Mayhem

Prohibition launched a deadly warfare between liquor smugglers and federal agents.

When America set out in 1920 on its "noble experiment," Prohibition, it was to unfold one of the most colorful, sordid, and ignoble chapters in the state's history—the Florida rumrunners.

The dikes set up against Demon Rum leaked profusely along the U.S. borders in the twenties, but never with such a flow as from the state's liquid gold triangle: Cuba, the Bahamas, and the shores of south Florida.

Schooners, motorboats, yachts, and freighters plied across the waters nightly on the short runs from Bimini or Havana, pouring their illegal hootch into the plush Gold Coast oases from Palm Beach to Miami. Blood often flowed as freely as the booze, as thugs waited on shore to relieve smugglers of their valuable cargoes, hijackers waited to "pirate" them at sea, and all three waited for a coast cleared of the U.S. Coast Guard.

The era's characters were unique: Captain Bill McCoy, king of the rumrunners; Havana Kitty, the vindictive amorist; and if Hemingway's Harry Morgan in *To Have and Have Not* was fictional, a lug named Jiggs Donahue wasn't. They all flourished until the big syndicates squeezed them out.

The easy money flowed. Runners could make from several hundred to several thousand dollars per trip. A case of Cuban rum costing four dollars would fetch one hundred dollars on the beach. Flush tourists and Florida land boomers were eager to pay fat prices for fine British Scotch from the Bahamas or good Caribbean rum.

Too often, however, the easy lucre reached up to taint the law and those in high places. One curious sight was moonshiners in unholy alliance with respectable "drys" urging stricter enforcement; rum competition was too rough.

South Florida's coast with its inlets, lagoons, and mangrove swamps, and the Keys with their mangrove-fringed coral islands offered ideal concealment to runners. Good highways paralleled these areas, providing quick access to trucks. On the Gold Coast, even the U.S. government inadvertently provided free navigational service to Bimini runners, with the powerful

84

flashing aircraft beacons on which a runner could take a bearing to fix his position exactly, without compass.

The U.S. Coast Guard was sorely undermanned in the early years, effective by day with aid of a spotter plane, but hard pressed at night. Often the rum fleets, mostly speedy motorboats, would slowly move out of their "mouseholes" at Bimini, Cat Cay, or Gun Cay and wait for sunset. Then they would spread out fan-fashion, picking up speed, and scoot like so many water bugs, often cutting between two Coast Guard cutters to avoid the staccato rain of machine gun fire.

They also had a trick of "belling the cat." One boat would move up and go through the motions of loading from a ship in legally protected waters and then take off with a patrol boat in hot pursuit. After a bowshot warning, they would finally stop and display their empty boxes. Meanwhile, the real carriers loaded quickly and took off by another route.

Captain Bill McCoy, dubbed the founder of Rum Row, was called "the real McCoy" since he was known to offer quality booze at fair prices. When one of his other schooners was caught one day, he simply transferred his *Tomoka* to British registry, getting full legal protection. McCoy was finally caught and served nine months in Atlanta's federal prison. When he got out, the syndicates had moved in, so he retired. He died in Florida in 1948.

A Florida woman called "Spanish Marie" (known to Coast Guard crews as "Havana Kitty") would strut about among her crews with a revolver strapped to her waist and a big knife in her belt. She had taken over her husband's fleet after he had fallen overboard one night after excessive sampling of the cargo.

She was known to deal harshly with her many lovers if she discovered one philandering, such as fitting him for a "cement overcoat" and dumping him at sea (a popular murder art form of the times). The law finally caught her on a beach at Coconut Grove, south of Miami, as her crew unloaded its cargo.

Others found highly lucrative sidelines in smuggling narcotics and aliens (mostly Chinese at one thousand dollars per head) from Cuba. The notorious "Stingray Jake" Bunton was convicted when one of the "cargo" of eleven Chinese he had jettisoned during Coast Guard pursuit survived to testify in court. The bullet had missed the young man's head when the boat lurched, blowing only part of his jaw away.

A Tampa skipper running heroin out of the Dry Tortugas, a smugglers' haven sixty-seven miles west of Key West, thought he had jettisoned his cargo, but an alert Coast Guard crewman spotted one of the packets fouled in the captain's rudder stock—five pounds of uncut heroin, worth a fortune in the States. The skipper got ten years in Atlanta.

The red-haired Jiggs Donahue, one of the most elusive and colorful runners, got involved with rebels in Cuba and began running rum one way and guns the other. The ruthless dictator, Gerado "El Gallo" Machado, was especially unhappy over gunrunners and used his sinister secret police ("El Pora") to crush them. One night they caught Donahue. Later, the Coast Guard spotted Donahue's boat drifting in the Florida Straits. Aboard were the badly decomposed bodies of Donahue and his son, trussed up, with throats slit. El Pora had towed the boat to the Gulf Stream where they knew it would float northward as a "reminder."

When the big syndicates squeezed out these independents, there were new names and faces: Frankie Yale, Big Bill Dwyer, Al Capone, Mannie Kessler, Johnny Torrio, Solly Weissman, Frank Costello. They employed hundreds, operating on a regular business basis with their own departments of sales, distribution, transportation, purchasing, and muscle. A political department handled nothing but the payoffs to Prohibition agents, police, Coast Guard, customs officers, and assorted federal, state, and local officials.

They paid huge income taxes to ward off the IRS. They used high-powered, custom-built, seventy-five-foot craft that, at fifty miles per hour, could outrun most Coast Guard vessels. Huge truck fleets waited on shore.

In their clandestine "cutting" plants, they could turn one case of Scotch into four. Three parts grain alcohol and distilled water were often used, but occasionally, a cutter used a sulphuric-acid compound or creosote which, while an excellent timber preservative, does not exactly sit like milk on the stomach. Printing plants produced their own fake internal revenue stamps, labels, and wrappings. The overhead was high, but fantastic fortunes were turned.

Short of both manpower and boats, the Coast Guard was also hamstrung by the law, recalls retired Coast Guard Lieutenant Harold Waters, who once helped track the rummies. Judges mysteriously looked the other way; prosecutors unaccountably found a lack of evidence in even the tightest cases.

Finally, a special task force of young Justice Department attorneys and a top legal advisor quietly moved in, and smugglers soon started going to jail by the score.

It took a massacre at sea to bring about complete law enforcement. In August 1927, a rummy named James H. Alderman, arrested at sea by a patrol ship, managed to grab up two .45s in the pilot house. He killed the skipper, a secret service agent, and a crewman, and wounded several others before he was subdued.

Alderman was sentenced and hanged at the Fort Lauderdale Coast Guard base. The reaction was instant. Congress quickly appropriated funds for a dozen reconditioned high-speed destroyers and other equipment. Rummy boats were soon caught in a coast-long crackdown.

The Coast Guard Intelligence also had a highly effective "dirty tricks" department, Waters recalled. Its cryptoanalysis intercepted and decoded scores of rummy codes, making arrests very simple. The Coast Guard would cleverly dispatch thank-you notes, enclosed with sums of money, to the most trusted key men in various syndicates for their "helpful information," making certain that rummy overlords intercepted the notes. The rum barons rose to the bait. The purge of "traitors" began swiftly, and in due time, many a bewildered rummy skipper, secret radio operator, truck-convoy captain, and others were wearing "concrete coats."

In a short time, the Coast Guard had almost wiped out the rummy traffic. But the pinch hurt the tourist trade. The big resort hotels were vehement in denouncing the crackdown as a threat to the entire economy, as tourists moved on to plusher watering holes in Nassau and Havana. The land-boom easy money was also being spread around to "the right places." The Washington Coast Guard headquarters was soon getting surreptitious notes from solons asking it to "ease up."

The "drys" were vociferous but fundless. Their unholy allies, the moonshiners, implored congressmen, arguing that it was even more "patriotic" for tourists to buy their lethal varieties of fuel-oil-laden corn (rotgut) than the more palatable foreign stuff.

The amphibious planes went first, and then the destroyer divisions were ordered back to Northern bases.

Nevertheless, scores of rummies had been put out of business, and the Florida traffic never fully recovered. The repeal of Prohibition in 1933 ended, finally and mercifully, what Herbert Asbury called "The Great Illusion," with all of its attending euphoria, corruption, and colorful madness.

22.
Florida's First Black Outlaw

Herman Murray terrorized Gainesville and central Florida until his rampage was ended by an old acquaintance.

There was something almost ghoulish about the scene that September morning in 1891, as the crowd shoved, pushed, and elbowed on the depot platform, trying to squeeze into the small railroad car to get a glimpse of the corpse of the dead black outlaw, Herman Murray.

And then the crowd still outside spotted another black man, Elbert Hardy, the man who had felled Murray, standing in the doorway of a second car, cradling a Winchester rifle, and quietly smiling. "That's him!" someone shouted, and at once a roar of cheers went up.

Finally the sheriff and undertaker were able to wrangle the coffin past the scrambling mob and into a waiting wagon. The wagon took off quickly as a crowd of excited men, women, and children trailed in pursuit, on horse or foot.

It was the wildest scene in Gainesville's history up to that time, reported historian Jess Davis. The racial hostilities of post-Reconstruction Florida had something to do with the excitement, but in fact, Murray and his gang had been terrorizing Gainesville and much of north central Florida with robberies and murders for the past two years. Despite the most arduous efforts, sheriff and posses had failed to capture him. Now, incredibly, he was dead, and the sudden release of long-held tensions and fears induced in townspeople a delirium of relief.

Herman Murray was one of four sons and three daughters of Gilbert and Emma Murray, two of Gainesville's most respected black citizens. In boyhood he attended the local Union Academy, but his somewhat rebellious and restless nature prompted him, at age 12, to run away from home and go to Georgia. Nothing is known of his activities there, but in 1888, at 22, he returned to Gainesville and took a farmhand job with local merchant H. Pinkoson.

Then one evening, Murray, who had a girlfriend in nearby Arredondo, took one of Pinkoson's horses to go and see her. He stayed late, and when Pinkoson discovered one of his horses—and Murray—missing, he got up a search party to hunt for him. On his return journey, learning from a friend of the search, an apprehensive Murray left the horse with the friend to return it for him and fled on foot. But the party caught up with him. He was arrested, tried, and sentenced to three years for horse theft. He was sent to a prison work camp, but it could not hold him for long.

Within three months, Murray had formed a friendship with a white man from Northern Ireland, Michael Kelly, and two other Gainesville blacks, Tony Champion and Alexander Henderson. Together they plotted an escape. Enlisting the aid of five other prisoners, who created a scuffle to distract the guards one evening, Murray took an axe helve he had concealed in his clothes and pried loose a section of board in the prison barrack. After midnight they fled to freedom. Going in separate directions, they agreed to meet later in Tampa.

In Tampa, Murray worked by day in a hotel, but at night his gang embarked on a wave of theft and robberies. When suspicion began to fall on Murray, he took his gang north to the Gainesville area and there began a series of robberies and murders that soon left citizens so fearful they often would not venture from their homes after dark. Gainesville's frustrated sheriff, Lewis Fennell, scoured the area with posse hunts, but always in vain. Then, the morning after the gang had been foiled in an attempted store break-in, the sheriff got a tip from an informant that Murray and several of his men would meet that night at a woman's house near the train depot. The informant was gang member Henderson.

A stakeout was set up; the lawmen waited. Just before, the gang had shot and killed a Mr. McPherson, burned his barn, and robbed his house. Now, as they approached the meeting, the sheriff's men opened fire. Murray and others escaped, but Kelly and Champion were wounded and captured. That night, a mob of twenty-five men broke into the jail, seized the two men, and lynched them in a tree in a nearby grove.

By now Murray was heading northeast hunting for Henderson, whom he had learned was the informant. He got to Fernandina Beach, where he killed and robbed a man. Then he went to Jacksonville, where he nervily went to that city's police chief and got a job as a law officer. Failing to find his man, he left and went to Starke. Entering that town, he was accosted by a marshal and his deputy with guns drawn. Walking nonchalantly toward them, he quickly drew his pistol, fatally shooting both men before they could return fire. Fleeing to High Springs, he finally spotted Henderson. Henderson turned to run when he saw Murray. Murray fired once, killing Henderson. Still in a vengeful mood, the outlaw headed south to Archer, a town southwest of Gainesville, where he intended to "shoot up" several people who had once refused to hide his gang. Murray had terrorized many blacks whom he had forced to give him food and shelter at gunpoint. One such victim was later lynched by Gainesville's "respectable" white citizenry. And such incidents as these had earlier prompted three young Archer-area blacks—Elbert

Hardy, Wesley Thomas, and Perry Henderson—to take an oath either to capture or kill Murray. A fortuitous chance soon arose.

Hardy had been a boyhood acquaintance of Murray's, and this vague tie led Murray to Hardy's home late on the night of September 3, 1891. Murray demanded that Hardy accompany him, as an aide of sorts, for his intended "shoot-up" in town. Barely concealing his excitement, Hardy feigned mild protests and then consented. The pair walked down the main road; then Murray took a short cut into a path at Long Pond, two miles from Archer. It was three o'clock in the morning.

Hardy knew he had to act quickly. And he knew Murray would eventually kill him since he had no intention of joining in the "shoot-up." At that moment, Murray suddenly quickened his pace. Now or never, thought Hardy, as he slowed down his own steps. Then, in that instant that Murray turned his head to see where his partner was, Hardy fired one round from his Winchester rifle, the bullet entering Murray's upper back. The outlaw fell dead.

Within hours, the early morning train, bearing Murray's body for the short run to Gainesville, was on its way. Sheriff Fennell had been telegraphed at 8:30 A.M. and the news spread fast, electrifying the town. The local *Sun* quickly got out an extra with the banner head: "MURRAY SLAIN BY ONE OF HIS OWN RACE." But already the excited crowds were hurrying toward the depot. Later that day in a public interview, the hero of the hour, Hardy, would relate a modest, clear, and concise account of the previous night's events. That same day, Murray's body would be embalmed. He would lie for the next five days on exhibition in the courtyard square where people, white and black, came to view it.

It had been an epic occasion in the town's history. After all, there had been numerous white outlaws in Florida in those years, but a black desperado was a new phenomenon. Later, in quieter moments, people would ponder this and even wonder whether Murray really did intend to steal old Pinkoson's horse that night.

23.
Gambling and Politics Fell a Sheriff

Broward County Sheriff Walter Clark commenced a reign of gambling and politics in the 1920s—but finally lost heavily.

Walter R. Clark served as sheriff of Broward County from 1932 to 1950. (Florida State Archives)

Among the pernicious notions that periodically afflict social thought is that of the "easy-money" or "quick-fix" solution to society's problems. This notion becomes even more alluring when the costs of that society's obligations seem to rise faster than the willingness of the citizens to pay them. Consider what happened in Broward County (Fort Lauderdale) back in the 1930s.

After a triple blow in the 1920s—the land-boom bust, two punishing hurricanes, and the stock market crash—the county and its citizens were bankrupt. Few people could pay their taxes. Bonds went into default, and Broward's economy was stagnant. Hundreds had fled the area. Therefore, it was not surprising to find many of the remaining three thousand Broward residents eyeing—and slightly envying—the dollars that its more popular neighbor southward, Miami, was raking in from gambling—horses, casinos, lotteries, and slot machines.

Such a mood seemed propitious for the 1932 election as sheriff of 27-year-old Walter Clark of Fort Lauderdale. Clark shrewdly parlayed Broward's sentiment into an eighteen-year fiefdom of political power that would reach to the statehouse doors, and sometimes beyond. During his reign, Broward's portals would be opened to some of the nation's kingpins of organized crime, and every level of Broward government would be infused with a camaraderie of corruption.

In Miami, crime boss Meyer Lansky and his brother, Jake, eyed Broward County as virgin territory, and so the pair made a visit to Clark. Soon after, Jake was operating the opulent Colonial Inn casino in Hallandale. Word got around, and soon other casinos—all illegal—popped up, operated by such mob figures as Joe Adonis, Frank Costello, Frank Erikson, and Vincent "Jimmy Blue Eyes" Alo. There were the Club Greenacres, the Club Boheme, the It Club, and the Lopez and Valhalla restaurants. The Farm, or Plantation, opened in a packing shed in the midst of a vegetable field. But apparently its operator, "Potatoes" Kauffman, incurred the mob's displeasure. "Potatoes" disappeared one night, rumored to have drowned while trying to swim wearing cement overshoes. Soon enough lotteries (bolita), book houses (for Miami horse races), and slot machines began cropping up, some operating out of the back rooms of respectable retail stores. And the sheriff surveyed it all with tolerance, made all the more benign by periodic visits from gambling figures bearing tangible tokens of their gratitude.

Sheriff Clark epitomized the affable "good old boy." His genial manner was enhanced by a willingness to do small favors or get jobs for constituents, even as he used his expanding political power to help the whole county on projects pending in the legislature. Born December 11, 1904, in Fort Lauderdale, he operated a small butcher shop and grocery store before running for sheriff. His campaign ads touted him as "the first white male child born in Fort Lauderdale"—a false claim, he knew, but good politics. Taking office in 1933, he promptly made his brother, Bob, his chief deputy.

While the white citizenry generally found Clark to be a benevolent "boss," Broward's growing black population was exposed to a meaner side of him. "He was a headbeater," recalled L. D. Gainey, one-time head of the Broward Urban League. "Clark was a man to be feared if you were black." Clark expected all blacks to rise when he entered a room. One day John Wooten refused; he was later arrested on a vagrancy charge and died that same night in a jail cell. Clark explained that Wooten fell out of bed onto his head. Nor did the sheriff interfere in 1935 when a black field hand, Reuben Stacy, 37, was lynched by a white mob after being accused of the attempted rape of a white housewife. Clark prospered on the state's loose peonage laws. He routinely rounded up blacks on vagrancy charges. They were allowed to pay a thirty-five-dollar fine, which they rarely had, or work off the debt in area vegetable fields. Paying the workers a fractional token wage, the farmers then paid Clark thirty-five dollars for each prisoner.

In this period, the gambling interests carefully cultivated a "Robin Hood" image, noting that they took money only from wealthy natives and tourists. They often gave donations to charities and civic projects. They gave much more generously to political campaign funds, especially Clark's. The relatives and in-laws of other members of the body politic were often rewarded with sinecures in the gaming industry. By the 1940s and World War II, Clark had skillfully woven the many-threaded strands of gambling and politics into a tightly knit tapestry of power within the state's Democratic party structure. It would soon serve him well.

Despite the lush gambling largess, Broward County had by now acquired a notorious reputation as a lair of organized crime. Finally, on July 22, 1942, Governor Spessard Holland suspended Clark from office for failing to enforce the gambling laws. But the Florida senate had to confirm such suspensions. Here Clark pressed all his power buttons and called in all his political chits. At the close of the next spring's legislative session, the senate met in a closed "executive session" and voted on June 1, 1943, to reinstate Clark. He received back pay along with his job.

The sheriff was now emboldened to cut a larger slice of the gambling pie. And, with the Lanskys' blessing, he operated a numbers lottery from his office and installed slot machines all over the county under the name of the Broward Novelty Company, with he and brother Bob each holding a quarter interest in it.

But with a fast-growing population and new people concerned about the mob's presence and government corruption, an assistant state attorney, Dwight L. Rogers, Jr., in 1948 was able to close down permanently Lansky's Colonial Inn and two other casinos. A key state witness, native Browardian Lee Wentworth, remained unfazed by a $25,000 bribe offer and, alternately, a death threat. A Lansky hood, calling on Wentworth one night, handed him a shoebox filled with $25,000, saying, "You know how these things end—either with a silver bullet or a silver dollar." Wentworth calmly retrieved a shotgun he kept by his door and told the caller he would count to five. The caller didn't wait; he and two other hoods, waiting in a car, sped away.

But most other gambling operators still flourished until the arrival in 1950 of lanky Tennessee Senator Estes Kefauver and his widely publicized national Senate Crime Committee. Clark appeared visibly discomfited when summoned to appear before the probers during televised hearings. Kefauver found this "astonishing sheriff" unusually evasive.

Yes, Clark knew of these places, but they were "clubs," not casinos. "I let them have what they want for the tourists down here," he added. Yes, Clark had heard "rumors" of gambling at these places "but no actual evidence of it." Yes, he knew some gamblers contributed to his campaigns, but he never "bothered" to find out how much. But Clark's calm evasiveness was shaken when Kefauver cited income tax records of a $35,000 annual income when Clark's official salary was only $7,500.

Evidence from the hearings prompted Governor Fuller Warren to suspend Clark from office. And in August 1950, Clark, brother Bob, and an associate were indicted on fourteen counts of illegal possession of slot machines and one count of conducting a lottery. At his trial, Clark hobbled into the courtroom on crutches, presumably from an arthritic ailment. He won acquittal on all counts.

But his victory was short-lived. In February 1951, Clark was stricken with acute leukemia, and he died the following April.

24. Panther Key John: A Centenarian Legend

A self-styled ex-pirate lived a chunk of Florida history until his accidental death at age 122.

Ex-pirate John Gomez died in a fishing accident at the age of 122, but left behind a legend. (Florida State Archives)

He was offbeat, a breed out of time and place, the stuff of color and legend, this mysterious Methuselah who nomadically ranged along Florida's west coast, from Key West to Cedar Key, for the entire one hundred years of the nineteenth century.

Ex-cabin boy to the notorious pirate José Gaspar ("Gasparilla") and then a pirate himself, "Old John" (Juan) Gomez would become a sailor, U.S. ship's pilot, Indian fighter, fisherman, hunter, woodsman, guide, farmer, and even a resort operator before his accidental death by drowning in 1900, at the vigorous age of 122. He definitely was not your ordinary senior citizen.

He was remembered by almost every pioneer citizen who ever lived on Florida's west coast in that century, and by written or spoken word, they regaled posterity with stories of Gomez's exploits, especially the darkly intriguing episodes of his piratical past. Thus, there came to be as many John Gomezes as there were tellers of him. But through sifting of fact, legend, fancy, and credibility, there emerges a fairly plausible life record of this simple but legend-studded character; a composite necessarily sketchy but perhaps as close to the authentic Gomez as anyone is likely to get.

Gomez was reportedly born on the Portuguese island of Madeira in 1778. The family moved first to Spain (where the young Juan recalled being thrilled at the sight of Napoleon on parade in Madrid) and later to Bordeaux, France. From there, a teen-age Gomez signed on a ship bound for America.

After landing in Charleston, South Carolina, he fled the ship's "cruel captain" and went to St. Augustine. There he joined on another vessel, but the ship was seized by the pirate Gaspar; Gomez was taken prisoner and made a cabin boy. Whether from youthful desire for adventure or lack of choice—or both—the zestful, robust youth apparently rose in ranks enough to be permitted a little part-time buccaneering of his own.

Odette Phillippe, a young naval surgeon for Napoleon who fled to America after a brief imprisonment in the Bahamas by Lord Nelson, recalls his first encounter with Gomez. Phillippe, preparing to settle on the Indian River, was on a supply trip to the Bahamas when pirates boarded his ship. Learning his profession, they ordered him to treat a number of sick pirates; he did, and they recovered. "Their leader, John Gomez," Phillippe related, "was so grateful that he presented [Phillippe] with a chest filled with golden treasure" and released him. Another time, when Indians attacked Indian River settlers, Phillippe fled the area in his boat. Again John Gomez turned up, with another shipful of fever-ridden pirates. By now, Phillippe considered himself "un-official surgeon" to the brigands. This time Gomez drew out a map to show Phillippe. "Here," the pirate pointed, "is Espiritu Santo Bay [Bay of the Holy Spirit], Tampa Bay. If there is a God, surely this is his resting place. There is but one bay to compare with it—Naples. You can find no place like it." Phillippe believed—and moved. He built a home near Safety Harbor, planted a flourishing orange grove, and prospered. (Phillippe Park, near that town, is named for him today.) He would meet Gomez again many years later under more amicable surroundings.

The pirate José Gaspar reportedly captured and sank thirty-six ships in just one eleven-year period in his heyday. The French vessel *Orleans,* carrying a forty-thousand-dollar cargo, was warned in September 1821 by U.S. naval officials of "one Gasparilla, a noted desperado of blackest dye." Too late. Gaspar seized the vessel and afterwards wrote a note, preserved in state records, to a U.S. naval officer who was aboard the *Orleans:* "Sir: Between buccaneers, no ceremony. I take your dry goods, and in return I send you pimento; therefore, we are now even . . . I entertain no resentment, [but] nothing can intimidate us." That is, nothing except the U.S. Naval Squadron under Commander David Porter, which gradually eradicated all pirates remaining in the Gulf-Caribbean area. In 1822, Gaspar got too close to what he thought was a large prize British merchantman; it was instead a disguised U.S. warship. The pirate ship was riddled, but before she could be boarded, Gaspar, seeing the end of his career, wrapped an anchor chain around himself, plunged into the water, and drowned. Ten of the crew were caught and hanged; a few, including John Gomez, swam to Gasparilla Island at Boca Grande, the pirate's main lair. From there, Gomez swam to the mainland and fled into the Everglades.

The subsequent years are sketchy, but Gomez related that he wandered about the southwest region aimlessly, living with friendly Indians at times and surviving on fish, oysters, and game. Later, he claimed to have joined Colonel Zachary Taylor as a volunteer scout, in time for the decisive Battle of Okeechobee against the Seminoles in December 1837.

Gomez later wandered northwesterly, arriving in the little settlement of Keysville, south of Plant City in Hillsborough County. Hungry and wearing only rags, he found refuge with a poor widow, Mrs. Sara Shavers, and her widowed daughter, Mrs. Martha Weeks. The two women took him in, fed him, and made clothes for him. Having nothing to give the widow for her kindness— except himself—he did so. He proposed, she accepted, and the couple lived happily in Keysville and elsewhere until the widow's death in the 1850s. Mrs. Weeks, who lived to be 113 until her death in 1940 at Lithia, just west of Keysville, recalled her stepfather as "good-natured, honest, and a willing worker." He was of medium height, thick-torsoed, and powerful, and although he was pushing his seventies, his thick, curly hair and beard were still coal black. He rarely wore shoes or hat, and the soles of his feet resembled gnarled, heavy leather.

After his wife's death, Gomez first wandered toward Cedar Key and then Crystal River where, for a while, he fished for a living. He then came to Tampa and worked as a ship's pilot in the Egmont Key passage. On the side, he worked on the development of a picnic and fishing grounds resort at Pass-a-Grille Beach in Pinellas County. For a brief while, it became a favorite holiday resort, especially for troops at Fort Brooke in Tampa, and one of its most enthusiastic promoters was an elder pioneer at Safety Harbor— Odette Phillippe. Here a historian notes: "To everyone but Phillippe, John Gomez was a mystery . . . [but] Gomez never denied his piratical past."

Nevertheless, Gomez's attempt to live a clean, honest, unsullied life became clouded again when he became enamored of another widow, in Tampa, and she of him. Meanwhile, a jealous former suitor of the widow, named Williams, returned to Tampa and threatened Gomez. As Gomez told it: "I yere talk in town that man Willums come back. He say he kill me. One day I see Willums come 'long the road. I take my gun. I say, Willums, I no wanta you come in here. He say, I come in, I killa you. I say, Willums, donta come in da gate. Willums, he coma in da gate. I shoota him, and he staya there. I coma 'way."

After this, Gomez fled to Key West and, during the Civil War, served as a ship's pilot for the U.S. Blockade Squadron. His superior, Commander C. H. Rockwell, was intrigued by this strange, aging Portuguese, "a perfect pilot, who knew familiarly every shoal, rock, oyster bed, creek, inlet, mud bank, fishing ledge, channel, wild bird roost and deer track" on Florida's west coast. Rockwell wrote of the "swarthy, silent" Gomez thusly: "He was always perfectly clean and neat but his clothing was tropical and free and he wore shoes rarely. At first sight he would be passed by, but if once one could penetrate beneath the bark there was a rich yield of a life of adventure. His language was calm and slow; I rarely saw him vehement. But there was a secret, slumbering force about the man which savored of helpfulness and power."

At the war's end, Gomez dropped out of sight again, but apparently in these years he had found a home—permanently—in the wild, sparsely inhabited Ten Thousand Islands south of Fort Myers. Captain W. D. "Bill" Collier, a settler on Marco Island who remembered meeting Gomez during the latter's Pinellas resort days, met him again in 1871 when Gomez appeared at Collier's trading store for supplies. He learned that Gomez had settled on Panther Key (now officially Gomez Key), some fifteen miles from Marco. Here he fished and farmed and married a woman (fifty years his junior); they would remain devoted to each other until his death in 1900. In 1880, Gomez, in partnership with a Captain Horr of nearby Horr's Island, attempted to raise goats, but panthers ate all the goats—thus the original name, Panther Key.

The centenarian became a popular if still mysterious figure among settlers in the Fort Myers area and was referred to as "Old John, the last of the pirates." He could still neither read nor write, but he spoke seven languages and he would often relate episodes of his early days. In 1885, at age 107, he was a robust, walking advertisement for Florida's healthful climate, and he maintained that he had never taken any medicine in his life. A contemporary noted: "His voice was clear and full and he gestured freely as he talked, with the animation of a young man."

During the last ten years of his life, he still earned his livelihood from fishing, but Lee County saw fit to award him a supplemental income of eight dollars monthly. The couple lived contentedly in their two-room palmetto-thatch hut, but once, remarking on his age to a neighboring visitor, C. Roy Watson, Gomez lamented: "God has forgotten me; it is past my time to die."

His time was near, but even two years before his death, Kenneth Ransom described Gomez: "His complexion was . . . a dark, rich color of century-old mahogany, set against bushy, thick white hair and beard . . . a face seamed and lined but keen and full of vigor."

On July 12, 1900, shortly after U.S. census taker of Punta Gorda, the Rev. George Gatewood, recorded Gomez's age at 122, making him possibly the oldest man in America, the old centenarian went netting for mullet in a nearby pass. The next day his body was found hanging out of his skiff, drowned, his feet entangled in his netting and an anchor line.

It seemed an absurdly incongruous death, especially for a man who had survived such an adventurous, strenuous, and hazardous existence over so remarkable a lifespan.

But he had left behind him not merely his young wife of 71 but also a multifaceted legend of his time and place and century. So much so that, even today, older residents of the west coast recall the fascinating tales of their childhood, passed on to them by parents who remembered "the last of the pirates" and one of the most colorful characters in Florida's history.

25.
A Political Octopus Takes a Sprawl

W. D. Chipley juggled railroads, Bourbonism, and politics in the late nineteenth century until his tentacles got tangled.

During the heyday of Florida's railroad development in the latter nineteenth century, the rail czars could at times move state legislators and even governors about like figures on a Tammany Hall chessboard. Indeed, when a liberal reform in the 1880s began to crack both the gridiron of Southern Bourbonism and the railroads' grip on government, its vanguard battle cry was "Chipley in the West . . . Plant in the South . . . and Flagler in the East."

The three certainly were formidable. H. B. Plant had only to shake a town's dust from his shoes (Cedar Key), and it could shrivel into economic atrophy. Henry Flagler had the legislature pass a special act so he could divorce his wife. But it was Pensacolan W. D. Chipley who most aggressively used the power of his railroad empire to force even governors, such as E. A. Perry and Francis Fleming, to assist his causes.

Chipley's hometown newspaper, the *Pensacola Commercial,* once warned him editorially: "Look here, Major Octopus, you can't talk politics, run the state of Florida, do a general land office business and run a railroad at the same time. Your tentacles will get tangled."

Finally they did. In his last-ditch effort to stem the tide of liberal reform sweeping the state in the 1890s, Chipley reached for a power seat almost within his grasp, the U.S. Senate. But he lost, and the bitter contest probably cost him his life just a few months later.

William Dudley Chipley was born in 1840 in Columbus, Georgia. Educated at a Kentucky military school, he was able to rise quickly to the rank of lieutenant colonel in the Rebel ranks during the Civil War. Wounded twice, he was finally captured and imprisoned for the war's duration.

Chipley was involved in a few unsuccessful postwar business ventures before joining the management of several Southern railroad systems. In 1881, he was named vice president and superintendent of the newly organized Pensacola & Atlantic Railroad. He also served as P&A's general land agent. The railroad company had already been given a federal land grant of 2.8 million acres to build a railway from Pensacola to Chattahoochee, a midway point that would unite east and west Florida by rail and give west Florida access to major Atlantic-seaboard rail systems. But Chipley also was trying to secure a large pre–Civil War land grant given to a railroad that became defunct long before, thus forfeiting its right to the grant. It would have given P&A virtual ownership of a major portion of the Florida panhandle.

In this same period, the shrewd railroader had become chairman of the state Democratic Executive Committee, a position that enabled him in large part to screen lawmaker candidates on the basis of their railroad sympathies.

But by this time, the issue of huge land grants to railroads had fractured the state into two major political factions: the railroad and corporate interests versus the liberal populist movement then gaining strength in the state. The latter group was led by U.S. Senator Wilkinson Call, nephew of the former territorial governor, Richard Keith Call. The liberal ranks included reform stalwarts like Frank Pope, John Stockton, William Jennings, and Napoleon Broward (the latter two later became governors). This faction labeled the land grants "land grabs." It also charged the railroads with employing discriminatory freight rates and using out-of-state seaports to the exclusion of Florida ports for shipment of such products as phosphate and citrus. It later was able to prove these charges and correct them with the establishment of a state railroad commission, which Chipley's now-powerful political machine had been able to defeat twice in prior legislatures.

In 1888, when Senator Call introduced a resolution in the Senate calling for the forfeiture of all expired land grants and opening them instead to the public for homestead claims, Chipley made Call a personal target. In a bitter fight to block his election to a third term in 1891, Chipley induced a portion of state senate electors to absent themselves from the balloting, but Call won anyway. Chipley then had Governor Fleming declare the election illegal, but the U.S. Senate, the final arbiter, officially seated Call.

Prior to this, Chipley had completed the railroad's Chattahoochee link with the east. This would remain his most distinctive personal achievement. It had also enhanced his power base: When the 1896 election arrived, he was able to enlist most of the state's press in an all-out effort to unseat Call. Running for the seat himself, Chipley tried to dilute the liberal bloc by voicing support for U.S. presidential candidate William Jennings Bryan, a populist. With slightly less candor, he even hinted he would support a state railroad commission (a strong and effective one was enacted a year later). The balloting took cliffhanging contours as the legislature roll-called through twenty-five successive ballots, with votes switching like quicksilver. On the evening of the final vote, Chipley seemed to be the victor. But the liberals, seeing Call's certain defeat, persuaded him during a night-long caucus to drop out in favor of a moderate liberal compromise, Stephen Mallory of Pensacola, who was a longtime foe of his fellow townsman. It worked. Three key lawmakers switched to Mallory and led him to a 55 to 44 victory.

Although Chipley expressed satisfaction over his "sole purpose" in running, namely, "to retire Wilkinson Call from political life," he bitterly denounced in private the vote-switching "treachery that came in to rob me of my victory."

Thus, the end of an era had come. The liberals finally had wrested state government control from the "corporate and railroad interests" and would remain in power the next fifteen years. But it also marked the end of a career. Deeply affected by the strain and bitterness of his crucial defeat, Chipley, the last of the railroad political czars, died suddenly a short time later, on December 1, 1897.

Heroes and Heroines

26.
The Pioneer Teachers of Fortitude

Working conditions were primitive, sometimes hazardous, and the pay was poor for Florida's early schoolteachers.

Instead of an axe or rifle, she wielded the pine tree version of a hickory stick; instead of rough and homespun, she usually wore a trim and crisp shirtwaist dress.

But Florida's early schoolteacher was every bit as much a pioneer as the gaunt and stalwart figure we commonly depict for the breed. The wilderness she conquered was demanding and at times hazardous. And she felt blessed if she could stretch her meager paycheck from one month to the next.

This was especially true in that turn-of-the-century era, roughly 1890 to 1910, when most of Florida was still rural and "book larnin' " was still in the early stages of public acceptance. Education in the abstract, of course, like liberty and motherhood, had long been extolled with solemn lip service, but not until 1885 did a new state constitution require the legislature to provide a free public school system and counties to levy a school tax to pay for it. Even so, it was hard to dispel a lingering frontier attitude that often could not grasp the value of a product one could not see, buy, barter, or sell. Hence, fiscal foot-dragging at the local level often required a teacher to have the stamina and dedication of a singular type of pioneer, a pioneer who was, more often than not, a lady.

During the 1890s, Miss Alice Brickell, the first teacher in the first public school in Dade County, must have had such dedication. Her pay was simply her room and board, and she traveled by boat several miles each week to her Lemon City classroom, a room in the house of the county sheriff.

Ivy Cromartie, 18, had it a little better when she journeyed into the woods of Fort Lauderdale in 1899 to teach the children of the half-dozen settlers' families there. She boarded with a school trustee, received twenty dollars a month, and had a new twenty-by-thirty-foot classroom, to and from which she trekked through the woods three miles each day. Later, after becoming Mrs. Frank Stranahan, she pioneered the first classes for Seminole Indian children, even though the "classroom" was often only a log and a tree stump. Over the years, she became Broward County's first and foremost educator.

105

But getting the school dollar in those years was often like pulling bears' teeth. In Orange County, a school official recalled how the county tax collectors "seemed always reluctant to part with the funds belonging to the schools, and formal demands upon [them] and threats of legal proceedings within 15 days were frequent."

The effects of such fiscal stonewalling were quite visible, especially in Duval County, where in the late nineteenth century a grand jury found most county schools to be "primitive one-room shacks, often in disrepair . . . and in a disgraceful sanitary state, lacking even outhouses."

Sometimes an outsider had to come in and fill the breach. In one such instance, a little-known but historic episode occurred in Florida: the first lawful school integration. In 1890, the American Missionary Association organized the Hand School in Orange Park in Clay County. It taught primarily black children but was also open to whites, a number of whom attended because there were no other schools around. Vandalism and harassment of the school by some white residents led to an 1896 state law making it illegal for whites to teach or go to school with blacks, and vice versa. The school stood firm and challenged the law because it accepted no state

Florida's early schoolteachers worked in primitive conditions, often for only room and board. (Florida State Archives)

funds, and the national AMA took the case to the Florida Supreme Court. In September 1897 the high court struck down the statute, and the integrated school operated peacefully thereafter—until 1917 when a re-emergent Ku Klux Klan terrorized the staff and burned down the school chapel. This forced the Hand School to close permanently.

If poor facilities and teaching tools could tax a teacher's ingenuity, the occasional frontier lifestyles of her charges could as often tax her fortitude. A not uncommon scenario was one reported in an Ocala newspaper in the 1890s: "The citizens of Bucalew Heights and around Lake Como are much annoyed by the manner in which certain boys . . . disport themselves— throwing stones, shouting and firing pistols and guns, some of the shots of which come uncomfortably near passersby. Last week the boys . . . shot the pet dog of Mr. Mayo's son. Such conduct is very wanton and must be stopped."

But parents, too, were not always above a little "wanton conduct." In the phosphate boom town of Dunnellon, during a meeting to organize the first school, a citizen reported that "Mr. H. and Mr. F. had a slight misunderstanding over a building. Harsh and hard words were passed. So was an oil stone from the hands of H. to the head of F., who dodged, seized a handsaw and made a slash at H., who, in warding off the blow, had the palm of his hand seriously slashed."

The single-minded love of teaching had to be strong in the spirit of the pioneer teacher. Salaries were uniformly wretched and, between sexes, shamefully disparate. In Santa Rosa County in the 1900s, male teacher Fons Hathaway (a future state political figure) received forty dollars a month; two equally qualified sisters, Maude and Cora Coleman, earned twenty dollars a month. Between 1890 and 1910, the peak average teacher salary would reach only $44.69 a month. Since the average school term in this same period was less than five months (4.85 months), a single teacher had to cramp her lifestyle severely to get through the year.

Adequate lodging in those days was usually rare, and teachers were commonly "boarded around," usually at the home of some pupil's parents. But these were not always felicitous arrangements; at times they could be the proverbial "last straw." Fresh from college in 1909, Alice Fry recalled her first teaching post in the Manatee County settlement of Rye, where she boarded in the shack-like dwelling of the parents of five of her pupils, ages 7 to 19. Arriving for her first day at the small school two miles away in the woods, she found the local trustees cutting new posts to prop up the building, the old posts having rotted away. They could now safely enter, and after a trustee "kindly shook the rats' nests" out of her desk, she set about her classes with "a few ragged books."

She found the beginners much averse to learning, the youngest, age 7, informing her that "he was going to be just as mean as he could be, and he usually was." There were occasional pranksters, like the 11-year-old who wrapped a dead snake around her neck from behind. But she was thankful none of the misdeeds was as serious as befell her male predecessor, who had been attacked with a hunting knife.

At her lodgings, the family fare was "mostly grease and grits" with an onion added for "a little variety," and sometimes some oranges and sugar cane. Her tiny room off the outer porch, with a small prop-open shingle window, left her little room for anything but sleeping. This, too, could be a problem. When the roaches were not fearsome, the father would sometimes begin playing "weird strains" on his fiddle at all hours of the night. The mother was quieter, spending most of her time chewing tobacco which, fortunately for bystanders, she "expectorated with great precision."

Otherwise the host and hostess were a very taciturn pair who "seemed puzzled and startled by my 'good morning' and 'good evening' greeting." Finally, especially when the incessant rains came the following spring, Miss Fry felt that she "had had about enough. I made a bargain with myself. If it rained the next day I would go home. It did and I did."

But with only a little variation of scene, condition, or characters, Miss Fry's "boarding around" experience was not exceptional for most teachers of that early day.

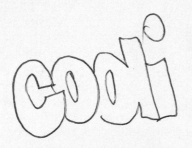

27.
A Florida Shipwreck Inspires a Classic

Author Stephen Crane found his own red badge of courage off the shores of Daytona Beach in the 1890s.

The slight figure garbed in old work clothes moved in anonymity through the milling crowd on the Jacksonville wharf and ascended the gangway of the seagoing tugboat *Commodore*.

No one recognized 25-year-old Stephen Crane, although his book, *The Red Badge of Courage*, published a year earlier in 1895, had already made him a celebrated national author. He was now embarking on a Florida voyage that would have fateful consequences for Crane and the future of American letters.

Florida has hosted, and influenced, a variety of artistic migrants over the years—Harriet Beecher Stowe, Marjorie Kinnan Rawlings, and John James Audubon, to name a few—and they often have sung the state's praises. But Crane, who was in and around Florida often in the 1890s, had more ambivalent feelings about the state. Once, uncertain of his recent book's future, he swore that "if *The Red Badge* is not all right I shall sell out my claim in literature and take up [Florida] orange-growing." On another occasion, his first sight of Jacksonville could hardly have pleased that city's boosters: "The town looks like soiled pasteboard that some lunatic babies have been playing with." Tampa was "nothing but . . . sand, sunshine and quinine pills [for malaria]." Key West's dubious distinction was a local gambling kingpin "straight out of a dime novel, moustache and all, with bunches of diamonds like cheap chandeliers on each hand."

But the shores of Daytona Beach would leave the writer with far more memorable impressions.

Stephen Crane was born November 1, 1871, in Newark, New Jersey, the last of fourteen children born to Rev. and Mrs. Jonathan Townley Crane, he a noted Methodist minister. Although an avid reader, young Crane did not take easily to formal studies, and after a brief stint at Syracuse University, where he excelled only in literature and baseball, he went to work for a New York newspaper, *The Press.* His first novel, completed when Crane was 19, portrayed the wretched existence of a young girl in the city's slums. The story's grimly realistic style prompted publishers to refuse it, so Crane used his own funds to print copies of it. Still, it caught the attention of two literary figures of the day, Hamlin Garland and William Dean Howells, the latter praising its "quality of Greek tragedy." The two men would help and encourage Crane thereafter.

At 23, Crane completed *The Red Badge of Courage*. The enthusiastic response after it appeared in newspaper serial form led to its being published by Appleton Company. The book immediately won critical acclaim as "the most realistic war novel ever written," "a masterpiece of deliberate, finished art . . . bright, fresh and honest." The story of a young man's encounter with battle and death during the Civil War possessed such stark realism of detail, mood, and setting that several Civil War veterans insisted they had known Crane at Antietam. It became a best seller on both sides of the Atlantic; in Europe it won Crane the attention and future friendship of such writers as Joseph Conrad, H. G. Wells, and Henry James, the American expatriate.

In winter 1896, when Crane arrived in Jacksonville, the city was the scene of a flurry of filibustering on behalf of the Cuban revolution against Spain. Crane was on assignment for a New York news syndicate to cover the conflict. Although he wore a money belt containing seven hundred dollars worth of Spanish gold, he insisted on working passage as an ordinary seaman at twenty dollars a month on the *Commodore*. The vessel was one of many carrying Cuban volunteers, arms, and ammunition to the island.

As it sailed up the St. Johns River that New Year's Eve 1896, the *Commodore* struck a sandbar, and although it was pulled off at daybreak next day, the impact had loosened the vessel's seams. Several hours later, in the heavy Atlantic seas some eighteen miles offshore, the vessel took on water and the engine room was quickly flooded, preventing operation of the pumps. Captain Edward Murphy, hoping to make a run to shore, ordered the boilers fired to capacity, but the waters soon quenched the fires and Murphy gave orders to abandon ship.

Crane declined to board either of the two large lifeboats. He stayed behind to assist Murphy, who sustained a severe shoulder injury while helping to get the boats lowered and clear. Then Crane, Murphy, oiler Bill Higgins, and cook Charles Montgomery boarded the last boat, a small ten-foot dinghy. From a distance, they later watched helplessly as seven men in one of the lifeboats returned to the vessel to retrieve some provisions and were trapped and drowned as the *Commodore* sank.

Beneath dullish gray skies and in heavy swells churned by brisk and chilling northeast winds, the men took turns rowing and continuously bailing water to keep the small craft from swamping. Later that evening, the two lifeboats had reached shore at New Smyrna Beach, but for some reason, the occupants failed to notify local residents of the dinghy's situation, wiring news to Jacksonville instead.

By nightfall the small dinghy rode within six inches of the waterline. Throughout the night the now-exhausted men continued to row and bail. Heavy seas, winds, and gray skies were still with them at daybreak, but they had come within a half-mile of the shore at Daytona Beach. But before them curled a long line of high, seething breakers, a perilous barrier to shore. They had spotted three men on the beach but failed to get their attention. If they remained where they were, the small craft was certain to swamp, so the captain decided to try to run the breakers. The frail dinghy shimmied erratically through the swift, roaring rollers, and then, about 150 yards from shore, a mountainous crest tipped over the craft, dumping its four occupants. Crane tried desperately to hold onto oiler Higgins, who had been struck unconscious by the boat's gunwale, but the rushing water pulled Higgins from his grasp and the oiler's lifeless body washed ashore soon after.

Submerging then surfacing, on and off, in the powerful undertow and boiling surf, the men soon spotted a figure running down the beach toward them. It was resident John Kitchell, who stripped off his clothes and rushed into the surf's edge to drag to shore the semiconscious cook. He then went out to Crane, who had doubled over with cramps, and pulled him to the shallows. Finally he reached the exhausted Murphy, and soon all three survivors were huddled on the beach.

The experience in the waters off Daytona Beach would remain with Crane. In powerful imagery it had come to symbolize to him a universal condition of man: his fragility when in conflict with the monumental forces of the natural world, forces of hostility or indifference affording no special favor to humankind. And thus, to Crane, the four men in the boat became Everyman, all of them in the same boat, and their only strength against such forces lay in their mutual attention to the condition of the other.

When Crane's story, *The Open Boat,* was published the next year—dedicated to his three companions—it was praised as "a flawless piece of paradox and symbol." The *New York Times* London editor, Harold Frederic, wrote: "No living English prose writer of his years approaches his wonderful gift. . . . " Writer H. G. Wells called it simply "Perfection." It has since joined the classics of American literature.

One can only speculate on what Crane's later years might have contributed to American letters. Unfortunately, his harrowing Florida experience, which served as such a brilliant muse of literary creation, was also the harbinger of tragedy. The Florida waters had left Crane with a nascent tubercular condition that would lead to his death in June 1900 at the tender age of 28.

28.
Chief Coacoochee's Great Escape

The Seminole warrior's daring break from an "escape-proof" prison enabled him to rally his war-weary people.

Seminole Indian Chief Coacoochee ("Wild Cat") was a brave, flamboyant, and resourceful leader. (Florida State Archives)

It was a dramatic and daring escape, squeezing through the smallest aperture in the five-foot-thick cell wall of the ancient, "escape-proof" fortress at St. Augustine.

Historians are still uncertain of all the details of how Seminole Indian Chief Coacoochee ("Wild Cat"), seventeen subchiefs and warriors, and two women made this "impossible" exit. But they are certain of one thing: It prolonged by four and a half years one of the longest and costliest wars in U.S. history, the Second Seminole War (1835–42).

It was a stinging blow to General Thomas S. Jesup, the U.S. Army commander who, until then, was certain that the war was all but over. A substantial number of Seminoles had already surrendered or been captured, and only a month earlier, the famous Osceola and other tribal chiefs had been seized during "flag of truce" talks (an episode that Jesup would still be trying to justify twenty years later). But now Coacoochee, son of the revered chief King Philip, could join with leaders still at large—Tiger Tail, Sam Jones, Alligator—and rally their forces together.

An enraged Jesup was certain the group "could not have escaped without aid from without." But there was no such aid; it was an inside job, executed by one of the boldest and most ingenious of the Seminole tribal chiefs.

Coacoochee possessed some magnetic traits of character. About 32 years old, five feet eight inches tall, he had the slender, tough, and agile frame of a "prince of the forest," befitting the son of a king and a mother

112

who was sister of a major chief, Micanopy. Historian John T. Sprague, an officer who fought four years in that conflict, described Wild Cat this way: "His eye is dark, full and expressive, his countenance extremely youthful and pleasing. His voice is clear and soft, speech fluent . . . a mind active and ingenuous, clear and comprehensive . . . governing his band in a firm but politic manner."

The chief was also endowed with a vivid imagination, at times lending his behavior a certain flamboyancy. Once his men captured a traveling Shakespearean theater group. Much later, when meeting with Colonel W. J. Worth to discuss peace terms, Coacoochee arrived garbed in the costume of Hamlet; beside him stood "Horatio," and behind both lurked "Richard III."

Coacoochee and a small group of his people had been captured in early October 1837. They were imprisoned in a thirty-three-square-foot cell at Fort Marion, formerly the huge Castillo de San Marcos built in the 1600s by Spain. The chief's father, King Philip, captured earlier, was in a different cell. There were no sentinels posted at these cells since officials believed that their sheer massiveness made them escape-proof.

Aside from a thick door, there was only a small aperture about fifteen feet overhead to let in light and air. Just below it was a ledge about two feet wide. Farther below was a wide platform rising three feet from the floor. On the first day inside, Coacoochee climbed onto a friend's shoulders from atop the platform, grabbed the ledge's edge, and hoisted himself upon it. He made eye measure of the five-foot-long, wedge-shaped opening which narrowed to the wall's exterior, twenty-three feet above the fort's moat, to an opening some eighteen inches wide but only eight inches high. In addition, two iron bars stood vertically near the embrasure's interior opening. The bars posed a problem, but Coacoochee was convinced that a human body could squeeze through that outer eight inches.

Historians differ on how one of these bars was later removed. Some insist that a file was somehow smuggled into the cell by sympathetic local blacks who worked around the fort and knew Coacoochee's half-breed Indian black aide, John Cavalo. Others accept the official investigative report which claimed that "time had corroded the iron and they [the Indians] wrenched it from its place." Nevertheless, removed it was. Meanwhile, over the weeks, the group tore and tied together, rope-fashion, the burlap forage bags on which they slept. And each night, the moon's phases, long familiar to the outdoor tribes, were checked because Coacoochee wanted to time the escape for a moonless night. That night came on November 19, 1837.

The slenderness of the average Indian made U.S. soldiers appear corpulent by comparison. On this last day, the Indians also ate little if any food, hoping to shed even a fraction of additional girth. Even so, as he squeezed his body through the small outer aperture, Coacoochee recalled that "the sharp stones took the skin off my breast and back." The burlap rope had been securely tied to the remaining iron bar, its length pushed out to the moat below. Coacoochee clutched the rope as he slowly inched out head-foremost downward; with feet clear, he quickly descended. Then, one by one, they all came through—some easily, others with great effort and bloodied torsos. The last one came down just before daybreak. The whole operation remained undetected and the group made its way rapidly eastward to the St. Johns River, then finally due south to the Lake Okeechobee area where they would join Sam Jones, Alligator, and Tiger Tail.

The escape so enraged General Jesup that he threatened to execute King Philip if his son did not give himself up. The general finally cooled down but kept Philip under sentinel guard.

Jesup had reason to fear the consequences of Coacoochee's escape. Now strongly united, the Indians continued sporadic but successful hit-and-run raids until, in late December 1837, Colonel Zachary Taylor led a force of almost 1,000 men in a Christmas Day attack on the Seminoles at Okeechobee. The Indians—400 of them led by Coacoochee, Jones, and Alligator— were well entrenched on a wooded hammock overlooking a large grassy swamp. It would be the last formal pitched battle of the war. The Indians fought fiercely for several hours but were finally forced to withdraw in the face of sheer numbers and fire power. Although heralded as "a great victory" for Taylor, it was a somewhat Pyrrhic victory because Taylor's forces suffered 26 killed and 112 wounded; only 25 Indians were killed or wounded. Thereafter, the war continued as before, with the Seminoles keeping close to the Everglades for concealment.

But by 1841, the war had taken a heavy toll on the Florida natives. Unable to plant crops, they suffered chronic food shortages; starvation became a threat. Ammunition, too, was scarce and getting scarcer.

Coacoochee became appalled as he contemplated the grim, slow attrition facing his people in a deadlocked contest against vastly superior forces. He recalled later that, after his escape, he and his men decided they would all die in Florida. "This caused great suffering among our women and children. I was in hopes I should be killed in battle, but a bullet would never touch me. I had rather be killed by a white man in Florida than die in Arkansas."

But finally he concluded: "The whites are too strong for us; they make powder, we cannot. I could live like a wolf, but our women and children suffered when driven from swamp to swamp." And so, in 1841, Coacoochee arranged to come in for surrender talks with Colonel Worth at Fort Brooke.

A poignant scene occurred in his first encounter with Worth near an Indian detention camp in the area. Coacoochee's small daughter, whom he had long supposed to be dead, came running out of the camp toward him with hands outstretched. In one of her hands she held some powder and bullets which she had collected for him and kept hidden while in captivity. At this sight, the proud chief wept openly.

By fall of that year, Coacoochee and some three hundred of his people embarked at Fort Brooke for the trip to Arkansas. Nevertheless, when Colonel Worth officially declared war over in August 1842, some two hundred Seminoles remained hidden deep in the vast Everglades. Of these holdouts, Worth said in effect: Leave them alone; they will come in sooner or later. But they never did, and their descendants remain there today.

29.
The Circuit Riders Tame the Frontier

Methodists on horseback were bold and fearless in bringing the Gospel to a wild and isolated Florida territory.

They were, for the most part, bold, fearless, and strong in the faith as they rode alone over the trackless frontier wilderness of territorial Florida.

Relentless and plodding as they moved over forest, hammock, river, and swamp, they endured dangers and hardships in their zeal to bring "the glad tidings" to red, white, and black men alike. They belonged to that phenomenal breed who arose all across the frontiers of early America—the Methodist circuit riders.

It seems a curious and glaring omission that the strongest moral influence in weaving the civil and social fabric of early Florida is negligibly mentioned, if at all, in the tomes of modern history. But in the sometimes violent and anarchistic milieu that was much of territorial Florida, they were considered "the moral courts" of that land. Noted historian William W. Sweet declares more succinctly: "No single force had more to do with bringing order out of frontier chaos than the Methodist circuit rider, and among no other class of men was the herioc element more finely displayed."

The idea of the circuit rider was itself unusual: The church of that day disdained what seemed to them a rough and crude ministry, one perhaps even "unchurchly," especially when that church might be a forest clearing, a dirt-floor cabin, a courtroom, barn, blockhouse, or stable. But how else to reach so many souls scattered in isolation, thought Francis Asbury, the Wesleyan Methodist who initiated the practice in the latter eighteenth century and by 1808 had five hundred circuit riders fanned out over the edges of the new republic. John Wesley and George Whitefield had already turned England upside down by taking their Methodist gospel to fields, mines, and homes, thus incurring the boundless wrath of the rigid high church of England, which accused the Methodists of "enthusiasm," a term then denoting any claim to the biblical experience of Pentecost.

By 1821, Methodist circuit riders were ready to bring their message to newly ceded U.S. territories, which had been officially closed to the Protestant faith by Spain for more than 250 years.

Asbury

116

200 mile

Florida riders went out to this new region from three main district bases: Pensacola, Tallahassee, and St. Augustine. The work was hard and demanding. The pay was meager at best and often short of bare expenses. A rider carried only clothes, books, simple rations, and a sack of corn for his horse. It was a lonely journey over a two-hundred-mile circuit where for **200** miles neither house nor human was seen. Cold, rain, or tropical heat could bring ague or fever, and if rations ran short, one had to depend on a chance "parishioner" for hospitality. The fare was often similar to that offered one rider: "Musty corn bread . . . and the tough lungs of a deer fried in rancid bacon grease." But the ardor and faith of these itinerant preachers were usually a match for such rigors and hardships.

One of the early riders, John Slade, often referred to as the father of Florida Methodism, was not atypical. To keep his appointed rounds, he thought nothing of once plunging on horseback into a rain-swollen river in bitter cold, arriving at a small cabin where, with icicles formed on his clothing, he preached with warmth to a gathering of poor white settlers. But to Slade, "the value of an immortal soul could not be estimated." Historian George G. Smith described Slade as tall, well-formed, "with a voice at once strong, clear and musical. He was endowed with an intellect of high order, possessed great moral and personal courage, and preached Christ with power . . . clear and comprehensive." Even in "wayworn and weather-beaten" later years, Slade's long, flowing white locks recalled to one elder "the image of an old patriarch or apostle . . . the fire in his eyes still undimmed."

Riders found many black people receptive to their teaching. Young Joshua Glenn found only one Methodist when he arrived in predominantly Catholic St. Augustine in 1823, but within a year, he had organized a church there of forty black and twelve white members. Riders went to the Indians, too, but sometimes their Christian message was not so well received. Even Isaac Boring, a man considered possessed of strong common sense and invincible pertinacity, entreated in vain with Seminole leader John Hicks to let him preach to Hicks's tribes. Chided Boring: "Persons who would not hear the good word and continued to do bad displeased the Almighty and when they died would go to the bad world." Hicks replied that "many of the whites did not attend the good talk, and that they were as wicked as himself." Boring wrote later: "What a lamentable truth." Still he prayed that soon "these children of the woods shall joyfully hear the gospel."

One of the most fearless preachers to ride the Florida circuit was John L. Jerry. In the darkest days of the Second Seminole Indian War when many settlers were killed, families were massacred, and no man dared travel alone, Jerry remained on his lonely ride undaunted. Historian Smith recalled him as "a man of courage and zeal, and neither tomahawk nor scalping knife

code

drove him from his work." Emerging from the war unscathed, Jerry had his
own explanation: "The people say the reason I was not troubled was because
the Indians knew me, but I say God protected me." Rev. Jerry spoke with
such fire and conviction that both soldiers and citizens would journey many
miles to hear him.

A religious awakening seems to have swept over most of mid-north
Florida during the late 1830s, and this was enhanced by the popular camp
meetings that drew families from miles around to pine wood clearings, usually near a spring, for the "most exciting event going on." For many isolated
frontier families it was a chance for socializing as well as spiritual renewal.
Circuit preachers often spoke four times a day, and amid laughter, tears,
singing, dancing, and shouting, meetings went on for several days or more,
as long as "the spirit led them." But such gatherings were not always without risk. Such was the case with one protracted meeting in Alachua County
when the worshipers suddenly found themselves surrounded by some seventy-five Indian warriors. Just as inexplicably, the warriors withdrew, and
only later did Rev. R. H. Howren learn that the red men had planned to attack
but "seeing such an unusual stir among the people, they became alarmed
and withdrew."

Tallahassee had put together a Methodist church, but the town generally, one rider observed, was often the scene of "wild dissipation, and the
gambler and duelist were there." But the presiding district elder and rider,
Josiah Evans, although of rough and plain exterior, was considered "daunt-
less, energetic and spiritual" and was never timorous about handling toughs
and rowdies or disciplining errant church members.

Still another problem beset that area, as described by a veteran rider:
"Cotton was high. Speculation was wild. Paper promises were abundant.
The county was wild in its pursuit after wealth, but God was providing
something better than money—a great revival—and to prepare the way for it
the rod of a terrible chastisement [loomed]." Whether of divine origin or
not, a great "chastisement" did befall this area not long after: The mighty
Union Bank failed and wiped out scores of its most affluent citizens.

But the circuit riding days in Florida—and the South—were marked for
decline following a bitter controversy over the removal by the main Methodist Conference of a slave-holding official. Methodism prohibited slave
owners from holding church office. The action against the official prompted
Southern dioceses, including Florida, to form in 1845 their own "Methodist
Episcopal Church, South." In turn, some conscience-troubled circuit riders
withdrew into a form of lay ministry, and others went north. During the Civil
War itself, Methodist membership suffered its sharpest decline.

By the latter nineteenth century, the circuit rider had vanished from the
scene, recalled only in story and legend. But Floridians can recall these ded-

icated men with some pride and fealty; rarely had so few done so much to bring "order out of frontier chaos" or to set the moral tone for a young territory as it moved toward statehood.

30.
Captain Brannan Holds the Fort

Acting quickly and without orders, the Union captain seized Key West's Fort Taylor overnight for a critical Civil War move.

Bold or heroic acts and decisions during the Civil War rarely adorn the pages of history unless they are vividly defined by shot and shell-fire—and preferably accompanied by gore.

But on the eve of that great war in a faraway, lonely army outpost in Key West, amid a hostile hotbed of secessionist intrigue, an obscure army captain, acting without orders from his Washington superiors, decided on his own to "hold the fort" before the first shot was ever fired. His farsighted act proved to be one of the most important command decisions of the war: It secured the Union's vital "Rock of Gibralter" and, as much as any single act, greatly hastened the conclusion of that tragic conflict, doubtlessly saving countless lives.

When all other Southern forts and naval bases fell easily into the hands of surrounding Rebel forces in the early days of the war, Key West alone enabled the Union to command the seas in both the Gulf and South Atlantic and choke off lifeblood supply lines to the South with devastating blockades. It also enabled major attacks to be launched against Southern ports, such as Commodore David Farragut's historic victory in Mobile Bay.

The wealthy and powerful slave-holding secessionists could have seized Fort Taylor in Key West harbor with little effort during the months preceding Fort Sumter—and they had every intention of doing so. The only U.S. presence was a tiny force occupying the army barracks at the opposite end of the island from the fort. There was also a small contingent of laborers with the U.S. Corps of Engineers who were making construction repairs within the fort after its heavy damage in a hurricane years earlier. It was unmanned otherwise.

Captain James M. Brannan of the U.S. First Artillery, stationed at the barracks with his under-strength company of forty-four men, was already outnumbered in sheer force. He could never have retaken the fort had the secessionists occupied it. The latter, in turn, considered the captain a negligible threat to their designs; they could bide their time until hostilities actually began. The artillery unit was virtually isolated from any outside reinforcements, and any such that might arrive could be easily detected and almost as easily resisted, since the fort was designed only to repel attacks from the sea. The secessionists therefore felt secure in the belief that they had it covered both ways. Captain Brannan, at least, would be no problem.

As early as 1831, the strategic value of Key West's location and fine harbor was recognized when Commodore David Porter, who had destroyed the last pirate strongholds in the Gulf and Caribbean, wrote the secretary of the navy: "The advantages of Key West's location as a military and naval station has no equal except Gibralter. . . . It commands the outlets of all trade from Jamaica, the Caribbean Sea, the Bay of Honduras, and the Gulf of Mexico, and is a check to the naval forces of whatever nation may hold Cuba." By 1845, the government was similarly convinced and began construction of Fort Taylor after setting up the army barracks post.

In 1860, the port of Key West contained 2,913 souls—160 free Negroes; 451 slaves; and another 2,302 men, women, and children—mostly white adult males. Aside from commercial fishing and shipping, the town had prospered greatly from the shipwreck salvaging business. Merchants, lawyers, and allied interests had also generously enriched themselves from this lucrative trade as the dangerous currents and reefs of the Florida Straits for years yielded up millions of dollars in booty from wrecked vessels. The temper and sympathies of that community's leading citizens were perhaps best summed up in the attitudes of one of its later judges and self-styled historians, Jefferson B. Browne. They were the "cultured Southern gentlemen" who yearned for the Bourbon splendor of an elitist-ruled South and were likened, in Browne's imagery, to feudal barons of Magna Charta days, only the threat then was not King John but the "despot" Abraham Lincoln. As the national war clouds darkened, these men were heatedly voluble in their rhetoric of resistance to "Federal usurpation." Aside from the Browne family, they included influential figures such as William Pinckney and Judge Winer Bethel (both later imprisoned for treasonous covert activities) and Florida's U.S. Senator Stephen R. Mallory, known more commonly as "Cat-o-nine-tails" Mallory for his advocacy of floggings for sailors who infracted naval rules. Mallory would soon become the Confederacy's navy secretary.

Although Browne claimed that Key Westers who remained loyal to the United States were men "of meagre importance," they included courageous voices counseling temperance, such as that of Colonel W. C. Maloney, Sr., and Federal Judge William Marvin, who would later ably serve as provisional governor of postwar Florida under appointment by President Andrew Johnson.

In his own mind, Captain Brannan was certain that war would come, and the Union's vulnerable position in Key West disturbed him. Word of the various plots and intrigues seething among the town's leaders reached him, and he knew that Fort Taylor was in danger of being seized at any time. He knew that this would be a great strategic loss to the United States, and he also knew that his token force, greatly outnumbered, could not possibly retake it. The small force had been stationed there originally to forestall Indian attacks during the Seminole War; no one then envisioned any major civil uprisings.

But Captain Brannan was a solid West Pointer, a veteran of the Mexican War, and trained to act on orders from higher command and not without such orders. He had until then received no orders whatever about what to do in the event of civil war. He might have to turn over his barracks, supplies, and the fort itself, as so many U.S. post commanders, surrounded by superior local forces, later would do. This dilemma prompted him, on December 11, 1860, to write at once to Washington for instructions whether he should "endeavor at all hazards to prevent Fort Taylor from being taken or allow the State authorities to have possession without any resistance on the part of my command."

However, as the days passed and secessionist threats and intrigue increased within the town, the captain sensed an imminent danger to the fort. He also knew it might be weeks before he heard from Washington, and by then it would be too late. He finally concluded that he would have to act without authority, and at considerable risk to himself and his men. But he saw no choice.

On Sunday, January 13, 1861, the captain made certain that the day would be no different from any other Sunday. He and his men attended local church services as usual; they ambled about the town, having their dinner and mingling in casual social ways, as was their custom. And the day ended with its usual, uneventful routine.

But on the midnight of that Sunday, as the town slept quietly, Captain Brannan moved swiftly. He and his men scoured and loaded up everything in the barracks post that wasn't nailed down—food, water, weapons, ammo, and general supplies—and set out on the four-mile march to the fort. They had previously cut a crude, rocky road around the town, and this enabled them to reach the fort, unload, and secure themselves before sunrise. The captain then immediately set up two sand revetments to cover the single landward approach to the fort and reversed emplacement of ten of the citadel's big guns, training them on the town to repel any landward attack. He then sent another message at once to Washington, requesting immediate reinforcements and the presence of at least one or two warships in the harbor. The great prize had been taken and he was determined to hold it.

Next day, the town buzzed with excitement over the seizure. The secessionists were shocked, then angry, seething with a myriad of schemes to attack. They had been taken completely off guard; all of their well-laid plans were—at least temporarily—aborted. They learned also that the captain had seventy thousand gallons of water and food provisions to last four months. They were also aware that their numbers in force were close to twenty to one and that a well-executed attack could very easily succeed.

And so they dallied, hotly disputing among themselves their conflicting plans—direct attack, harassment first and then assault, or siege. They opted for the latter since, with every Southern state now officially seceded, war was a certainty and the fort could soon be starved into surrender. But it was a fateful choice.

Washington had by now affirmed the captain's action and had also notified Major William French of the Fifth U.S. Artillery in Texas. In order to avoid surrender of his command in his isolated post, Major French swiftly marched his men and arms down to the Rio Grande where, at Point Isabel, they embarked for Key West, arriving on April 6, 1861. This well-armed and superior force quickly moved into the fort and secured every strategic surrounding point in the harbor.

As historian Browne lamented: "Whatever hope the faithful ones may have had that they might ultimately wrest Ft. Taylor from federal control was destroyed." Warships later arrived, and when the war began, Union forces were now able to occupy the town and hold it under strict martial law.

The captain's decisiveness in securing Key West for the Union made it the only naval base in the South which was never occupied or attacked by the Confederates. It assured the Union access to the Gulf for its crucial victories there, such as Farragut's attack on Mobile. Without Key West, more importantly, the devastating blockade of Southern ports would have been virtually impossible; the Union kept more vessels there than in any other port in the country. Ironically, the blockade runners, who had perpetuated heroic myths of their escapades on behalf of the Rebels, were mostly an unsavory, profiteering lot who actually helped to drain the South's funds and resources. For example, one of the South's most desperate commodity needs—salt—cost the privateer $1.50 a sack in Nassau, but he demanded up to $150 a sack when it reached a Southern port. Or they would pay the often ragged and starving Rebel forces twenty cents a pound for their cotton and sell it in England at two hundred percent profit.

The effectiveness of the Key West–based blockaders was staggering. In total, they brought into Key West Admiralty Court 299 blockade runners, with cargo, most of it out of Havana or Nassau. Next to the relentless General U. S. Grant himself, the securing of the Key West "Gibralter" may have been one of the greatest single factors to hasten the war's end.

Or, as University of Miami historian Vaughn Camp, Jr., observes, history overlooks the captain's role since "no bullets sung past his ears, no bombs burst over his head" as he carried out what he conceived to be his duty. "Nevertheless," Camp adds, "the resolution of Captain Brannan's dilemma remains one of the most important command decisions of the Civil War."

31.
He Led in Perilous Times

Despite death threats and corruption, Governor Harrison Reed guided Florida through the stormy trials of Reconstruction.

Harrison Reed was Florida's first full-term Reconstruction governor (1868–72).

As headlines blare of indictments, jury probes, or the latest allegations, we tend to think today that our state political structures are being fouled irreparably by little nests of nefarious men engaged in scandalous abuse of public trust for personal gain.

But this may be a healthy sign of housecleaning compared to other days in Florida politics, such as the turbulent period in post–Civil War Reconstruction when a governor could wonder if his very office might be "occupied" next morning by political gangs or, indeed, if his life and limb would remain intact for the term.

Florida's first full-term Reconstruction governor, Harrison Reed (1868–72), did in fact face such a situation. His own lieutenant governor literally tried to steal the office from him, and Reed was possibly the first and only state executive ever set up for assassination.

But in that seething post–Civil War turmoil, demagoguery, bribery, cheap whiskey, cash, cigars, and gunpowder were as often the political tuning forks of the electoral process as were any of the more orderly civil procedures.

When the state delegates convened to elect a governor and draft a new state constitution, three factions were at odds: the radical Republicans; the native Rebels, many of whom were disenfranchised for their roles in the secession and who soon formed a Democrats party; and a more moderate Union-Republican party, called the Reed party.

The radicals were composed mainly of Union men, or carpetbaggers, who had strong support from the Freedmen's Bureau which was set up to aid the Negro in developing his personal welfare and newly won citizenship. The Democrats were often native planters, Cracker farmers, former Confederate officers, plus fringe elements that were often covertly sympathetic to the Ku Klux Klan. Reed's party opted for a center in this maelstrom.

Of mild manner and conservative bent, Reed hoped to play a conciliatory role in the midst of often bitter and intriguing warfare. He failed. As historian Allan Nevins observed: "He appointed some Democrats to important offices along with Negroes and imported Republicans, took care to give the state a sound judiciary, surrounded himself with a good cabinet and discouraged appeals to prejudice. The result was that he displeased every group."

It was a motley swarm of delegates who thronged Tallahassee's City Hotel across from the capitol in early 1868. Heated caucuses held forth, whiskey flowed, and just about anyone would take a bribe from anyone who offered it, and for any favor. The greater number of delegates were impoverished men, and each party outdid the other to fete them with food, liquor, and lodgings. Many a former slave tasted champagne and smoked fine Havanas for the first time.

But the two major factions—Radicals and Reed's—clashed, and it took the intervention of General George Gordon Meade, the Gettysburg hero, to assure a fair and impartial session. Reed was elected governor by a large vote, and the new constitution—granting franchise to black and former Rebel alike and providing a liberal framework for progress—was overwhelmingly adopted. Reed was sworn in June 8, 1868, and it looked for a time as if the moderate-progressive movement would temper the times and accelerate postwar recovery and development. This was a short-lived dream.

The man elected as lieutenant governor on the same ticket (against Reed's own preference) was one William H. Gleason. Gleason was a protégé of T. W. Osborn, a crafty wheeler-dealer type who had lent grudging support to Reed at the convention. But he was to become Reed's arch antagonist when the governor proved less than pliant regarding an Osborn and Gleason proposal for a secret deal to exchange state bonds for scrip (the form of money paid all state and local government personnel) at a handsome profit that they promised to share with Reed.

In another Osborn "deal," a check for five hundred dollars was sent to state Senator A. A. Knight to secure passage of a bill to incorporate a savings bank in which unlimited amounts of state funds could be deposited without any adequate security. It sailed through both houses within twenty-four hours, and Knight rushed it to Reed for signature that midnight. But

Reed merely took it under study. He promptly vetoed it the next day, and with the bill's dubious features now exposed, the senate dared not override him.

It was the first of many vetoes to incur the wrath of the Osborn clique. And that same year, when Osborn finagled a seat as U.S. senator, he used that powerful post to attack Reed throughout his term.

Reed then antagonized Rebel Democrats by organizing black as well as white militia to resist the Ku Klux Klan. He purchased two thousand rifles in New York for this militia, but Klan members attacked the train carrying them and threw most of them off.

With the ranks of his enemies now swelling, attempts were made by various factions to threaten and intimidate Reed in hopes of forcing his resignation. When these failed, a conspiracy developed to depose him by violence and seize the capitol. The insurgents sent up signal rockets each night from their City Hotel quarters and frequently fired guns or rifles at or near Reed's residence. Their efforts were thwarted by the presence of Adjutant-General George B. Carse, aided by loyal Leon County Sheriff Munger, who guarded the capitol for forty-six days and nights with a volunteer armed force.

Failing here, a group of Osborn men, on November 3, 1868, pushed through the House a resolution to impeach Reed, but it failed for a lack of a quorum when reported to the senate. Nevertheless, Gleason and George J. Alden, Reed's perfidious secretary of state, interpreted the resolution as a de facto suspension of the governor, permitting Gleason to act in his place. Gleason then set up his "governor's office" in the City Hotel while Alden promptly swiped the state seal from his own office and gave it to the usurper to stamp documents which he issued periodically. This went on for several days while armed police guarded Reed's office day and night.

On one occasion, as reported by the black historian John Wallace (a contemporary of these events), Gleason slipped into the office in Reed's absence and made himself at home in the executive chair. Adjutant Carse discovered him and ordered him out. Gleason refused, at which point Carse lunged at him with a drawn revolver. "Gleason wore a fine beaver hat, which went one way while he went the other, retreating in double quick time to the seat of his hotel government," Wallace wrote.

Reed finally counterattacked. He first axed the traitorous Alden and named the distinguished black senator, Jonathan C. Gibbs, to replace him, greatly enhancing his lagging support with the freedmen. Reed then asked the state supreme court for an opinion on the illegal impeachment proceeding and, on November 24, 1868, was given full support as legal governor by the justices.

Finally, he hit Gleason directly by challenging his right to be lieutenant governor since Gleason had not been a resident of Florida for the three years prior to his election, as the law required. Reed won, and Gleason was ousted on December 14, 1868.

Another less-heralded intrigue during this harassment period was the conspiracy by three of Reed's enemies to have him assassinated. The gunman selected for this purpose was the notorious Luke Lott, a hellion from Calhoun County. Lott soon appeared in the capitol and made little secret of his avowed intent, but a Tallahassee planter, William D. Bloxham, heard of the mission and intervened. He finally persuaded Lott, by one means or another, to abandon his project. The slinger was last seen in Jackson County, shooting up objects—both animate and inanimate—possibly in some fit of pique over his frustrated "big-game" plans. Bloxham was to become, twelve years later, one of Florida's distinctive governors.

Successive impeachment attempts dogged the remainder of Reed's term, with Osborn's ring and other factions making it almost a ritual order of business in- each legislative session. With his great federal patronage power as a U.S. senator, Osborn tightened his hold on the lawmakers. Thus, while Reed successfully beat down the ouster efforts, he faced a continually hostile legislature and hence failed to effect any major achievements or basic reforms.

But Reed was no radical or adventurer. He liked the state, saw its new-frontier aspects, and worked for its development. He remained in it after his term ended, residing in Jacksonville with his wife and son until his death in 1899.

It might almost be enough to say that Reed held the extremely volatile spirits of the period in check, serving as an effective buffer for those counterposing forces that might easily have set the state's progress back into violence, bloodshed, and anarchy had Reed not held the very shaky ground on which he stood as Florida's first full-time Reconstruction governor.

32.
The Mighty Oak Falls to Politics

John Quincy Adams fought to save north Florida's great live oaks, but political intrigue aborted his efforts.

We tend to think of the environmental movement as a strictly modern phenomenon, in which packs of Audubon and Sierra Club Davids suddenly arose to meet the Goliaths of pell-mell and devastating development.

But Florida's first conservationist was active more than 150 years ago, and that he was also president of the United States lent considerable clout to his activism.

Nevertheless, the zealous efforts of John Quincy Adams to save what was then one of Florida's greatest natural treasures—the live oak—were met with political intrigue and personal malignity, and most of his plans would die aborning in a political charnel house.

In the 1820s, great forests of huge live oaks swept majestically across the north and northwest sections of the state. The mighty oak's tough and durable timber was more valued than any known, especially for shipbuilding. But these forests were being systematically plundered by freebooting lumber and shipping interests. In fact, by 1827, Naval Secretary Samuel Southard told Congress that more than half the timber in accessible Florida coastal areas had been ravaged; along the St. Johns River, forests had been stripped bare up to fifteen miles inland.

This timber was a vital strategic material to the young democracy's naval defenses. An oaken vessel was seaworthy for half a century or longer. Oak is extremely hard wood, close-grained but buoyant, and the angular shape of its limbs for ship hulls made it a highly prized naval acquisition—so much so that in 1799 John Jay initiated federal funding of $200,000 toward preserving timber lands. Another law in 1817 forbade the sale by government of any lands containing live oak and red cedar.

But these laws were loosely enforced, if enforced at all. They failed to stop shipping and lumber barons from bringing in whole teams of woodcutters to pillage Florida's rich stands. The cutters, dubbed "Live-Oakers" by naturalist John J. Audubon, usually were imported from large Northern cities. They would move onto a site, hastily set up living shanties, and start cutting rapidly, mainly between December 1 and March 1, when the tree sap is completely down. The valuable timber drew premium prices, especially overseas.

President Adams, long an avid student of plant and tree cultures, was much disturbed by Secretary Southard's report. He decided to act at once to save Florida's live oaks "from the certain destruction to which they are tending." He spurred Florida's territorial delegate, Joseph White, to push through Congress authorization for Adams to establish a sixty-thousand-acre plantation on mainly public lands adjacent to the navy yard at Pensacola on Santa Rosa Island. The farm would not merely preserve existing stands but would also bear planting of thousands of new trees. He also initiated scientific studies of the oak for a better understanding of its cultivation and growth processes.

There was another live oak enthusiast who owned sixteen hundred acres of the proposed tree farm site, Henry M. Brackenridge, then district judge for west Florida. Brackenridge gladly agreed to sell his acreage provided he could keep a small orange grove on the tract. But Adams was so impressed by the judge's considerable knowledge of tree culture that he appointed him to superintend the farm. Brackenridge agreed to do so, serving without pay. Laborers were brought in for clearing and planting, and the farm soon became a thriving experiment.

The judge quickly proved himself to be perhaps the nation's first pioneer forester. (His studies and practices in forest management are still in use today.) The Deer Point project, as it came to be called, was soon in "a flourishing condition," Adams observed, with 100,000 trees, both existing and newly planted. The judge also quickly proved his contention that "no other tree so improves with care as the live oak."

But this pioneer effort to save the state's great oaks was almost doomed after the bitter presidential election of 1828, which Adams lost to Andrew Jackson. The new administration took a skeptical view of conservation, deeming it also as something competitive with, or adversely affecting, private commerce.

More pointedly, the acrid personal antagonism spawned in the volatile campaign left the new regime looking for any hint of scandal in the old. Thus, when a disgruntled ex-employee fired by Secretary Southard claimed that federal funds for the tree farm were used for private benefit, the new naval secretary, John Branch, leaped on this morsel. He ordered the suspension of the Deer Point operations until a navy commission could investigate it.

In the meantime, Branch and an aide, Amos Kendall, made attempts in Congress to besmirch both the farm and the individuals involved. When the commission finally reported finding no evidence of misspent funds or any misfeasance, Branch simply ignored it and contrived his own report.

Judge Brackenridge fought back, accusing Branch of "willful misrepresentation" and "a dishonorable suppression of the [commission] report, because it would have refuted and falsified his own." To Branch's innuendos that Judge Brackenridge may have gained private financial benefit, the delegate produced papers and documents showing that the sixteen hundred acres were sold to the government "for one-fifth its value." He also demonstrated that the value of the timber was far greater than the seven thousand dollars spent annually for the farm's operation. The judge even offered to rescind the contract and buy the acreage back at the same price at which it was sold. But a sympathetic Congress declined this offer.

Adams himself was incensed and lashed out at "the base purpose" of the secretary. "All is to be abandoned by the stolid ignorance and stupid malignity of John Branch and of his filthy subaltern, Amos Kendall," Adams fumed.

But the Deer Point tree farm soon would die. A dilatory Congress did not act on the conservation issue until 1831, when it enacted a law for forest preservation that specifically forbade the cutting by private parties of any trees on public lands. Nevertheless, the lawmakers failed to rescind Branch's termination order. Shortly after, when Branch was replaced by Levi Woodbury, Brackenridge renewed his efforts to save the tree farm but drew only a promise from Woodbury that the existing plantings would be cared for; the project itself remained abandoned.

But the 1831 law, like the previous laws, became just another shadowy, toothless parody of itself, and soon enough, the Live-Oakers were back in Florida in force, chopping away in earnest.

When his bench term expired in 1832, a disgusted Brackenridge left Florida for good and returned to his native Pennsylvania. Years later, in the latter nineteenth century, when the United States opened large tracts of north Florida to homesteading, most of the remaining huge stands of live oaks would be chopped down indiscriminately. Today, all that remains of the Deer Point experiment is that 1831 law and a smattering of government lands near Pensacola.

33.
Florida's Yankee Benefactress

A prime catalyst of the Civil War herself, Harriet Beecher Stowe nevertheless returned to help promote a vanquished state.

Harriet Beecher Stowe became one of Florida's most zealous promoters. (Florida State Archives)

Florida's early promoter giants—the Disstons, the Flaglers, the Plants— were mostly of one breed: all wealthy, all powerful, and all male.

But the person who most qualifies as the state's first eminent promoter was a female and, at that, a tiny, unprepossessing woman who seemed the most unlikely person ever to want to go live in the Deep South right after the Civil War.

To concerned Northern friends, the decision by Mrs. Harriet Beecher Stowe to buy a home in Florida seemed at best unwise, especially considering that, only a decade before, any Southerner possessing her scathing antislavery book, *Uncle Tom's Cabin,* might have been, and often was, run out of town or worse. It was as if, say, her minister brother, Henry Ward Beecher, had in prewar days gone to homestead peacefully in "Bloody Kansas," where he had sent so many crates of "Beecher's Bibles" (Sharpe's rifles) in the "free-state" warfare.

And now this singular lady, whom President Lincoln once jokingly greeted as "the little woman who started this big war," was going to live in a region that had suffered no little from its defeat in that war. But the once-obscure New England housewife-writer, whose powerful indictment of a "peculiar institution" was to shake two continents and help rip a nation asunder, was unflappable in her resolve. Thus, the most famous woman in America of that time became also one of the most zealous promoters of the virtues of living in the flower state; and her efforts were no doubt the greatest single contribution to the flourishing growth of Jacksonville, as well as other parts of the state in the years to follow.

Mrs. Stowe first came to Florida to visit her son, Frederick, who had tried, unsuccessfully, to operate a cotton plantation at Orange Park on the St. Johns River.

Fred, who was trying to recover from the illness and effects of having, as a young officer, caught an earful of shot-iron in the Gettysburg carnage, later left Florida.

While visiting Fred that spring of 1867, Mrs. Stowe, already delighted by the magic of stepping from winter into May, came upon a cottage for sale at Mandarin which included a thirty-acre orange grove, all perched right on the banks of what she later termed "the most magnificent river in America," the St. Johns. The enchantment took quick effect and she purchased the property that same year.

Contrary to fearful well-wishers, Harriet was welcomed by her neighbors near and far. The Jacksonville and St. Augustine press accented the cordiality in warm social notices, remarking also that the celebrated authoress had searched out "the real feeling of the people in her somewhat extended journeys all over Florida and found them so kind that they would surrender their own sleeping accommodations to her." But it might be pertinent to add here that the lady's simple homeliness and directness of speech and manner, her modesty and genuine concern for human welfare—whether Southern, Northern, black, or white—had endeared her as often to enemies as to friends. Not untypical a remark by her was her self-descriptive comment at the height of her celebrity in England: "I am a little bit of a woman . . . about as thin and dry as a pinch of snuff."

By the spring of 1868, Harriet was ensconced in her cottage and would soon enlarge it considerably with extra rooms and a veranda, and part of the house front built around a giant live oak tree. Her letters at this time to husband Calvin Ellis Stowe and twin daughters Eliza and Harriet glowed with accounts of the fruits, flowers, and sunshine of her new winter home. And in fact, it may have seemed a small, peaceful corner of heaven to a woman so long embroiled in the hectic, wearying, dizzy turbulence of prewar and war days. She expressed this feeling once when it came time to return for the summer to her Hartford, Connecticut, home: "I hate to leave my calm Isle of Patmos, where the world is not, and I have such quiet long hours for writing. If I had my say wholly, I wouldn't come North at all. I am leaving the land of flowers on the first of June with tears in my eyes."

The family joined her the next winter, and Harriet also persuaded cousin Spencer Foote, a Civil War veteran, to bring his family to live at Mandarin and manage her large grove. By the time the family arrived that year, Foote had set out even more trees in the flourishing grove, along with peaches, lemons, and grapes. With typical Yankee business acumen, Foote also did not hesitate to remind buyers of whose oranges they were purchasing by stenciling each fruit box headed north with the full name of the grower.

Aside from her writing, Harriet had other varied interests at Mandarin. She helped set up a school for black and white children and adults, strongly convinced of the need for education of the newly freed people. She also sought the aid of Florida's Episcopal bishop with an eye "to establishing a line of churches along the St. Johns River" to assist in this educational task. Although she could not persuade her brother, Charles Beecher, to leave his Northern parish and become clergyman for this project, she so sparked his interest in Florida that, not long after, he bought a plantation across the state at Newport on the St. Marks River, just south of Tallahassee, and became a respected settler in the area. His presence may have assisted somewhat the public welcome tendered his sister when she visited him later. Tallahasseeans drove her about the city sightseeing, honored her at a dinner, and had her welcome several hundred people in a receiving line on the capitol steps.

Husband Calvin found Mandarin as idyllic as promised. The noted biblical scholar, who had just completed his magnum opus *Origin and His-*

The Stowe family on the porch of their residence in Mandarin. (Florida State Archives)

tory of the Books of the Bible, became in retirement a contented fixture on
the cottage veranda, settled in his rocking chair and surrounded with scholarly tomes. Such a fixture that Harriet noted of her beloved "rabbi": "His
red skull-cap served [river] mariners as a sort of daytime lighthouse." He
was content to leave the neighborhood picnics, wood hikes, and river trips
to the rest of the energetic Stowe family.

Visitors were already trickling into the river region. Notables like William Cullen Bryant returned north to extoll the beauty of Florida. Harriet's
next-door neighbor in Hartford, a young and then unknown writer named
Samuel Clemens and his wife, Livy, visited the Stowes, and the future Mark
Twain was hard-pressed to leave "the great river."

But it was not until 1872 that Harriet began a series of travel articles on
Florida that might have thrown any modern commerce chamber into a frenzied euphoria. Her trips about the state by mule-cart had culminated in a
group of vivid on-scene portraits of the state's people, flora, fauna, climate,
and water. Published throughout the North under the title *Palmetto Leaves,*
the book became one of her most popular works. Up to this time, the North
knew nothing about the state, aside from an occasional news item. But this
book was the first saturation of promotional writing on Florida ever to reach
the country at large.

It was also unique in that it was completely unsolicited; to Harriet it was
as natural as any other writing she had done, a love labor. Moreover, unlike
later, more famous promoter appeals, she addressed the nominal average citizen, one of more modest means who might come to settle in with family and
help build the area. No grandiose talk here of giant development tracts or
railroads; only mocking birds, great live oaks, wild flowers, fertile lands,
and lazy rivers. She could bring fresh whimsy to her portraits, such as: "If
we painted her [Florida], we should not represent her as a neat, trim damsel,
with starched linen cuffs and collar: she would be a brunette, dark but
comely, with gorgeous tissues, a general disarray and dazzle, and with a sort
of jolly untidiness, free, easy and joyous." She could even suggest "grand
tours" for visitors, reciting steamboat fares, schedules, and points of scenic
interest.

It is difficult to gauge fully the results of this unique and massive advertising. Nevertheless, in only the first year after *Leaves* appeared, Harriet
could write to a friend that fourteen thousand tourists had been through the
area that year—a remarkable figure in that the native population of the whole
northeast area of the state barely reached this number. The crowds continued
to come.

However, the good lady publicist might have regretted her innocent promotional efforts at times. Tourists often flocked over the grounds of her Mandarin home, prompting Mrs. Foote to lock the gates at the sight of a steamer.

An ugly commercialism reared its head as steamers sold seventy-five-cent excursions to Mandarin, causing a scandalous invasion of privacy that was finally halted. Once a brazen woman marched right up on the front porch where Calvin was sitting, introduced herself, and added: "But I would have preferred to meet Mrs. Stowe." "So had I, Madam," retorted Calvin. "So had I—a thousand times." Worse yet, a few professional "Stowe-haters" suggested that Harriet colluded with the boats and even appeared in a pose of writing on her porch whenever a boat drew near!

However, the Stowes passed their years at Mandarin mainly in relative tranquillity, in spite of the sudden and rapid boom in the growth of Jacksonville proper. But by the early 1880s, first a great frost, which wiped out their orange grove, and finally Calvin's increasing ill health kept the Stowes from Mandarin for lengthy periods. When Calvin died in August 1886, Harriet sold all her Mandarin property and home, except the orange grove. Declining health kept her at home in Hartford until her death in 1896.

Harriet was probably never fully aware of how great had been her influence in advertising Florida to the country, turning it from an obscure down-under tip on the map into a beckoning, lush, tropical paradise to which tens of thousands would flock to help build a state over the following decades. She herself would doubtless have viewed it as a fitting Christian act to help restore a prostrate, defeated brotherland to its feet; Florida's first promoter was merely the Good Samaritan.

34.
The Seminoles' Friendliest Foe

William S. Harney was the ablest of Indian fighters, but he proved to be the red man's one—and often only—white friend.

He was their most formidable foe in battle, but for most of the nineteenth century, the Seminole Indians regarded William Selby Harney, whom they called Man-who-runs-like-the-deer, as their one—and often only—friend among white men.

In fact, had the United States heeded Harney's counsel, it might have cut short one of its longest and costliest wars, the Second Seminole War (1835–42). His superiors called then Colonel Harney their "bravest and most effective officer" in that war, but no other officer exerted so great an effort to resolve the conflict peaceably, an effort that almost cost him his life.

Harney's long, lone crusade against mistreatment of the American Indian actually began in Florida years earlier during the First Seminole War. Born in 1800 in Haysborough, Tennessee, and commissioned at 17 as a U.S. Infantry Second Lieutenant, Harney first gained distinction chasing pirates from the Mississippi Delta, forcing Jean Lafitte and his gang to flee to the Caribbean. He then joined General Andrew Jackson in raids on Seminoles in north Florida, and it was there, after viewing the devastated Indian villages and starving women and children, that the young officer began to question a government policy that viewed extermination of the Indians as the price of progress.

From here he was posted to the midwestern frontier, where he gained a widespread reputation among Indians for his fairness in protecting them from treaty violations and exploitation by both private traders and Indian agents.

Soon after his marriage to Mary Mullanphy, Harney went to fight in the Second Seminole War. Some twenty-five hundred Seminoles, led by Osceola, had been fighting the entire U.S. Army to a standstill in Florida's swamp and jungle. Harney believed it was duplicity and treaty-breaking by white men that had initiated the conflict. As U.S. casualties mounted, Harney worked arduously to persuade Commanding General Thomas Jesup that the Indians would honor a treaty permitting them to remain in the vast Everglades area, far from white settlements. But when a meeting was arranged

137

with Osceola and other chiefs at Fort King to discuss the proposal, General Jesup seemed suddenly swayed more by political expediency than high purpose. He violated the flag of truce and arrested the Indians. Osceola later died in captivity; the others were transported westward. Jesup was relieved of command.

Although dismayed and disgusted by Jesup's betrayal, Harney found Army Chief Alexander Macomb now more than eager to listen to his peace proposals. Macomb approved a treaty giving Seminole chiefs Sam Jones, Billy Bowlegs, Chekika, and others a sizable Everglades region, plus a trading post to be built on the Caloosahatchee River, near present-day Fort Myers. But this time betrayal would come from higher quarters.

At dawn on July 22, 1839, Harney and eight of his men awoke just in time to escape a massacre, as Jones and Chekika led 160 braves in a raid on the trading post site: eighteen soldiers and civilians were slain. Only after reaching a Biscayne Bay army post did the stunned Harney learn the cause of the attack. Powerful Florida politicians had pressured U.S. War Secretary Joel Poinsett into writing a letter assuring whites that the treaty was "only temporary." The chieftains had learned of it; thus their furious response. An angry Harney now stormed up to Washington and confronted Macomb, demanding that Poinsett be officially investigated. But the politically astute Macomb flatly refused, and Harney returned to Florida.

Later, with ninety men in canoes, Harney moved deep into the swamp and surprised Chekika's camp. The chieftain was slain and most of his men captured. This single act prompted some chiefs to surrender their tribes at Tampa for relocation westward. But many other Seminoles, including Billy Bowlegs, stayed behind. Years later, in 1855, Harney would be called in specially to settle a minor Third Seminole outbreak under Bowlegs. But first he forced assurances that "Washington won't make a liar out of me again." Harney then persuaded Bowlegs to move to the Arkansas River, but not before he secured a handsome cash settlement for the chieftain and all his tribe members. Yet a large number of Seminoles stayed behind—and remain there to this day. They were, finally, the only American tribe to win its war with the white man.

Harney went on to become a national hero—and a brigadier general—for his brilliant rout of Santa Anna's army in the Mexican War. Then, as western U.S. commander, he continued his efforts to secure and protect Indian treaty rights against the onslaught of land-hungry settlers. At one point he pleaded to Washington superiors: "It is not yet too late for us to requite, in some degree, this unfortunate race for their many sufferings, consequent to the domain of our peoples." During the Civil War, political connivance forced Harney into inactive status, an injustice that President

Lincoln later lamented as "one of the greatest mistakes of my Administration."

But at war's end, Harney was made a major general and specially honored for his "long and faithful services." His remaining years were spent pleading for the Indian's fair treatment.

In the 1880s, Harney retired to a home on Lake Eola at Orlando, where he died May 8, 1889—then the oldest living U.S. Army officer and one of its most unsung heroes. But the Indian tribes of America remembered the Man-who-runs-like-the-deer and honored him posthumously with a new name, Man-who-always-kept-his-word.

35.
Doc Webb: Merchant Prince and Hero

Builder of the "craziest drugstore in the world" in St. Petersburg, Webb also became one of the most effective consumer champions ever.

"It's the craziest drugstore in the world," its patrons often boasted.

Perhaps—but it was much more. It was the original shopping mall decades before the modern mall was conceived; it was a "festive marketplace" that might make its modern counterparts seem stiff and contrived; above all, it stretched the term "free enterprise" to wonderfully insane dimensions, delighting throngs of customers.

But then, some people thought now and again that James Earl "Doc" Webb, creator of The World's Most Unusual Drugstore in downtown St. Petersburg, might be missing a cylinder or two himself. Who else would sell you shirts or dresses or furniture at half-price, fill prescriptions below cost, hawk one-dollar bills at ninety-five cents each, serve a two-cent breakfast and throw in with it a colorful mix of beauty pageants, animal shows, and circuses? Here was a J. C. Penney or F. W. Woolworth gone berserk. Such madness enabled Webb to take a one-room shack in 1925 and over half a century turn it into a multimillion-dollar emporium with seventy-two stores sprawled over ten blocks, creating with it a St. Petersburg landmark and a national legend of sorts.

To thousands, especially the poor, elderly, black, and young, he was more than a merchant prince: He was a hero and a consumer champion.

Some of Webb's most significant achievements on behalf of consumers were in the courtroom. In 1949 he was the main party in a case in which the Florida Supreme Court ruled the state's fair-trade, or price-fixing, law invalid. And in 1951 he helped persuade the U.S. Supreme Court to rule all state fair-trade laws unconstitutional. The rulings may have saved the American public millions by holding down prices.

What's more, for twenty years Webb led the fight to stave off Florida's first sales tax.

Born on August 31, 1899, Jimmy Webb was an early enterpriser. At age 9, he sold bread, milk, and vegetables along his paper route, and he also mowed lawns or sold lemonade or orangeade curbside. When the family moved to Knoxville, Tennessee, Jimmy quit school to work in a bowling alley by night and a drugstore by day. The seven-day grind sent him into nervous collapse. But he bounced back, and at 20 he became part owner of the drugstore.

Working in an era before the Food and Drug Administration, Webb concocted his own medicinal remedies and sold them to the public. He brewed up a muscle liniment he called "Sorbo-Rub" and a laxative concoction of Epsom salts, herbs, and water called "Indian Wahoo Bitters." Webb sold all he could bottle of both. Customers began calling him Doc, and he kept the nickname. Soon came "Doc Webb's 608," a V.D. elixir, at $5.50 a bottle.

Medicine sales soared and so did Webb's savings. But meanwhile, an early marriage had broken up. Webb had two children, Eleanor and James Earl, Jr. At the urging of a former co-worker, Hayworth Johnson, by then in St. Petersburg, Webb headed for Florida during the crest of the land boom in 1925.

Webb formed a drugstore partnership with Johnson in a little 17-by-28-foot building near the railroad tracks at Ninth Street and Second Avenue South. Business was good until the boom burst and hard times loomed. When Webb began cutting prices, Johnson, fearing that bankruptcy was imminent, sold out to Webb and returned to Knoxville. Webb held on. He renamed the store Webb's Cut Rate Drug Company, then went on a price-slashing spree. His prime interest then, he later recalled, was customers, not cash. He ran colorful promotional ads, offered prizes, and cut prices to pennies above cost. The customers flocked in.

Bust years deepened into Depression years when Webb decided a drugstore could sell more than drugs. Soon he was selling tobacco, clothing, gasoline, food, tires, typewriters, and hardware. His cafeteria offered twenty-five-cent dinners and two-cent breakfasts (one bacon strip, one egg, grits, toast, and coffee). With his flair for vaudevillian hoopla, he featured talking "mermaids," dancing ducks, kissing bunnies, tightrope-walking roosters, and, in his parking lot, beauty pageants and mini-circuses. In the gloom of the 1930s, people found laughter and relief at Webb's, along with bargains galore: men's shirts, 68 cents; coffee, 19 cents a pound; cigarettes, 5 cents a pack; 1,000 one-dollar bills at 95 cents each. Business boomed. Webb soon had his first million, and in 1934, he found time to marry Arretta Brooks of Knoxville.

But Webb's Depression-era success did not endear him to other merchants in town. A group of them came to him one day and asked him to "cooperate"—that is, stop the price-slashing at his store. Webb responded, "You run your business and I'll run mine." The group then formed a merchant's association from which Webb was pointedly excluded. Webb happily survived the exclusion.

Merchants weren't his only detractors. One day Webb sold 7,000 fifty-cent tubes of Ipana toothpaste for thirteen cents each. This prompted favorable news stories as far away as New York. But Mr. Bristol of the Bristol-Myers Corporation, the toothpaste's makers, was not amused. He warned Webb to stop the "giveaway" sales. Webb refused and Bristol-Myers sued. Webb won the case, along with a series of others brought against him by suppliers.

Webb's customers cheered him on. To most of an enthused St. Petersburg, Webb was not only a symbol of the city's recovery but a consumer champion as well. Their loyalty to him was graphically illustrated when Webb took out a two-page newspaper ad saying he needed $200,000 to expand his store to a full city block. Within the next thirty hours the entire issue of preferred stock was subscribed by patrons.

The store steadily expanded during the thirties and forties, and Webb soon was selling almost everything a customer could want, from photo and electrical supplies to paints and roofing. There also were floral, gift, barber, and coffee shops, a travel bureau, and a beauty salon. In the late 1960s, one could even get a chicken or fish dinner for about a dollar in the cafeteria. This, along with half-price prescriptions, literally enabled many fixed-income elderly residents to survive. (At his death, Webb generously endowed the senior citizens' center named for him.)

Webb's popularity also gave him substantial political clout. Beginning in 1929, he would lead the fight over the next twenty years to foil imposition of a state sales tax. In 1938 he began battling the state's fair-trade law, which he viewed as merely a euphemistic permit for profiteering.

By now both his unusual drugstore and his court battles were finding their way into the American press, usually, but not always, favorably. Said the staid *Fortune* magazine, "[Webb] is an anachronism. He considers government protection of independent business both unnecessary and immoral . . . and is moved to wrath by the mere mention of minimum price-fixing, whether official or otherwise." Renowned correspondent Ernie Pyle admired Webb's limitless nervous energy: "He is sharp as the serpent's tooth . . . flexed, fixed, strained for the leap . . . he keeps winding up, like an airplane motor in a dive."

Webb's energy did seem to bound from some perpetual inner coil spring. He seemed perpetual motion personified, whether cavorting with a bevy of high-wire beauties in his parking lot circus, leaping onto a counter top to demonstrate his fitness from taking his store's vitamins, or dashing to his loudspeaker to announce: "For the next thirty minutes we will sell $25 toasters for $13.95" or "Today only, Swiss watches, $6.88." Even his sole recreation was fast-paced; in his 50s and 60s he excelled at tennis.

By 1970, Webb's City covered ten city blocks. Tourists from as far away as Wyoming went out of their way to see if The World's Most Unusual Drugstore really was that; they rarely were disappointed.

In 1972, perhaps perceiving the trend toward mushrooming suburban malls and dying downtowns, Webb retired and sold out to a Texas syndicate. The syndicate had no Doc Webbs, and despite all efforts, this American landmark closed in August 1979. A city mourned.

It mourned even more when Webb himself died in 1982. The loss seemed the more poignant, for St. Petersburg somehow knew that the like of Doc Webb and his "crazy" drugstore would never be seen again.

36.
A Female Physician with a Pioneer Spirit

Dr. Eleanor Simmons braved convention and the wilderness to care for Dade County's residents in the 1890s.

The fugitive killer lay badly wounded in the small wood shack. Meanwhile, in the darkness some distance away, several posse members waited in front of the bayfront home of the W. H. Hadleys. None dared go near the shack. It was three o'clock in the morning.

Soon, after treating one of the killer's victims, a slight figure emerged from the Hadley home and approached the group. "Men, I am going to the wounded man [in the shack] to do my duty as a doctor. Please do him no harm while I am in there." Then, walking to the shack, the doctor called out: "Mr. Lewis, this is Dr. Simmons. Can I do anything for you?"

"Yes, I am all shot up. Come in quick. If anyone comes with you I will kill him." The doctor then entered the shack.

Time passed. The waiting men grew anxious. Sam Lewis had proven to be a quick-tempered killer. He had killed two Lemon City men earlier, and the wounded man in the Hadley home would die later. The doctor was an attractive and petite blonde woman weighing a mere 110 pounds—and the only practicing doctor in Dade County.

But the lady from Coconut Grove was like a bit of velvet over leather, with the resilient inner strength it took for a woman even to study medicine in the nineteenth century, when woman doctors were about as welcome to the profession as a carrier of malaria. A male doctor had once summed up the attitude of his colleagues by declaring: "When a critical case demands independent action and fearless judgment," a woman doctor just does not have the male's "virile courage" to meet it.

And so in this sultry night in August 1895, as these men of "virile courage" huddled nervously at a safe distance away, this "inadequate" lady removed three bullets from the leg and thigh of the outlaw. She refused Lewis's plea for enough chloroform with which to kill himself (he feared a lynching), and instead, before leaving, persuaded him to surrender; later, when daylight came, he did. But so far as the doctor was concerned, it was all in a day's work, simply her duty.

Eleanor Galt Simmons was born to Dr. Joseph and Louise Galt in Delaware County, New York, in 1854. Her physician father imbued her with a love of medicine, and after a thorough private education, she entered the nation's only such school for women, the Woman's Medical College of Pennsylvania, taking her doctor's degree on March 13, 1879.

In those days, women doctors were only a bit removed from pariah status. Miss Galt surely remembered how Elizabeth Stone Blackwell, America's first woman doctor, had been repeatedly denied rental office space in New York City in 1849, and how at her own school some years earlier, several hundred male medical students had assailed thirty women students with harassments. She was not unaware of the odds; she just merely ignored them. This temperament enabled Miss Galt to open practices in both New Jersey and New York, and later she became first assistant at the Woman's and Children's Hospital on Staten Island. Soon afterwards, she met and married Captain Albion R. Simmons (a former Civil War Union captain), who then practiced law. When a warmer climate eventually became essential to the captain's health, the couple moved to Coconut Grove in Dade County in 1892.

Dade County then reached up to the Palm Beach area and had only about 500 settlers; some 250 of these lived in the Grove area. It was still largely frontier wilderness, but the Simmonses were happy to find such a unique and cosmopolitan settlement—a colorful cultural mix of teachers, writers, artists, European counts, native Crackers, and Bahamian blacks, with frequent visits from Seminole Indians. The couple built a sturdy coral-rock home and a similar office structure for the doctor on the shore of Biscayne Bay. The bay's crystal-clear water teemed with fish and shellfish, wild game was plentiful, and with its balmy tropical climate—in which the captain's health improved rapidly—the Grove retained something of an idyllic aura.

Dr. Simmons was Dade County's first woman doctor and, for most of the 1890s, its only doctor. Conditions were primitive, but she adapted well to the role of "saddlebag doctor." She was on call day or night, ready to throw her bags across a horse's back and canter over the rough terrain of pine woods, scrub palmetto, or marshland to reach a scattering of isolated homesteads, either near the small settlements of Miami and Lemon City northward or close to the jungly Everglades westward. Sometimes she journeyed by boat or cart, but the traveling was always slow and arduous. The doctor once lamented to a friend that getting around was so difficult that her patients were either dead or fully recovered by the time she reached them. But she made herself available at any hour, serving white, black, or Indian equably. The Indians were especially drawn to the "squaw doctor" and were often seen camping outside her door, waiting to try out her "wonder" medicines. Her cases were mainly routine—broken bones, fevers, wounds—but once she had to employ a little frontier psychiatry on a woman who literally had been driven insane by the piercing nightly screams of a panther near her cabin.

Despite her rugged circuit, the doctor always appeared well groomed and conservatively clad in an ankle-length dress and high-buttoned shoes. She was described as "friendly, easy to talk to and walked with a quick step."

She seemed to be, one friend remarked, a moving example of her own favorite quotation: "By their works ye shall know them."

As for Captain Simmons, in an area hardly suitable for any substantial law practice, he turned to the manufacture of guava jelly and wine and other exotic fruit preserves. It turned out to be an enterprise that met with modest success. In fact, his products would eventually reach markets as far away as Europe.

But the doctor was active in other areas, too. When not giving lectures on emergency home medical care or baking a favorite recipe of green mango pie, she was deeply involved in the works of the Housekeeper's Club, a cultural and social group that would beneficently, and indelibly, stamp the Grove's eclectic character.

In 1898, the doctor had her hands full with a scourge of typhoid fever that plagued Spanish-American War troops in camp at Miami. In 1899, she diagnosed the first case of yellow fever in an epidemic that placed Miami under armed quarantine and caused fourteen deaths out of 220 cases. Soon after, the doctor herself was attacked with severe peritonitis. Even so, a local newspaper reported, "she has refused to give up her practice, even while suffering acutely in riding about the country to attend patients." She was relieved only after undergoing surgery at a U.S. Marine hospital in Key West.

Fortunately, by the 1900s, a number of doctors had settled in the Miami area. But the strenuous and rugged years had taken their toll, and after her operation, the doctor's health gradually declined. She finally had to reduce her practice to being physician to a couple of Grove schools.

Nevertheless, she remained abreast in her field. She once greatly impressed the local medical society (of which she was a charter member) by presenting a paper on "Bacteriology," then still an embryonic study pioneered earlier by Louis Pasteur.

But her health continued its decline. Finally, in 1909, she was diagnosed as having "tuberculosis of the brain," and she died on February 2 of that year.

It seemed that all of Dade County turned out to mourn her. "A woman of wonderful mentality, a lovable and charitable personality," eulogized the

Miami Metropolis. It might have added a woman who pioneered against the odds on two fronts—a wilderness medical practice and the detractions of her own profession—and quietly surmounted both.

War and Peace

37.
From Dove to Hawk in 1898

Florida stood alone in condemning the Spanish-American War,
but her motives proved less than altruistic.

The colorful boom-time excitement that gripped Florida during the Spanish-American War of 1898 has been exhaustively recorded.

But it has completely overshadowed the lesser known fact that, during the two years of jingoistic clamor for war from both Congress and the nation's press, Florida stood virtually alone in its vehement opposition to that war, right up to the eve of its declaration on April 25, 1898—this despite the state's major role in the war's prelude. Even when the battleship *Maine* (for causes unknown to this day) blew up in Havana Harbor on February 15, 1898, killing 260, the state's press refused to sensationalize the disaster or conclude that it made war inevitable. Elsewhere, the press, especially the powerful New York newspapers under Hearst and Pulitzer, were busy fueling a national war delirium.

Indeed, Florida seemed to shine forth with a clarion voice of reason amidst an emotional bedlam, much in the spirit of outgoing President Grover Cleveland. He was much maligned for informing a group of Senate war hawks earlier: "There will be no war with Spain over Cuba while I am president," adding, not impertinently, "I happen to know that we can buy the island of Cuba from Spain for $100 million, and a war will cost vastly more than that."

Nevertheless, the reasons behind Florida's antiwar stance were somewhat less altruistic than those motivating the seemly practicality and sturdy conscience of President Cleveland. Florida's business, civic, and political leaders and its press were fearfully certain that a war would result in the annexation of Cuba to the Union, thereby posing severe competitive problems in rival trade areas such as fruits, vegetables, tobacco, cigars, sugar, and especially tourism. Of the latter they were convinced that the state would become merely an overnight stop for Havana-bound tourists. They also believed such a war would be primarily naval, leaving defenseless coastal cities at risk from Spanish shelling and despoiling the tourist trade.

What then compelled the state's establishment to switch from dove to hawk, literally overnight, when war finally came?

Despite their opposition, most Floridians were quietly certain by early 1898 that the febrile national mood would lead to conflict. This prompted the

Jacksonville *Times-Union and Citizen,* on March 2, to demand that the army begin fortifying Florida's coastal cities, even as the editor still insisted there was "no war in sight." The writer noted the cities' complete vulnerability to bombardment or even landings. The *Miami Metropolis* scoffed at such fears, derisively suggesting that Jacksonville had defense enough in "the water hyacinths" that clogged the St. Johns River, making it impassable for ships.

But within the week, Tampa and other coastal cities, including Miami, took up the cry for defensive batteries. A flurry of letters and telegrams went out to Florida congressmen and to Army Secretary Russel Alger. Alger's polite response explained that there were no guns available, no funds with which to buy them, and no time in which to build such installations.

Tampa persisted, unsuccessfully, until it got a little help from a friend who knew a friend. On March 22, rail tycoon Henry B. Plant, whose railroad and steamship line were based in Tampa, wrote a chatty "Dear Russell" letter to Alger, reminding him that the United States already owned the islands of Egmont and Mullet Keys. Each needed only to be equipped with a battery, and the entire Tampa Bay harbor entrance could be commanded. Within three days, the army approved installations for both islands; Tampans were exultant with relief.

This touched off a statewide scramble for defenses. Jacksonville, Miami, and other east coast cities would remind Tampa that they also had a friend or two. J. E. Ingraham, chief of Henry Flagler's Florida East Coast Railroad (FEC), hurried up to Washington to meet personally with Alger. Another friendly chat ensued. On April 4, the army announced plans for batteries for all major Florida coastal cities.

But approving installations and actually building them proved to be a disjunctive proposition. Delays seemed to be the order of the day until the impatience of the citizenry turned to alarmed concern when, on April 11, President McKinley asked Congress for authority to use armed forces in Cuba. For protection, cities began forming volunteer home guard units while demanding from the state adjutant general rifles for training.

But a bigger scramble awaited. On April 15, the army selected Tampa as its southeastern supply depot and army encampment. Within forty-eight hours, the first troops began pouring into that city, with thousands to follow quickly. Tampa became an overnight boom town, bustling with new buildings and other facilities. Hundreds of workers had to be imported from around the state and outside. Merchants sold goods faster than they could stock them. And with both civilian and military payrolls swelling local coffers, the town was giddy with an unprecedented prosperity.

Naturally, the spectacle of such lush times did not elude the covetous glances of other towns. FEC Vice President J. E. Parrott angrily notified army officials that Jacksonville, St. Augustine, and Miami had facilities for campsites superior to Tampa's. This was not quite true, but his message was understandable in that his was the only rail line serving passenger and freight traffic down the east coast. Orlando, Gainesville, Tallahassee, Pensacola, and other cities also began swamping the Tampa headquarters of Commanding General William Shafter with requests for campsites, even if it meant taking troops away from Tampa.

Tampa, even though bursting at the seams and hardly able to contain a population that jumped from twenty-five thousand to sixty-six thousand, fought against any and all attempts to divert troops, proclaiming in effect: "We want it all!"

But the cigar city—perhaps fortunately for her sake—did not get it all. Lakeland, thirty miles eastward, got a small camp of five thousand; Jacksonville, offering the inducement of free land and utility services, got a much larger camp of thirty thousand. Henry Flagler himself had to intervene to get camps for Fernandina and Miami. In Miami, the tropical heat, combined with the crude "bucket" sewage system and resultant water pollution, made typhoid fever cases soar. Conditions generally prompted one soldier to write home: "If I owned both Miami and Hell, I'd sell Miami and go to live in Hell." Both Miami and the Fernandina camp, with similar problems, were shut down within six weeks, hardly repaying the FEC for its time and expense.

Yet in spite of the prosperity that was infused throughout Florida, the state's press, while welcoming the protective presence of the troops, remained adamantly opposed to an invasion or occupation of Cuba. The *Tampa Times* still assailed "belligerent" speeches by Washington officials; the *Miami Metropolis* denounced the "loud-talking jingoists"; and the Jacksonville *Times-Union* gloomily predicted that, within ten years, Florida would become "only a way station [for tourists] on the road to Cuba." Other editors were equally glum about the state's long-range economic future.

But then something happened at the last minute that would trigger in Florida's fourth estate what might best be described as an editorial somersault. When the resolution approving the April 25th declaration of war passed Congress, there was attached to it the famous Teller amendment, which, among other things, stipulated that the United States would not annex Cuba. The state's newspapers were almost joyous as they heaved a collective sigh of relief. Thereafter, they were just as unanimous in voicing an enthusiastic support of the war. In fact, their pages would soon echo a bellicosity that would make even Hearst's *New York Journal* sound slightly tepid.

And thus occurred the transmutation of the state as it emerged overnight from the fearful cocoon of peace to become not a butterfly but a militant hawk, happily aware that it was indeed a "splendid little war" after all.

38.
The Song of the Suwannee River

Rich in folklore, the Suwannee is a rare natural asset and a silent chronicler of Florida history.

"It is a river to be sung . . . God has created a river lovely as a song," wrote the noted journalist and statesman Jonathan Daniels, describing a journey he once made down the Suwannee River.

And so it is. Millions have sung of it since it was immortalized in 1851 by Stephen Foster. Most of these singers have never seen the river, or know exactly where it is, or even if it really exists. Foster himself probably never saw it. He was in Pittsburgh trying to write a song about a Southern river, and his tentative choice, the Peedee River in South Carolina, just did not sound romantic or euphonious enough. Reportedly his brother spotted on the map the winding river in north Florida; its name and meandering course appealed at once to the composer. Since then it has become a kind of Everyman's river, evoking memories of any river one has ever known.

But the Suwannee would be a major Florida distinction even if Foster had been tone deaf. In the nineteenth century it was a flourishing steamboat river that became a vital economic artery for the development of north-central Florida. In the twentieth century it has become that rare anomaly among rivers—that is, the Suwannee is a survivor. In the 1970s, a two-year task force of twenty-five federal and state officials announced that the Suwannee was the only major river in the southeastern United States that remained unspoiled. Ironically, this achievement is due in large part not to man but to the river's singular natural defense against the ubiquitous Florida developer—periodic flooding. This proves at least that poetic justice is a viable notion.

Thus the Suwannee is one of the few natural settings out of Florida's past that is still around. True, much of the wildlife is disappearing: the panther, bear, fox, alligator, razorback hog, and great indigo snake. And the fat colorful steamboats have long since given way to the sleek and slim canoe. But its winding banks are still shaded with river birches, live oaks, water oaks, sweet gums, cypress, and pine. And from their limbs one still hears the choruses of the pine warbler, the flicker, the bluebird, the pileated

woodpecker, the tufted titmouse, and the Carolina wren. And in the glowing
dusk of an evening on the river, as one native said of it, "it is a hush, a lull
in the life of civilization."

The Suwannee rises out of the vast, brooding miasma of the Okefenokee
Swamp that squats over the Georgia-Florida border north of Lake City, a
source that is 120 feet above sea level. The river picks up speed and creates
a rapids at Big Shoals north of White Springs. The Shoals is the largest
white-water area in Florida. The Suwannee then winds lazily first in a wes-
terly then an easterly arc, finally moving southwesterly to the Gulf, some
266 miles through eight Florida counties. It is fed by a host of creeks and
rivers along the way—the Santa Fe, the Ichetucknee, the Alapaha. It also is
cleansed by some fifty-five natural springs that pour into it millions of gallons of water daily. But during prolonged rains, the quiet river turns into a
turbulent boiling mass, flooding high and deep over its banks and far into the
woods. Loose logs perched high up in tree limbs mutely remind viewers of
past floods. This, then, is the Suwannee's savage defense against "progress," holding at bay the subdivisions, the glitzy motels, the neon glare.

The steamboat came to the Suwannee as early as 1836, but the river's
tricky shallows, shoals, and tree-root snags confined boat traffic to the lower
river until the state made navigation improvements in the early 1840s. The
136-foot sternwheeler *Orpheus* initiated the steamboat era with a journey
upriver as far as the thriving market settlement of Columbus, across the river
bank from Ellaville but no longer in existence today. At this time a steady
migration of settlers into north-central Florida would make the river a vital
economic artery for the entire Suwannee River country. In this same period
Cedar Key, fifteen miles south of the Suwannee's mouth, was rising to prominence and prosperity as the state's major west coast port and the main trans-
fer point for trade with both Key West and New Orleans. The port would
prosper even more after the Civil War with the arrival of several large pencil
factories (Eberhard-Faber, Eagle, Dixon), using the great stands of cedar
trees near the Suwannee's mouth and along the nearby coast for pencil-
making.

Other boats soon followed the *Orpheus*. One of the most notable steam-
boaters was Captain James Tucker, who came to the Suwannee in the 1840s
and built the 120-foot *Madison*. With a U.S. mail contract in hand, he began
a thriving twice-a-month service from Cedar Key to Columbus. Tucker operated a floating country store for farmers and settlers in the scattered small
villages and isolated farms along the river country. It was exciting for settlers
to hear the sharp blast of the *Madison*'s whistle, audible from miles away
and giving them plenty of time to bring their cotton bales, produce, hams,
venison, cow and deer hides, beeswax, honey, chickens, eggs, and other
items to the river landing. Tucker carried a general line of merchandise
picked up at Cedar Key which he sold or traded to the settlers. He would stop

at various landings—Branford, Troy Springs, Luraville—all the way up to Columbus. When the state refused officially to declare the Suwannee navigable because no boat had gone up as far as White Springs, the last major settlement on the river just northwest of Lake City, Tucker declared he would put the *Madison* in White Springs "if I have to run her up there on wheels." Heavy flood rains helped him although he lost his stacks and pilothouse to now-lowered tree limbs. But he made it up and back, and the river was officially declared navigable. During the Civil War, Tucker sank the *Madison* at Troy Springs to keep it out of federal hands. Its hull is still visible there today.

The Suwannee bustled with boat traffic and commerce after the Civil War. A succession of steamboats—the *Wawenock*, the *David L. Yulee*, the *Bertha Lee*, the *City of Hawkinsville*, the *C.D. Owens*, and others—shared in a brisk and flourishing river business. One colorful steamboater was Captain Robert Absalom Ivy, whose most popular boat was the *Belle of Suwannee*, a two-deck sternwheeler that featured a bridal chamber on the upper deck, lavishly furnished and finished in mahogany. No Suwannee country wedding was complete without a honeymoon cruise on the *Belle*.

But the most renowned river authority was the black mulatto pilot, Dan McQueen. Born a slave at Old Town in 1860, McQueen began steamboating at age 11 as a dishwasher on the *Wawenock*. He worked on the *David Yulee* for three dollars a month for six years and then became its mate at forty dollars a month. It was said he knew every tree, snag, shoal, and alligator hole on the river. River lore has it that he once piloted the *Belle*, which he helped Ivy build, through eighteen inches of water. He also had a master's license and captained other boats. When off duty, he taught at a black school in Old Town.

By the 1890s, the railroads began to draw away the thriving river trade, and the picturesque steamboat era went into decline. Meanwhile, the depletion of the cedar forests closed up Cedar Key's pencil factories. This, along with Henry B. Plant's selection of Tampa over Cedar Key for his railroad terminus, hastened that port's decline. As if to punctuate dramatically the end of an era, the great hurricane of 1896 smashed into Cedar Key and cut a giant swath northeasterly across the state to Fernandina. Many lives were lost and much destruction followed, with many steamboats splintered to pieces.

Nevertheless, the loss of the Suwannee's role in the economic development of Florida seems more than compensated for by the public's gain in the twentieth century of one of the few natural and unspoiled sanctuaries remaining in the state.

If the legislature thought enough of the river in the 1930s to make "Suwannee River" the state song, then perhaps in the 1980s it might actively push the proposal for the federal government to buy any remaining private property along the Suwannee's banks and have it declared "a wild and scenic river." Such a move would surely keep the river's romance alive.

39.
When Greed Infected Rogue Florida

In the 1920s, promoters luring Northerners into dubious Florida land deals sparked a bitter backlash that hit the state hard.

Florida has long been the chosen mecca for Northern tourists and vacationers; countless thousands flock to its balmy sands and waters annually.

But there was a period more than sixty years ago when the state became something less than the tropic Elysium of its colorful publicity blurbs and more suited to the moniker "Rogue Florida," a land to be shunned, a place where flourished a virus that could prove mortally hazardous to one's financial welfare. Throughout the North and Midwest especially, there arose such a crescendo chorus of Florida-bashing that the governor himself felt compelled to march northward with a platoon of prominent Floridians to answer the state's detractors.

The period, and the occasion, was that manic phenomenon called the Great Florida Land Boom (1921–26), when much of the state was gripped by a giddy fever of get-rich-quick land speculation. Tens of thousands of people were pouring into the state, from factory workers and stenographers to grandiose developers, lured by heady tales (sometimes true) of fortunes made overnight, where the most modest chunks of Florida sand could be parlayed into instant riches as the prices of lots and acreage soared to even a hundred times their value. Hucksters were fanning over the country peddling fifty-foot fronts of "a Wee Bit of Florida Heaven," while at home a mere ten-dollar "binder fee" could buy you a ride on a fantastic Fortune Express.

But this headlong exodus to a golden El Dorado was triggering five-alarm reactions up North, especially in the financial community, where the cold yardstick of currency—and its drain-off—could instantly measure its impact. For example, Dana S. Sylvester of the Massachusetts Savings Bank Association reported that about 100,000 depositors of that state's three million accounts had drawn out an estimated twenty million dollars for Florida investment. These were, he added, "mostly people who cannot afford speculation." Indeed, as the *New York Times* observed, withdrawals from Northern, midwestern, and western banks had been "enormous." In many states, bankers were taking out full-page newspaper ads warning Florida-bound speculators they could lose their shirts, if not their life savings, to "pirates of promotion."

After sending its commerce director, Cyrus Locher, down to study the boom firsthand, Ohio lawmakers passed "blue sky" laws forbidding real estate agents from selling Florida property in Ohio, since its citizens had no way of knowing the reliability of the venture. Typical of sales offers was something called "Manhattan Estates," touted as "not more than three-fourths of a mile from the prosperous and fast-growing city of Nettie." Further inquiry revealed no such city; Nettie was the name of an abandoned turpentine camp. Locher reported that land sales were based not on actual worth or productive value but strictly on resale and quick profits. Such boom values would surely go bust, he predicted, producing "headaches all over America."

In Chicago, banker Walter Greenbaum urged the Investment Bankers Association of America to draft a national "blue sky" law because Florida land schemes "were being floated all over the country and involved a total of 20 million lots, which would require a population of 60 million people in Florida (half the U.S. population) to support."

Minnesota Immigration Commissioner Oscar Smith warned Minnesotans to think twice about becoming victims of "the most monumental real estate boom that has ever been artificially produced in the United States." When it bursts, he added, "and it will just as sure as the sun shines . . . it will carry down with it hundreds of thousands of innocent victims."

But despite these Northern salvos, the frenzy of buying and selling in Florida continued unabated. The feverish activity was heaviest on the southeast Gold Coast, but it had gripped the southern half of the state across to the west coast with equal fervor. To match Merrick's grandiose Coral Gables or Young's Hollywood-by-the-Sea, D. P. Davis in Tampa was selling millions of dollars in lots (which were still under water) faster than he could dredge up two marshy mudflats in Hillsborough Bay to create his posh Davis Islands. And even before "Dad" Gandy's new bridge over Tampa Bay opened in 1924, in both Tampa and St. Petersburg wild speculation in properties along the main roads leading to the bridge sent acreage zooming from fifty dollars to as high as ten thousand dollars. The scene repeated itself southward, in Sarasota, Fort Myers, and elsewhere.

But a less-visible potential time bomb lurked beneath the boom's rainbow shimmer with the scores of "shoestring" subdivisions mushrooming from coast to coast. In *Barron's* magazine, William Bartlett warned investors to beware of buying Florida municipal bonds of any kind since most of them were public improvement bonds whose sponsors simply got out the vote, without any thought of "pay day." Ninety percent of these lots, he predicted (presciently it seems), would not be worth the taxes due on them. For example, to accommodate developers, Fort Myers annexed itself to eight times its size and then persuaded voters to approve bond issues totaling $3.5 million. But the sprawling sewer and gas mains would end up serving only palmetto clumps and overgrowth. In the hard postboom years, Fort Myers, along with some 150 other Florida cities, would stagger into financial default, unable to carry its heavy boom-time debts.

As if to deepen this fiscal quagmire, in a burst of euphoric madness aimed at luring wealthy migrants, state lawmakers hastily revised the constitution to prohibit two of its few solid and equitable revenue sources: income and inheritance taxes.

But the state was beginning to smart under the barrage of Northern diatribes, driving one Gulf Coast newspaper to shriek in a front-page banner, "Shut Your Damn Mouth!" The *Miami Herald* denied there was any boom at all in the "western sense" but simply a healthy increase in land values that was engendering prosperity and new development, achievements which, echoed an effusive Governor John W. Martin, "are but heralds of the dawn."

Nevertheless, the governor was concerned enough in 1925 to take an entourage of prominent Florida investors such as Barron Collier, August Heckscher, S. Davies Warfield, T. Coleman DuPont, and others up to the Waldorf Astoria in New York for a "Truth About Florida" meeting, to which were invited leading representatives of Northern states and the Northern media. The Floridians protested the "unfair attacks on a healthy economy" and insisted that most of the rise in land prices was on a "solid basis." They blamed the excesses on "curbstone" real estate promoters and "binder boys" but affirmed that policies were being effected to curb these "renegades."

Several months after this meeting, Florida newspapers were happily remarking on the sharp decline in this "defamatory propaganda." But it did not occur to the press that the "propagandists" may well have considered their mission accomplished. By early 1926 there was a conspicuous slump in real estate activity. This was viewed only as "a breathing spell," but it was more like a terminal warning bell because the "lull" soon nosed over into a headlong plummet. By September it had smashed itself onto a rock-bottom market. Businesses went bankrupt, banks tottered, and both small and giant developers were wiped out across the state. The golden bubble had burst and the Great Florida Land Boom was over.

There was no need now for dire warnings about "Rogue Florida." The rogues of realty themselves had written the concluding chapter, and it came with horrendous finality.

40.
Feuding Generals Stymie a War

The vitriolic feud between two generals in the Seminole War may have cost two nations an early peace.

The two officers had been vitriolic antagonists for years. General Edmund Pendleton Gaines once described General Winfield Scott as a vain pretender whose character was "chiefly composed of puerilities," while Scott termed Gaines "an imbecile," one only "fit to be a dry nurse in a lying-in hospital."

Thus it seemed that having both men in the same theater of war—the Second Seminole Indian War (1835–42)—was certain to invite a military version of Murphy's law, "If anything can go wrong . . ."

And it did. In fact, it may have cost the single opportunity to conclude that war in its earliest weeks instead of its becoming one of the longest and costliest wars in U.S. history.

Both generals had distinguished themselves in the War of 1812 and elsewhere. Gaines commanded the Western Department of the U.S. Army and Scott the Eastern; in Florida, their commands divided roughly down the peninsula center.

The ruggedly independent Gaines, 59, was marked by his candor. A veteran Indian fighter, he still sought as often to protect the red man from white depredations. He once infuriated President Andrew Jackson by questioning "the justice or policy of wresting from the Indians all those rights which Washington and Jefferson and Madison had recognized and cherished."

Scott, 50, unlike Gaines, had little experience with Indian warfare. Fond of the panoplies of rank, he brought to Florida his band, elegant furnishings, wines, and other luxuries, but his eighteenth-century European-style military tactics would prove woefully unsuited to Florida's climate, jungly terrain, or elusive foe. Yet he was picked to command the Florida war.

Long incensed by white encroachments on their lands, repeated U.S. treaty violations, and now the efforts to force their removal westward, the Seminoles reacted with fury. General Gaines was in New Orleans when he learned of the "Dade Massacre" on December 28, 1835, the slaying of Indian agent Wiley Thompson, the razing of sixteen St. Johns River plantations, the killings of frontier settlers in isolated homesteads, and the general panic in the territory. He decided at once to go to the aid of then territory commander General Duncan Clinch at Fort King near Ocala.

Sailing with eleven hundred men, Gaines arrived at Fort Brooke, Tampa, on February 10, 1836. He had heard but did not officially learn until then of Scott's appointment in Florida and his own assignment to go to the troubled Texas-Mexican border. But realizing that Scott's arrival would be long delayed and viewing the situation as critical, Gaines decided at once to march to Fort King. (Clinch meanwhile had moved most of his men twenty miles away to Fort Drane.) Gaines paused in his trek at the grisly death scene of Major Francis Dade and 107 of his men only long enough to hold a burial service.

Assured earlier by the quartermaster that sufficient rations (120,000) had been sent to Fort King, Gaines was chagrined to find that they had not arrived. He had no choice but to return to Tampa. He requisitioned 12,000 rations from Clinch at Fort Drane and set out on a different return route westward, hoping to encounter the Seminoles at the Withlacoochee River. But his attempt to ford this river on February 27 was met with a hail of fire from the opposite bank, and he soon learned that nearly all of the main Seminole force, under Osceola, was there. He set up a fortified camp back from the river's edge, Camp Izard, and would fight off repeated Seminole attacks over the next eight days.

Gaines saw at once here a major chance to subdue the Indians if he could keep them occupied and possibly end the war. Though facing a severe food shortage, Gaines's troops agreed to hold out, and the general rushed a message to Clinch to bring his men and provisions to Camp Izard where he planned to effect a pincer movement to the rear of the Indians. Time passed and no word came from Clinch. By now, Gaines had lost five killed and forty-six wounded, and his men were eating the last of their horses and mules. Fortunately, the Indians were suffering some attrition, too, and they contacted Gaines for a peace parley. Osceola offered to cease any attacks or raids if Gaines promised to let the tribes remain unmolested on the south side of the river. Gaines replied that he was not empowered to do so but would refer the proposal to the officer in charge of "diplomatic arrangements," a veiled dig at Scott.

Meanwhile, Scott finally reached Florida on February 22, making camp at Picolata on the St. Johns River. He found that neither his transportation nor his volunteer units had arrived. But he was especially riled at "the interloper," Gaines. He spent much time writing to the War Department complaining that Gaines had spoiled his plans "to close the war in a single season" and that Gaines had taken "nearly all" the rations at Fort King and was now under Indian siege at Camp Izard.

Clinch's delay had been due to a message from Scott on March 1 ordering Clinch not to aid or join the beleaguered general. Clinch, legitimately under the command of both men, faced a delicate decision but finally leaned to the "humane" one. Even before Scott relented somewhat on March 4 and sent Clinch permission to aid Gaines if deemed necessary, Clinch was on his way to Camp Izard.

But as Clinch's troops drew near the camp and saw a large body of Indians there—unaware that the talks were in progress—they fired a volley at the band, forcing them to scatter back across the river. But in the days ahead, the Seminoles kept their promise of a cease-fire. Two days later, Clinch, Gaines, and his near skeletal troops reached Fort Drane. Gaines, satisfied that the enemy "had been met, beaten, and forced to sue for peace," turned over command to Clinch and prepared to leave for the west. The day before he left, Scott finally arrived at Drane, but little more than "a cold salutation" passed between the two rivals, to the relief of their subordinates.

When the Seminoles learned that the man in charge of "diplomatic arrangements" was instead now coming to "annihilate" them, they separated into small mobile groups, waging an effective guerrilla-style war thereafter. So effective were they in eluding Scott's five-thousand-man offensive that the frustrated Scott would soon after withdraw from the Florida command.

At a court of inquiry later that year, Scott blamed his failure on "the unexpected intrusion of General Gaines." He also claimed, falsely, that Gaines had tried to make a separate treaty with Osceola. Justifying his "intrusion," Gaines wryly inquired whether the Indians had assured the president "that they would suspend their massacres and conflagrations until 'the gallant General' [Scott] should complete his plans to . . . subdue them?" He asserted that he had stopped frontier raids and forced the Indians to sue for peace while Scott was dallying on the Oklawaha River "indulging in the luxury of a steamboat cabin." With droll sarcasm, Gaines noted the reason for Scott's late offensive. "It seems it rained . . . and the movement was deferred . . . possibly because the little steamboat was not there. It can hardly be urged that I caused it to rain." But Gaines unleashed his full wrath at Scott's order forbidding Clinch to aid him at Camp Izard, which made Scott "the *second* U.S. General officer who has ever dared to aid and assist the open enemy," the first being General Benedict Arnold. The court chided Gaines for this "invective" but finally, to Gaines's exasperation, exonerated both officers for any specific failure of effort.

Nevertheless, Camp Izard was the first and only time that virtually the full Seminole force was in one place, and had Clinch not been delayed, a pincer movement may well have been effected, resulting in the defeat and capture of most if not all of the Seminoles' main warrior groups.

And thus did the piques and vanities of men supersede the hard requi-
sites of war and peace, with consequences of tragic and costly duration.

41.
When Florida Was an Idyllic "Free State"

For over a century, the state stood as a beacon to runaway slaves who found security and freedom within her borders.

On an autumn morning in the year 1687, a small, weathered longboat pulled up to the harbor shore of Spanish St. Augustine and from it stepped a bedraggled group of black Africans—eight men, two women, and a child.

They informed the town's governor, Diego de Quiroga, that they were runaway slaves from Saint George in England's Carolina colony, they were seeking asylum, and they desired instruction in the Catholic faith. Sympathetic but uncertain in the matter, Quiroga decided to feed and quarter the group at his home until he could be advised by the royal court at Madrid.

The little band of fugitives was surely unaware of it, but they were about to write an ironic but obscure chapter in Florida history, a story that remained largely unwritten since its very obscurity was the key to the survival of those who lived it. But for more than a century, like a small beacon glimmering within the dark pall of human slavery over two hemispheres, Florida was to become a virtual "free state" to the victims of that bondage. Generations of blacks would flee to the virgin wildlands of north Florida, form settlements, raise families along with herds of cattle and horses, and even cultivate thriving plantations of their own. In St. Augustine itself, there would be established the first officially free black community in America: Gracie Real de Santa Teresa de Mose, or simply Fort Mose.

Throughout this period, English colonial frontiers in South Carolina and Georgia were regions of tension and rivalry among the British, French, and Spanish, with each seeking control of the eastern half of North America. Spain especially resented English intrusion into the Carolina-Georgia region which the Spanish had claimed earlier as a part of Florida.

While Governor Quiroga waited to hear from Madrid, a Carolina emissary came to the city to claim the slaves. Since the slaves had been recently "baptized," Quiroga refused to return them and instead paid the emissary 150 pesos for each black as compensation. He then put the eight men to work on the new fort, the huge Castillo de San Marcos.

Madrid first approved Quiroga's actions and then later, in 1693, issued a royal cedula authorizing up to two hundred pesos to be paid for runaways who would then be set free. In 1699, King Charles II dropped the compensation clause and decreed simply that full protection be given "to all Negro deserters from the English who fled to St. Augustine and became Catholics." The king's actions, of course, derived less from humanitarian impulses than from the desire to aggravate a detested colonial rival. Even so, Spanish colonials in the Americas owned only token numbers of black slaves, mainly for domestic work, and in general were more liberal in their treatment of black bondsmen.

The policy had its intended effect: English colonials were more than disturbed. Word of a "freedom land" had reached their settlements much earlier, and slaves began to flee in numbers to Florida. Many simply bypassed St. Augustine and went deep into the Florida forests where they found friendly cooperation from another band of "runaways," the Seminole Indians. So enraged were the English that, during the Spanish Succession War in 1702, Carolina Governor James Moore led troops and Yemassee Indians on raids to wipe out Spanish mission posts near Tallahassee and lay siege to St. Augustine itself. But the great San Marcos fort, now completed, proved impregnable, forcing Moore to retreat.

By the early 1700s, runaways became as much a threat as a problem to the English. Slaves who had not gone to Florida would head into the frontier's wilderness interior, forming groups called "Maroons." Occasionally these groups would boldly raid isolated plantations, and yet they stubbornly defied capture. English planters soon came to fear the slave more than the Spaniard. As one of them lamented: "Our Negroes are very numerous and more dreadful to our safety than any Spanish invader." Indeed, slaves often outnumbered whites by more than two to one. Around 1715, there were some forty thousand blacks in the Charles Town (Charleston) area alone. Insurrection conspiracies among slaves were also frequent but were generally unsuccessful. One of the most serious was at Stono, twenty miles south of Charleston, where dozens of slaves seized provisions and arms and marched southward, freeing slaves as they went. But a heavily armed militia caught up to them and meted out savage reprisals—hangings, beheadings, and burnings.

In this period also, another misconception about the African slave was flatly refuted by an English colonial who found "not the slightest hint of docility . . . submissiveness . . . contentment" among them. They were, he asserted, "fierce, hardy and strong" when enabled to fight.

This opinion was doubtless shared by St. Augustine Governor Manuel de Montiano. English-Spanish tensions heightened after 1731 when Spain's Royal Council of the Indies reaffirmed the 1699 decree granting full freedom to runaway blacks. The slow but steady arrival of the fugitives into the ancient city prompted Governor Montiano in 1738 to establish a large number of them into a fort-community, Fort Mose, strategically situated on a vital travel route at the head of Mosa Creek just north of the city. Some thirty-eight blacks and their families were settled there, creating the first officially free black community in North America. They were provided their own officers, arms, cannon, and food provisions until they could cultivate their own crops. The fort was well barricaded with sod, stakes, and sharp-thorned Spanish bayonet hedges, set into a moat three feet deep and fronting a six-foot-high earthen wall.

The governor found the blacks eager "to unite themselves to our arms" against the British. Such eagerness was amply illustrated in the "War of Jenkins's Ear" in 1740, when Georgia Governor James Oglethorpe invaded St. Augustine. In a feint, the blacks were first withdrawn from Fort Mose, drawing into it a large British contingent under Colonel Palmer. The blacks, with a force including both Spaniards and Indians, then made a surprise attack on their own fort, killing Colonel Palmer and virtually annihilating the entire British force. Elsewhere, the great Castillo fort once more proved impregnable, and Oglethorpe retired in defeat to Savannah. A Spanish coun-terinvasion in June 1742, which included a full black regiment, was repulsed when the invaders became bogged down in the Georgia coastal swamps. Historians generally agree that had the Spanish followed original orders to attack first Carolina's Port Royal, "proclaim liberty to the slaves," and offer them free Florida lands, they might easily have driven the English out of both Carolina and Georgia. In this period, there were there only about 6,000 able-bodied white Carolinians while, as one planter fumed, "[we have] 57,000 potential 'intestine' black enemies."

Yet, despite the Spanish cession of Florida to Great Britain in 1763 and after its re-cession to Spain in 1783, the steady dribble of runaways to Flor-ida remained unabated. They were met by the descendants of those who had escaped generations earlier, large numbers of whom had settled along the fertile banks of the Apalachicola and Suwannee Rivers where they had formed small communities with names like Big Hammock, King Hejah, and Mulatto Girl. Here they cultivated large farms, raised flourishing herds of cattle and horses, and prospered generally. They lived in harmony with the Seminoles and often intermarried with them. When hostile Georgians, hunt-ing for runaways, made raids into the region, black and Indian joined together to repulse them. They were, in fact, an authentic pioneer group.

But by the early 1800s, with both black and Indian suffering from white encroachment, U.S. military raids, and, finally, the cession of Florida to the United States in 1821, the "free state" would be no more. And thus ended a remarkable century-long idyll for the free Florida black, truly a historic anomaly.

42.
Ponce de León's Goldless El Dorado

Seeking gold, de León claimed his "island" of Florida, but the Indians wouldn't let him set foot on it.

Much official state literature still touts Juan Ponce de León, Florida's discoverer, as a somewhat romantic fellow, a dashing conquistador subduing the tropical wilderness even as he searched for a legendary youth-restoring spring.

The truth is that de León never so much as carved a settled beachhead on the territory he named *La Florida*—for years he even thought it was an island. In his four tries and as many battles, the Indians kept him out. What little he saw of his "conquest" was mainly from the deck of a caravel, the final score remaining Indians 4, de León 0.

Although he named the state Florida, he wasn't exactly thinking of flower power. And he cared even less for some mythical Fountain of Youth, then a current Indian legend. Far from finding life-restoring waters, Ponce's quest would ultimately cost him his life; he died in a final shootout with the fierce Calusa warriors near Charlotte Harbor. His quest was in fact the more mundane and popular one of his day: hunting for gold and silver, plus as many Indian slaves as he could find to mine them. Originally his search was for "a fabulous island" called Benini (Bimini) where Caribbean rumor reported such treasures lying in abundance.

At the time, de León was in something of a royal political fix. He had sailed with Columbus's second voyage in 1493, when Puerto Rico was discovered. After Columbus's death, Ponce won royal favor with his often bloody suppression of Indian revolts, first in Hispaniola (Haiti-Dominican Republic) and then Puerto Rico and the Lesser Antilles islands. Aided by bloodthirsty Spanish greyhounds—which Indians feared more than weapons—he duly enslaved the natives to work the rich gold mines of these islands as well as cultivate plantations. As his personal wealth grew, so did his royal preferment, and he was named governor first of Haiti and then Puerto Rico.

Meanwhile, however, back in Spain, Don Diego Columbus had filed suit in the palace court, seeking direction over the possessions his famous father had discovered. He won, and began at once to move his own political cronies into the islands' main administrative posts. Ponce was ousted overnight. Chafing at such premature retirement, de León decided to find some possessions of his own to exploit, and a sympathetic King Ferdinand granted him a patent to do so. Thus, on March 3, 1513, de León set sail from Puerto Rico with three ships on a northwest passage.

On Easter Sunday, March 27, some twelve miles north of today's St. Augustine, de León discovered what he thought was not Bimini but a much larger island. Because it was Easter (the Feast of the Flowers), he named the "island" *La Florida*. He then sailed southward along the coast, ever on the lookout for prospective Indian "mine workers" to dig out the gold he was certain his island possessed. Along the way, noting that his ships were making little headway despite strong northeasterly winds, he soon discovered the course of that powerful undersea river, the Gulf Stream; this find would one day determine the homeward route of the great Spanish treasure flotas.

Soon he came upon the area Indians called Mayami and observed a large number of natives on shore waving and beckoning to him. Convinced he had an easy batch of mine-working "recruits," Ponce waved back and then took some men and rowed to shore. But as he drew close, the Indians suddenly let fly with shafts and arrows, wounding two soldiers before de León could beat a hasty retreat. Unbeknownst to him, Caribbean slaves who had escaped to Florida years earlier had related to the southern tribes fearsome stories of the strange-looking visitors in shiny metal suits who had horrendously altered the lifestyles of many Caribbean populations.

That night, de León sailed a little southward, hoping to find firewood and fresh water. He failed to notice some sixty Indians who followed him by land. As he tried to get to shore, the Indians attacked again, but this time he got away without casualties and even captured one Indian whom he would use as a pilot. Sailing along the jutting coral of the Florida Keys, the rocks from a distance reminded him of suffering human figures, and he called them *Los Martires* (martyrs), a prophetic enough label in view of their future role as a "ship's graveyard." Sailing perhaps further than intended beyond Key West, he came upon some islands which, while lacking water, had an abundance of loggerhead turtles. Appropriately, he called them the Dry Tortugas, taking about 160 of the amphibians along with him for fresh meat.

It was late May when de León reached the area of Charlotte Harbor. Once more he observed Indians on shore waving welcoming greetings, but this time the wary cavalier just remained on his caravel and waved back. This lure failing, the Indians piled into twenty canoes and headed toward the ships. Two of the craft circled round and made for the anchor cables, hoping to cut them, while the main body attacked. But arrows proved no match for the crossbow and harquebus, and the Indians were soon beaten off, de León's men capturing four of them. Two of these were released to go to their chief and tell him Ponce only wanted to trade with him. They returned next day to inform de León that their chief was on his way in person, bringing large gifts of gold. Ponce's expectations were so roused at this prospect that it was not until he saw first twenty, then eighty more canoes packed with Calusa warriors heading toward him that he realized the trap set for him. Once more a bloody battle ensued, but once more Spanish guns and crossbows forced the Indians finally to retreat.

But by this time, de León had had enough of the Calusas. Weary, running short of supplies, and disheartened over his inglorious failure to conquer his "island," he returned to his home in Puerto Rico. In the following years, a Spanish scouting voyage skirting up the west coast reported to de León that his "island" was really the mainland. Another ship he had sent to search for the elusive Bimini reported finding it but no gold or silver. (Actually the ship had discovered Andros Island.)

But de León's failure to exploit his discovery haunted him. Especially rankling was the rising fame of Hernando Cortez, conqueror of Mexico's fabulous riches, and this finally roused Ponce's dormant spirit to try again. This time, fitting two ships to capacity with stores, arms, and men, he sailed once more for Charlotte Harbor in February 1521. This time also, he vowed, there would be no guileful greetings waved back and forth; on arrival, he boldly disembarked his men and landed on the mainland shore. But the ever-vigilant Calusas were ready, too, and soon they attacked in force with such savage fury that, within a short time, over half the Spanish troops were killed or wounded. Ponce was seriously wounded in his thigh, barely escaping back to his ship. The fatal arrow had not only struck de León's femoral artery but had broken off in his bone, and the surgeon was unable to remove it. With a small surviving remnant, the aging conquistador limped back to Cuba where, within a few days, he died of his wound.

And thus to a tragic end came the white man's first attempt to settle mainland America. But it might have been at least some grim consolation had de León known that a succession of would-be settlers after him—Allyon, de Luna, Narvaez, de Soto—would meet similar fates, and that it would be well over three centuries before Florida was finally and totally wrested from its original settlers. And it would certainly have displeased him no less to know that, in a sense, he had found "gold," or better—a land that would one day be one of the nation's most valuable chunks of real estate.

43.
The Achilles' Heel of Governor Warren

A cosmopolitan yet homespun populist, Governor Fuller Warren's essential guilelessness made him vulnerable to exploitation.

He was essence "Cracker Boy," with a commoner's touch and the twang of his native woodsy Florida panhandle. Still, he was a curious mix of cosmopolitan and homespun, silver-haired and silver-tongued, this colorful and controversial figure who was Florida's thirtieth governor (1949–53), Fuller Warren.

He was a porkchopper's porkchopper, but he assailed that machine's most cherished federal barony (in the reapportionment fight). He sipped the state's orange juice religiously but shellacked the citrus titans for shipping green and immature fruit to market, a quick-profit practice that also disrupted the entire industry. He stopped the annual slaughter and maiming of residents and tourists by getting cows off the highways. He could enthrall both tutored urbanite and untutored Cracker with his stentorian Elizabethan-type oratory pungently laced with the local idiom, in an extinct stump style that needed no prepared text or ghostwriter.

He might have been "a man of the people"—he doubtless was at heart—but while his political instincts were sound, his basically unsophisticated country soul proved vulnerable to the darker pitfalls of worldly political wiles, which almost cost him the governorship itself. Yet in more halcyon days, he imbued state politics with a joy, zest, and offhand populism that anticipated much of the "New South" of today.

Warren was bitten early by the political bug. Born in rural Blountstown in northwest Florida in 1905, the youngster once eluded farm and sawmill chores long enough to run for the post of legislative page boy at age 13. He lost, but the bite was infectious. While a student at the University of Florida, age 20, he ran for the state legislature from his Calhoun County and won, turning 21 in time to take and serve one term. Getting his law degree from Cumberland University, he moved to Jacksonville to practice law and also serve three terms as a city councilman.

He was elected to the legislature again in 1939 and at once began his campaign to remove cows from highways. In spite of the alarming toll of

171

deaths, injuries, and damages from cow-car accidents, the powerful Cattle-men's Association had effectively blocked any legislation requiring fencing since 1899. Cows would flock to the highway edges to graze on the high-quality grass and, on cool nights, liked to bed down on the heat-retaining pavements. An unwary motorist by night might not even see the warning sign until they hit the beast, and one cow could often bag two cars at a time. His bill failed, but Warren's rhetorical skill and enthusiastic spirit thrust him into the limelight, and in 1940, at age 35, running for governor in a field of eleven candidates, he finished third behind the eventual winner, Spessard Holland.

After service as a naval gunnery officer in World War II, he returned to the political scene, speaking volubly and employing one of his favorite out-lets, simple letters to editors, on a variety of issues, including his crusade against "Florida's Sacred Highway Cows." He plunged spiritedly into the 1948 governor's race with a grueling eighteen-hour-day stump speaking cir-cuit. But seemingly on forensic prowess alone, in a field of nine candidates, he beat out the conservative Dan McCarty to win the governorship.

Shortly after taking office, with a somewhat tongue-in-cheek banter, he published a small book on "How to Win in Politics," stressing the oratori-cal. In it, he advised aspirants to office: "I recommend the use of many adjectives, a plethora of adjectives. Never use a lone adjective where ten can be crowded in. The goal of most orators is sound, not sense, and an array of euphonious, alliterative adjectives makes mightily for sound. For example, instead of saying an opponent is a 'mean man,' fulminate in stentorian tones, 'he is a snarling, snapping, hissing monstrosity.' And instead of saying a girl has a 'sweet voice,' intone that she has 'a soft, susurrant, satisfying accent,' or 'a dulcet, melodious voice.' Or, instead of calling a vicious man a cad, really swing out and castigate him as a 'lying, libidinous, lecherous libertine.' "

He observed that when he spoke even squalling babes-in-arms were hushed. "I do not mean to say the infants in our audiences were interested, but I do record the fact that they appeared to be attentive," which fact, he was assured, won him the "baby bloc." Gesticulate wildly, he advised, or strike poses such as head thrown back, eyes turned heavenward. "This posi-tion carries the subtle suggestion of receiving inspiration from above."

But for all his drollery, Warren was astute and dedicated on major issues, often taking positions requiring bold fortitude. He was considered almost a traitorous "anarchist" in porkchop land when he came out for reap-portionment (one man, one vote). But he viewed the state as "rent and torn by sectional bitterness, stirred up by an unconscionable effort on the part of 23 men to oppress nearly 2,000,000 citizens."

In the powerful citrus belt, he lashed at "a few greedy men who are spoiling the market for smaller growers and those who work in the industry by shipping green, immature, inedible fruit." As governor, he would stop the practice with a new "taste-test" citrus code.

He instituted a "Pine Tree Prosperity" reforestation program, a massive effort of planting over sixty-five million pine seedlings which would greatly bolster the economy. He initiated sweeping plans for the highway systems, including the Jacksonville expressway and the Sunshine Skyway. Though he would never occupy it, he initiated plans for a new governor's mansion to replace the dilapidated "state shack" he was forced to live in, falling plaster and all. He would also find time to marry a Los Angeles girl, 27-year-old Barbara Manning, in June 1949. (The marriage, unfortunately, would dissolve ten years later.)

Warren's basic simplicity, so valuable a trait in confronting clear-cut issues, would prove debilitating in complex fiscal matters. For example, he campaigned hard against a proposed three percent sales tax, which he termed a "special interest" scheme to "broaden the tax base" at the ordinary family's expense. He advocated instead a severance tax on phosphate and other minerals. But when the legislature passed the measure, he signed it, lamely noting that it exempted "the necessities of life." And even though he was finally able to get the cows off the highway, his fuzzy grasp of fiscal complexities, which virtually forced him to sign the sales tax law, seriously impaired his political support base. In fact, his essential trusting nature, combined with this airy guilelessness in financial matters, would set him up for a cauldron's brew that would decisively damage his political career.

In 1950, U.S. Senator Estes Kefauver and his hard-busting national crime commission moved dramatically into Florida, conducting mass hearing in probes of the activities of organized crime in the state. Among the numerous sensational revelations came the disclosure that virtually three men alone were the kingpin financiers of Warren's 1948 governor's campaign, coughing up the then-staggering sum of over $600,000. The trio were C. V. Griffin, one of the state's most prosperous citrus growers; Louis Wolfson, a financial "golden boy" multimillionaire at age 36; and William H. J. Johnston, a dog-track owner (two in Jacksonville, one each in Miami and Tampa) and a horse-track owner in Cicero near Chicago. Johnston and Griffin had put up about $155,000 each, with Wolfson throwing in some $300,000. The latter also had in his strongbox a note for $100,000 signed by Warren plus a $125,000 life insurance policy on the governor, assigned to protect the loan. Johnston was a low-key, affable figure who moved in higher circles in Jacksonville's commercial establishment, but his political contribution had made him a very interested party in the gravy-ladling of state business, such as bonding, insurance, road-building materials, and so on. The Kefauver committee learned that Johnston had strong ties to the late Al Capone's Chicago mob. They also learned that, upon taking office, Warren appointed a Jacksonville private eye, W. O. Crosby, to investigate Miami's gambling syndicates, among which was the powerful S. & G. Syndicate, an operation with concessions at two hundred hotels and which grossed $26 million annually.

Crosby, whom the committee later linked to organized crime, joined Dade Sheriff James Sullivan in a series of gambling raids, but curiously, they only hit the S. & G. operation. (Kefauver testimony disclosed also that the sheriff's personal assets waxed beautifully in a short period, from $2,500 to at least $96,000 that could be traced.) S. & G. finally got the message and sold for $20,000 a one-sixth partnership in the syndicate to a member of the Capone mob, giving the latter a "Trojan-horse" opening into Dade's immensely wealthy gambling turf. And the raids suddenly stopped.

Evidence indicated that Warren had walked blindly into this sordid entanglement. He had made no background check on Crosby, accepting him "at face" on suggestion from his racetrack friend. In fact, the nasty infighting over lucrative state business had, at one point, forced the beleaguered executive into a hospital for a brief rest. But Warren's surly and defiant defensiveness only compounded his problems, as when he reinstated Sheriff Sullivan after the man had been suspended from office, and refused to appear before the Kefauver committee on grounds it violated states' rights.

An angry legislature by now had already drawn up articles of impeachment against Warren. A specially assigned committee found the articles "legally insufficient" and they were dropped. But Warren would never recover from the scandal.

After leaving office, he moved to Miami and practiced law. No evidence had ever shown him to have benefitted materially from his position, and no one had ever accused him of so doing. In fact, when he died of a heart attack alone in his Miami apartment in September 1973, his means were found to be severely modest.

But leading political figures in the state, led by U.S. Congressman Claude Pepper, joined Warren's beloved panhandle Crackers in mourning him when he was buried in his native Blountstown. He had provided a brief but colorful interlude in Florida politics, with a bold, refreshing tilt at the windmill of "machines" and special interests, a banner that would be taken up more successfully by two later governors, Collins and Askew. Paradoxically, his rural simplicity, trust, and candor, admirable traits in themselves, would serve finally to abort a career that a would-be page boy had so longingly dreamed of since childhood.

44.
Sarasota's Million-Dollar Belly Splash

A funny thing happened on the way to the town's great seaport dream—it got waterlogged.

Nobody was exactly sure why Sarasota wanted to be a great Gulf seaport, a deep-water port capable of hosting steamships from all corners of the globe. But it seems she always did, even in the earliest days when she was just a tiny fishing village with hardly enough freight traffic to fill a Model T truck, much less a ship's bottom. Nor did the existence of other entrenched and thriving Gulf ports—Galveston, New Orleans, Mobile, and closer by, Tampa—seem to faze the town. True, she was no metropolis, but give her time. She had vast tracts of land in every direction ripe for agricultural and industrial development, and her salubrious shores and climate made her an ideal tourist resort. She was a "natural" for a seaport; even a provincial dimwit could plainly see that.

In the delirium of the Florida land boom, when no scheme or project was too spectacular—or impractical—to leave untried, the port boosters finally got their chance. The city decided to cast its bread—a million dollars' worth—upon the waters of Sarasota Bay. But perhaps the old parable was slightly misunderstood, for instead of returning a hundredfold, the bread simply sank to the bottom, waterlogged, and was lost forever.

For years before the land boom, Sarasotans had made incessant appeals to Congress for enough funds to dredge a twenty-two-foot channel from the Gulf to her waterfront. But not until December 17, 1912, did their pleas elicit any response from Washington. And this response was negative, if not slightly insulting. Wrote Captain J. F. Slattery of the U.S. Corps of Engineers: "If a 20-foot channel were constructed to Sarasota as it is urgently requested, it is very problematical whether ocean-going steamships could be induced to call at the port and even if they did stop, it is doubtful that the saving that could be effected in freight rates would be sufficient to warrant this improvement . . . I find it impossible to get away from the idea that this deep channel is desired more for the purpose of exploiting real estate than for the purpose of navigation." Higher echelons in the corps concurred with Slattery. "Blind bureaucrats!" huffed Sarasotans.

However, in March 1914, the corps finally conceded to recommend a funding of $92,000 to dredge a seven-foot channel into Sarasota Bay by the Longboat Key inland waterway route. World War I interrupted the project, and it was not completed until the spring of 1921. But to Sarasotans, the project was a sop, little more than enough to handle a few small local passenger steamers.

That year, Sarasota had wrenched itself away from Manatee to become its own county. It had also been sideswiped by a punchy little hurricane that swept its waterfront clean of its clusters of dilapidated fish houses and rickety wharves. These events seemed to enhance port prospects.

But as the great land boom began to accelerate in the early 1920s, Sarasotans temporarily shelved the seaport plans and plunged with heady fervor into get-rich-quick speculation. It was a period of such euphoric aberrations that any modern-day drug addict might feel a twinge of envy at so many otherwise sober citizens getting such "highs" on real estate.

Especially in southern Florida, the frenzied buying and selling that sent prices soaring into the stratosphere left no square foot of dirt or water untouched. A $200 lot became a $2,000 lot almost overnight. A $50,000 land tract zoomed to $500,000 or more. "Binder boys" were kiting lots back and forth several times a day, each time at a higher price. People were indeed getting rich, from waitresses and stenographers to grandiose developers. New subdivisions mushroomed for miles around the town. Exhilarated by the prospect of an endless cornucopia of boom-time dollars, city fathers rushed a new city charter through the legislature enabling them to annex everything in sight—islands, keys, coastlines north and south and into the hinterlands. The town grew from its original size of two square miles to sixty-nine square miles, and the tax rolls swelled. Bond issues were floated with abandon to construct new city streets, sidewalks, and sewer and water mains.

By October 1925, real estate sales in Sarasota had soared to a phenomenal $11,420,000. Few realized this was the Last Hurrah; 1926 would be a grim year.

But in the giddy days of late 1925, Sarasotans once more returned to their seaport obsession. It seemed like the most propitious time to finally realize the dream. The town began to buzz with talk about the project. It could only boost the general prosperity and it would certainly be an economic cushion for any possible future slumps in real estate activity. In fact, it could be "one of the finest deep-water ports on the Gulf of Mexico," enthused the *Sarasota Times*.

But a port like that would cost close to a million dollars, and even in those flush times the city did not have even a small fraction of that kind of money. No problem, replied port boosters. Didn't the city own an electric plant and had not the newly created Florida Power & Light Company over in Miami offered earlier to pay Sarasota one million dollars for the plant? The city would still have the power service but could fulfill its destiny as a great seaport. It had everything to gain by such a venture.

Still, there were a few nagging questions posed by some wary citizens, such as what will those big steamships from all parts of the world be carrying out of the port? With patronizing patience, the *Sarasota Times* explained that such a question was being asked by "the uninitiated, those not acquainted with the potential" of the Sarasota region. "It is true," the editors conceded, "that the present tonnage which may be offered for export is small, but the possibilities for locating industries here loom high."

Moreover, the region's agricultural importance was growing fast. "Its back country is as rich as that in the Valley of the Nile and when it is developed, whole fleets of ships will be required to carry away the produce grown in this section." Boosters also noted that the state's monstrous building boom had required such immense quantities of building materials that the railroads, overwhelmed with 1,000-car bottlenecks, had placed an embargo on all Florida-bound shipments for an indefinite period. The port could make a fortune, they insisted, just bringing in building materials.

Another more objective question loomed. Old-timers familiar with coastal waters argued that the selection of the New Pass entrance for the harbor channel was a mistake because of the currents and constantly shifting sands there.

But who were these old-timers to argue with the city's prospective port planner, a former government engineering expert from Jacksonville, Colonel J. M. Braxton? Enough nit-picking! Delay was only taking money out of Sarasotan pockets. It was time to begin.

And begin they did. On January 12, 1926, voters approved 461 to 214 the sale of the power plant, and in March, a Florida Power & Light official delivered a check for one million dollars. Even before the check came, the city awarded a $799,990 contract to United Dredging Company of Tampa to dig the channel. The remaining funds went for docks and bulkheading. By late fall of 1926, the city had a brand-new harbor for ocean-going ships.

But people were not celebrating. During the months Sarasota was digging its future out of the bay, past excesses were digging another kind of hole, not only for Sarasota but all over the state. In the spring and summer, real estate activity had slumped sharply. There were few buyers or investors now, and prices, unable to go any higher without the momentum of fresh infusions of cash, first paused and then went into a dizzying free fall. The bust of the golden boom had arrived.

Desperate to salvage something, Sarasotans stampeded to sell their holdings— at any price—but there were no takers around. The tourist season was the poorest ever: Visitors, wary of the boom's exorbitant living costs, stayed home. Builders refused to continue building because of the city's "ruinous tax rates," and so the city voted 974 to 31 to shrink back from sixty-nine to seventeen square miles. As the bust deepened, people would find their life savings wiped out, businesses would go bankrupt, banks would fail, and the city would stagger helplessly under the massive bonded indebtedness incurred during its profligate days.

As Sarasotans surveyed the grim economic scene, their gaze slowly turned seaward. Our golden port! That should bring relief! But where were the ships? Peer as they might, they could not see a single funnel stack on the horizon. Nor would they, then or later. True, the harbor had a baptism of sorts. On March 18, 1927, an "ocean-going ship," the *City of Everglades,* all one hundred feet of it, gingerly picked its way through the channel (the tidal sand shifts were already creating problems) and delivered the port's first cargo: three tons of freight for a local merchant. And in the desolate years ahead, it is estimated that not more than fifty tons of freight would ever see Sarasota's docks.

For a long time thereafter, people remembered their "great seaport" with slight shudders, recalling the time they threw a million dollars into the bay and all it did was sink.

45.
Pensacola's One-Man Economy

The city came by an economic coil spring in the 1820s when Colonel Chase began a passel of fort-building around the Gulf.

The city of Pensacola at the western tip of Florida's panhandle, a bustling commercial-resort city today, may just possibly owe its existence to the long-ago efforts of an army engineer who single-handedly kept that city alive for more than a generation with a very simple (and slightly dubious) form of economic pump-priming.

The formula was simple. Find an "urgent need" for the building of a passel of forts all over the place—specifically, the entire Gulf Coast—wangle a series of lucrative army contracts for same, mix generously with millions of tons of penny bricks and a sudden glut of eager brick-makers, and presto, you have a thriving, going city.

Of course, the means by which Colonel William H. Chase of the Army Corps of Engineers performed this feat during Pensacola's ante-bellum days (1822–60) might today have earned him the severest official censure, if not actually a private room in the nearest federal house of correction. But in those days, the distinctions among military, government, and private interests were blurred at best, and their relations were often more informal, homey, and personal.

In fact, the benevolent colonel found the rewards of fort-building so richly copious that he decided to splash about in this plenteous fountain himself and thereupon plunged into a bit of banking, railroading, and real estate—just on the side, of course. His official function was simply to build forts and expend the cornucopian flow of federal money for the task, and these duties he performed faithfully and perhaps even zealously.

Then Captain Chase, a West Pointer, had ten years experience in constructing forts when he was requested by the Army Department in 1828 to build a fort at Pensacola. A naval yard had already been situated in this perfect, natural harbor, and therefore some protective facility was a clear necessity. He was then, and remained, the ranking officer of the Corps of Engineers for the entire Gulf Coast and had already engineered the building of forts in Louisiana and Alabama.

The village of Pensacola was the victim of a sort of battered-child syndrome, historically speaking, when Captain Chase arrived on Santa Rosa Island in the town's harbor in 1829. Even its distinction as America's first settlement has been eroded, if not erased, in history's pages. But some fifteen hundred colonists, under Spain's Don Tristan de Luna, created the town in 1559, six years before St. Augustine.

The settlement was abandoned two years later when a major hurricane devastated the colonists, but for the next 250 years, it would be razed, beaten, and knocked about as various parent countries—Spain, France, Britain, and America—fought over custody of it. In 1822, when its handful of settlers incorporated it in the year Florida became a U.S. territory, it just missed being the state capital. For a while thereafter, it remained a sleepy village of sandy streets, with a depressed economy and periodic outbreaks of yellow fever and other epidemics.

Chase was given a "kickoff" appropriation of $75,000 for the new fort, and his most pressing first task was to search for the millions of bricks he needed. One brickyard in Mobile had long enjoyed a virtual monopoly on contracts for fort bricks. But Chase discovered his first order of bricks to be of poor quality, as well as expensive (thirteen dollars per thousand). So he decided to encourage local citizens, including a business associate of his own, to get into the brick-making business. He would also introduce competitive bidding. This maneuver proved so successful that he soon had an abundant supply of bricks of "good quality and proper size" from ten area brick-makers, and at a reduced cost of ten dollars per thousand; he promptly informed the Mobile supplier that he would not need "anymore from your yard."

Officer Chase was in a hurry to get Fort Pickens finished. As he informed Army Secretary Lewis Cass, the unhealthy climate of the Gulf Coast, with its "melancholy evidences" of illness and death (mainly yellow fever) required expeditious efforts. Chase once—and his wife twice—were afflicted with this fever in the next few years, but both recovered.

But the captain did not foresee the profound impact his decision to build fast and spend rapidly would have on stimulating and reviving the town's economy. By the start of the 1830s, Pensacola would be riding a boom in the building and supply trades, with diversifying offshoots of allied commerce. As the principal dispenser of this golden flow, the enterprising officer saw no reason why it should not be put to even further beneficence. Formerly, he had deposited these government funds in a New Orleans bank. But in 1831, he saw fit to start the Bank of Pensacola, in which he became a major stockholder, and into which he at once deposited all federal money. It would prove a timely move.

In the decades prior to the Civil War, with two costly and bloody wars in living memory (with Britain), the young republic developed a defensive complex toward hostile European foes, real or imagined. Consequently, it indulged a rash of fort-building everywhere, and especially in its vulnerable "Mediterranean," the Gulf of Mexico, and Captain Chase had exclusive supervision over this latter area.

Fort Pickens was completed in 1834, at a cost of $750,000, but so rapidly had the engineer pumped wealth into the local economy that, by late 1831, he could report that all the fort's bricks had been delivered. In fact, the area brick-makers had a fat surplus of three million bricks laying around their yards. This awkward situation could prove seriously detrimental to a vigorously moving economy if something wasn't done soon.

But as this depressing prospect loomed, so likewise did Captain Chase's grave concern for his country's defense. He thereupon requested an initial fund of $50,000 to begin another new fort that was "vitally needed" to protect the other side of the harbor to be built on the site of the old Spanish fort of Barrancas; its old water battery could also be prepared. This essential project would only take about five million bricks, Chase pleaded. An ever-defense-minded Army Department quickly approved the project, and Fort McRee was soon underway. In this same period, Chase looked around once more and noticed that the harbor's channel seemed unduly shallow. Could not the government come up with $106,000 to dredge it a few feet deeper to accommodate larger warships of the future? It certainly could—and would.

Of course, haste can sometimes make waste, as Florida historian Ernest F. Dibble has observed. "Perhaps Chase's subsidizing motivation for starting this new fort," he wrote, "is evidenced by the fact that he hurriedly built Fort McRee on such a bad site that it was cracking apart by the time of the Civil War."

But the town need not have fretted over its economic future because its military Midas would be in charge of many forts from New Orleans to Key West during the entire ante-bellum period, and these would supply endless markets for Pensacola labor and materials. These would include forts as vital as Fort Taylor at Key West, as well as the most monstrous and expensive "white elephant" ever built: Fort Jefferson in the Dry Tortugas, which would require thirty years to finish, forty million bricks, and 243 huge cannons that would never fire a shot, not even in the Civil War.

Throughout the 1830s, Chase added railroading to his banking interests, and headed up the Alabama, Florida & Georgia Railroad Company, which hoped to lay a line from far north Columbus, Georgia, to Pensacola, sweeping in the lucrative inland cotton crops to its shipping port. He also became a large landowner and speculator and a leading real estate promoter. The "melancholy evidences" of the town's unhealthy climate suddenly disappeared, and Chase began extolling the area's assets with effusive ads in Northern newspapers. Buyers were attracted to a big land auction held in 1836, and almost a million dollars worth of tracts were sold—on paper at least. Chase's brother, Artillery Lieutenant George Chase, visited Pensacola, and brother William quickly pulled wires to get him restationed in that town, enabling George to assist him in both his fort-building and his personal business enterprises.

Pensacolans themselves, meanwhile, had become so used to this bustling prosperity that they could even at times indulge a yearning for the sleepier days. Or, as one editor wrote: "The sound of carpenters' hammers heard on every side, we regard as the greatest annoyance—a man can no longer adjust himself for an hour's siesta." Iron and railroad cars were imported from England. Laborers were brought over from Ireland, and although they "worked like beavers, they fought like devils" and were soon replaced with Dutchmen. The latter consented to work only after they were granted their customary midmorning and midafternoon beer.

But most of Chase's enterprises, including the railroad and real estate plans, failed when a delayed reaction struck in the wake of the financial panic of 1837. Yet this made him only promote more frantically new military projects on the Gulf Coast whereby he could rescue his city—and his private interests—from a looming slump.

In this effort he was mostly successful, mainly through his promotion of a "grand vision" of massive defense installations against the most formidable of any hypothetical enemies. By the 1850s, Chase was so immersed in his considerable business holdings that he refused to accept an assignment in 1856 to be a superintendent at West Point. He resigned from the army later that year. Pensacola at this time was the largest city in the state.

But, however munificent the U.S. Army had been to him, Chase felt much greater loyalty to the ties and interests that his career had so grandly afforded him. Thus, when the great war came, Chase switched over to the enemy and took command of its local area forces. He captured the Barrancas Barracks, Fort McRee, and the navy yard. But he could not take Fort Pickens. He once regarded it as his most impregnably designed work; ironically, he found this to be too true. His own work would soon turn on, and defeat, him.

Pensacola would not again know such an extended period of economic well-being until many years later when the panhandle's as yet untapped and vast pine tree stands were exploited, giving rise to a boom in lumber, turpentine, resin, and other naval stores. And it certainly would never again know the likes of its economic patriarch for thirty years, a shrewd benefactor who probably laid the city's permanent foundations, even if the manner in which he did so might today have earned him a very long number tag instead of a rank.

46.
An Eyewitness to Shangri-La

A. W. Dimock recorded for posterity the vanishing Eden that was turn-of-the-century Florida.

It is difficult to evoke the image of another Florida and another time, when a large portion of the state was a lush, unspoiled jungle garden, fresh and wild, with pristine waters and seashore, all of it teeming with such abundance and variety of fish, fowl, and animals as will never be seen again.

If this semitropical Elysium existed—and it did—we have to ask: But when and how did it all end?

Today, in retrospect, we can fix the turning point for Florida's vanished Eden as those years just before, and into, the turn of the century, when the twin assaults of "progress" and "development" were just gathering voracious momentum.

It is fortunate that at least one individual, a man with a naturalist's avidity, a sportsman's instincts, and an explorer's curiosity, would leave a lucid, graphic, and often eloquent record of that Shangri-La that did thrive and just as surely did vanish.

A. W. (Anthony Weston) Dimock was a successful New York banker-broker who in the early 1880s decided to chuck the wild Wall Street game of that era for the call of another wild. He would explore and hunt—not with a gun but a camera—one of America's last virgin frontiers, Florida's Gulf Coast and inlands from Homosassa Springs to Cape Sable. So potent was the spell of the land that he spent most of the next quarter-century studying and photographing it, leaving a unique recollection of it in a book titled *Florida Enchantment,* published in 1905.

In that era, of course, Dimock sadly noted another destructive assault on this natural paradise caused by "man's cupidity and woman's vanity." Hunters and poachers were annually slaughtering thousands of exotic birds in their rookeries for plumage that later would grace the headwear of fashionable New York matrons. (In one year alone, a New York milliner might buy $200,000 worth of such plumes.) In such manner the beautiful snowy egret, the blue heron, the flamingo, and many other species became extinct, or nearly so.

Nor did the alligator elude this slaughter; thousands were shot each year for skins. Dimock recalled when in one season alone, two hunters left in one pile one thousand gator skeletons, the skins bringing them from ten cents to one dollar apiece. "It is for this pittance, to a few of her citizens, that Florida permits the destruction of an attraction and asset worth millions," he lamented. Even then, that rare and ancient reptile—the crocodile—was all but extinct. Dimock was the first to photograph one in 1889 and capture a few for refuge in New York's Bronx Zoo.

Even so, most of that sparsely settled coast and inland was a sprawling canvas of color and awesome natural beauty, and Dimock eagerly explored it, mostly by canoe and skiff. In 1882 he was perhaps the first to catch with rod and reel "that wonderful silvery creature," the tarpon, at the Homosassa River's mouth, anticipating by several years its role as a prized game fish.

By fragile canoe he also battled predatory denizens rarely seen today but which often roamed regularly close to the Gulf shore. (Like naturalist William Bartram a century earlier, he found most of these beasts much larger than their progeny today.) He recalls the "delirious excitement" of harpooning a sixteen-foot sawfish, one whose fifty-two-tooth nose could split a canoe with a stroke. He dodged the powerful wings of an eighteen-foot-wide devilfish, which he also harpooned. Dimock captured and filmed a giant hammerhead shark, its hammer nose four feet wide. On the other hand, he could frolic with a gentler giant, a one-ton manatee, in the Harney River.

On land, the Florida panther (all but gone today) roamed freely. He might curiously inspect Dimock's small camping party from a cautious distance, then ignore it and nonchalantly go for a morning swim in a Gulf inlet.

As he traversed the Myakka River region, the Caloosahatchee, or Florida Bay and into the Big Cypress, Dimock photographed every variety of wildlife and much of the flora, from dazzling water lilies to the lush and abundant native orchid. He crossed the Everglades, "a region desolate . . . but fascinating," in three days to Miami, reveling in his freedom from "the disenchantments" of civilization. He and his companions happily got lost in the intricate maze of the Ten Thousand Islands, paddling four days in a canoe "amid a wilderness of keys without knowing, or seeking to know, where we were."

The explorer carried a gun only for food to eat—or for use against the deadly rattler which commonly grew to six or seven feet. If he found living out under the stars in this Eden idyllic, he also found her storehouse bountiful. One needed to spend only a dollar for matches, salt, pepper, cornmeal, and syrup. Nature provided the rest in richest menu. Delicious fruit grew wild everywhere: grapes, limes, lemons, bananas, sapodillas, cocoa plums, avocadoes, coconuts, tamarinds, and custard apples. One might broil a brace of ducks for dinner to go with the boiled cabbage palm and the ashcake baked in leaves. Or one could spit-roast venison, wild turkey, or the delectable limpkin (Indian hen). Big four-hundred-pound loggerhead turtles on the beaches often provided hearty breakfasts of steak and eggs. Offshore, luncheon was available—mullet, sea bass, trout, or the gourmet pompano. Even the appetizers were sumptuous and plentiful. Much coastline comprised just one vast bank of clams, from littleneck-size up to five-pound quahogs, for clambakes. Or one could roast a bushel of the small sweet oysters that grew profusely in bunches on every reef and mangrove tree.

But where "civil" life entered, the scene could turn ugly. Once entering a rookery to photograph the beautiful egret, he found that the plume hunters got there first; of fifteen thousand nests, only fifteen were occupied. "And the tourist-with-a-gun will destroy what the plume hunter has left," he predicted, only too accurately. But other rookeries were still thriving, and Dimock photographed thousands of birds of every species: the pink, brown, and white curlew, or ibis; the blue heron; the forktailed kite ("the most graceful of birds"); the snakebird, or water turkey; the roseate spoonbill; the kingly man-of-war hawk; and the chuck-will's-widow. "Great wading birds stalked every flat, solid acres of water fowl covered the bays and streams, trees were burdened and skies darkened everywhere by great flocks of birds of the most brilliant plumage or of the purest white," Dimock recalled, but he could not marvel at it without "the painful knowledge" that it was all doomed.

Even in the 1900s, Dimock could assert: "There is just one power that can bring back the glory of that lotus land, restock its waters and restore again its forests for the education and enjoyment of the whole people, to whom it belongs. That power is an active public sentiment."

And today, some eighty years and thousands of bulldozers, dredges, and draglines later, we see that this power is still the only force that might save the isolated traces remaining of that vanished Eden.

47.
A Nazi Strikeout in Florida

A German freighter seeking shelter in "neutral" waters at Port Everglades gave the European war a new dimension.

The epic events of World War II are of common chronicle today, but few may be aware that the first head-on clash between that war's two major antagonists—Franklin D. Roosevelt and Adolf Hitler—occurred in the obscure little southeast Florida harbor of Port Everglades, well before the United States entered the war.

The episode was a decisive blow to Hitler's maritime ventures in American waters. It also gave a burdened, frustrated president the exhilarating tonic of his first "action" against the ruthless dictator after having his hands virtually tied by a rabidly isolationist Congress.

The affair so enhanced FDR's fondness for Florida that he made plans to build a retirement cottage in the state at the war's end—plans aborted only by his death.

In late 1939, after Hitler's blitzkrieg of Poland leading to the swift and brutal conquest of most of Europe, Nazi U-boats and the merchant ships that often fueled and supplied them at sea roamed freely in the western Atlantic and Caribbean. But strong isolationist sentiment, raucously fueled by congressional leaders, powerful private interests, and much of the press, often drowned out the president's attempts to warn the American people of the ultimate danger Hitler's Germany posed to the entire Western Hemisphere. Congress even passed a rigid neutrality law that would hamstring efforts to aid Britain as that nation was fighting for its very existence.

But in September 1939, Roosevelt found a way to utilize this same law, enabling him to set up a "neutrality zone patrol" for U.S. warships, ostensibly to prevent belligerent vessels or submarines from "warlike operations" in North American and South American waters. The naval patrol was ordered to "report the sighting of any submarines or suspicious surface vessels" and to radio their positions periodically until they had left neutral waters. But Roosevelt ingeniously inserted a "kicker" in the directive. The vessels' positions were to be radioed *in English*. Many Nazi freighters happily reported their positions to the trackers, grateful for this "protection" by U.S. warships and blithely unaware that British warships quickly picked up the English broadcasts, enabling them to move in swiftly on these passing German targets.

By such means, on December 19, 1939, the brand-new diesel-motored German freighter *Arauca,* returning from Brazil on its maiden voyage, was intercepted off Florida by the British cruiser *Orion.* Under chase, the *Arauca* fled into the harbor of Port Everglades while the *Orion,* forced to hold its fire, took up a grim vigil offshore. The uninvited German guest soon drew officials and curious citizens who came from nearby Fort Lauderdale to the port to have a look at the visitors. The locals even got in on the act, according to local newsman Holt McPherson. One long-time Fort Lauderdale resident, a salty, elderly Englishman, "Commodore" A. H. Brook, set about gathering candy, cookies, books, magazines, and other items (including a detailed map of waters near the port) and delivered them to the *Orion*'s crew.

"Then all hell broke loose," McPherson relates, when U.S. State Department officials poured in to inform Brook and others they had violated American neutrality. "Hell, we ain't neutral," the Commodore responded. The officials were only partly mollified when the locals also delivered several cases of beer to the German crew, at which time the *Arauca*'s captain, Frederick Stengler, invited McPherson aboard to a Christmas party. The newsman reported how the "bouncy, enthusiastic" captain was elated over his narrow escape, boasting that his "covering" battleship would soon take care of the *Orion* and that Germany would have the war won before Stengler got home to Bremerhaven. "But his gutsy manner changed abruptly," McPherson later recalled, when informed that his "cover," the pocket battleship *Graf Spee,* had been trapped by three British cruisers and blown up near the harbor of Montevideo, Uruguay. Her captain had committed suicide.

The *Arauca* would remain at Port Everglades, under the watchful eye of Coast Guard and immigration officials, for all the year 1940. Then, in late March 1941, FDR and his closest confidant, Harry Hopkins, happened into the port as they returned from what would prove the last of their customary fishing trips off the Florida coast. The relaxed mood of President Roosevelt changed as he caught sight of a Nazi flag fluttering over American soil. He and Hopkins quickly learned of the nature of the *Arauca*'s presence; then Hopkins observed the dour expression on his chief's face slowly turning into the familiar broad grin. The president was recollecting the "short of war" policy drawn up less than three months before by his Joint Chiefs of Staff. Under a clause of this policy, he saw his first chance to strike out at both powerful isolationist critics at home and Hitler abroad. He also received word that the FBI had uncovered a plan whereby the crews of any Axis ships trapped in neutral harbors would sabotage and destroy the vessels.

On March 30, before boarding the train to take him back to Washington, Roosevelt broadcast an order for the immediate seizure of the *Arauca,* plus any other Axis ships then seeking refuge in American ports. Within four hours of the president's departure, the U.S. Coast Guard boarded the German vessel and removed its fifty-two men, including Captain Stengler, and detained them at the Coast Guard base in Fort Lauderdale. (As a result of this order, some fifty-three Nazi ships were seized in American ports. The *Arauca* itself later saw useful wartime service hauling shipments of nitrate between the United States and South America.)

Isolationist cries of "war mongering" were heard from both the Congress and the press, but they could do nothing. Hitler screamed. FDR chortled with delight. The Nazi dictator, in one of his periodic Reichstag harangues, charged that FDR had violated international law by advising "enemy naval forces of the movements of . . . *Arauca.*" The United States, he shrieked, was in "unneutral collusion" with the British and had cooperated to prevent the German vessel's escape.

Former FDR speechwriter and biographer Robert Sherwood reported that no single episode of those dark and perilous early war years had given the immensely burdened president more sheer pleasure and morale-boosting than the Port Everglades affair. It also strengthened Roosevelt's hand with Congress, especially after an enraged Hitler sent his monster battleship *Bismarck* to the North Atlantic seven weeks later to draw blood with the sinking of the American merchant ship *Robin Moor.*

Aides would later recall how FDR dreamed of—and even designed himself—a "hurricane-proof" retirement cottage which he intended to build on one of the Florida Keys after the war. But he never forgot the state that gave him his first down-home "action" against the menacing tide of Hitlerism.

48. John Ringling: Circuses and Fine Art

The circus king's love of art provided a magnificent legacy to art-loving Floridians.

Portrait of John Ringling by Russian artist Savely Sorine. (Florida State Archives)

Gaudy circuses and classic art would seem to be incompatible interests. But if circus king John Ringling had not had a shrewd talent for the former and a gifted eye for the latter, then Sarasota—and Florida—would have been deprived of the magnificent Ringling Museum of Art, one of the world's great art galleries. And Sarasota would not be the thriving and prosperous cultural colony it is today—a distinctive center for art, music, and theater.

In a sense, Ringling gave his life for his art. In the dark days of the Depression when duplicitous associates and relatives sought his financial ruin, he could have solved his financial woes by selling just one of his art treasures. But he had sworn to hold them in trust for "the people of the state of Florida." And he did. Once among the world's richest men, Ringling died in 1936 with only $311 in his bank account. But his estate, with the art collection intact, was valued at $23.5 million.

The son of German-Alsatian immigrants, Ringling seemed an unlikely art collector. Indeed, there were few aesthetic qualities about the rough one-ring circus that he and his six brothers later transformed into the "greatest show on earth" after taking over their chief rival, Barnum & Bailey.

But John Ringling had an untutored eye for beauty, and he was captivated by the great masterpieces he viewed while traveling in Europe to collect new circus acts. By the turn of the century he had become a collector, devouring books by authoritative art critics, haunting Europe's great museums, and training his eye to form, color, and technique. His proficiency was acutely demonstrated once when he and a friend paused to glance at a painting in a small New York art shop. Something about it sparked a vague déjà vu in Ringling. He bought the work for $200. Later, when the over-painting was scraped off, it turned out to be a Tintoretto with a true value of $50,000.

In 1909, Ringling and his wife, the former Mable Burton, visited Sarasota, then just a fishing and farming village of one thousand residents. They were enthralled with the natural beauty of the area and bought a winter cottage overlooking Longboat Key and the Gulf of Mexico. Soon other members of the Ringling clan arrived, transforming the town into a popular winter colony. Ringling, who had interests in oil, railroads, and assorted businesses, began buying local real estate, including the islands of Bird Key, Coon, Otter, St. Armands, and a few miles of Longboat Key, to which he built Ringling Causeway.

By the 1920s, Ringling's art collection was massive, and some pieces were rare finds indeed. He discovered four huge Rubens tapestries depicting biblical scenes "rolled up like old rugs" on the English estate of the Duke of Westminster. He paid the Duke less than $100,000 for them. Other rare treasures included Murillo's *Immaculate Conception,* Rembrandt's *St. John the Evangelist,* a replica of Michelangelo's heroic statue *David* (one of only three bronze statues cast from the original marble in 1874), plus a splendid array of masters such as Fra Bartolommeo, Titian, Franz Hals, Breughel, Velazquez, Goya, Reynolds, and Gainsborough.

After building his palatial three-story mansion, called Ca'd'Zan, on the Sarasota waterfront, Ringling built nearby the museum which he later bequeathed to the state. Constructed in the classic lines of an Italian villa, the rose-pink stucco structure consists of two long, low wings which enclose a mirror pool and a formal garden filled with bronze and stone sculptures. Marble columns support the court's rounded arches, and the flat, balustraded roof is lined with more distinctive statuary.

The Great Depression wiped out most of Ringling's holdings. And in 1932, he lost control of the great Ringling Brothers and Barnum & Bailey Circus when a trusted business associate and two other Ringling heirs (John was the last survivor of the seven brothers) managed to wrest ownership through the fast purchase of a note on which Ringling had defaulted. Although debt-ridden, Ringling refused to sell any of his art treasures. After his death in December 1936, his estate was tied up for years in a bitter tangle of lawsuits by relatives, creditors, and the IRS. When the dust had settled, the museum legacy to the people of Florida emerged intact.

John Ringling wanted people everywhere to see another kind of "greatest show on earth," one that just might be more enduring and beneficent.

49.
Judah Benjamin: The Confederacy's Dark Genius

Described as both brilliant and sinister, Judah Benjamin was reputedly the "brains of the Confederacy." (Florida State Archives)

Fleeing for his life, the Rebel secretary of state found a ticket to freedom in Florida.

He had been running day and night through Florida's "underground passage," sticking to the jungle-like woods and backroads—the most wanted man in America, with a forty-thousand-dollar price on his head, dead or alive.

And now, hiding out in the temporarily deserted mansion near Florida's southwest coast, he barely eluded capture when a surprise search party forced him and his aide to flee through a kitchen door and take refuge in the woods.

It was a novel—and dismaying—role reversal for the fugitive, for he was Judah P. Benjamin, the brilliant Confederate secretary of state, reputedly the "brains of the Confederacy." After the fall of Richmond, Virginia, he had fled southward with President Jefferson Davis and his cabinet, carrying government records and more than three hundred thousand dollars in gold, hoping to reach Texas and set up a new Confederacy west of the Mississippi.

But Benjamin had had a strong, and accurate, presentiment of capture and because of it had struck out on his own through the wilderness of Florida's interior. Taking a modest share of the gold, he told Davis he would meet him later in Texas, but in fact, he wanted only to get as far as possible from the United States. Pursuing Federal soldiers captured Davis and Confederate Postmaster John Reagan a few days later in Georgia. Benjamin, who had managed to escape, feared a harsh retribution if captured. No wonder. Fol-

192

lowing President Lincoln's assassination, policies aimed at "reconciliation" between North and South were swept aside in a storm of grief and outrage. Many Northerners agreed with a call by the *New York Times* for the "supreme penalty" for all the Confederate cabinet, declaring them guilty of "the greatest crime of the ages . . . aimed at the overthrow of the best government the world ever saw." Most of the cabinet members had been arrested at their homes or as they tried to flee, and now the Federal troops had issued a virtual all-points bulletin up and down both Florida coasts for Benjamin and Confederate War Secretary John Breckinridge. (The latter escaped but returned from Canada, under amnesty, three years later. Few cabinet members, in fact, served more than a year in jail.)

Aside from his "brains" sobriquet, Benjamin was truly an enigmatic figure, a sort of anomaly among Rebel leaders. Born to Sephardic Jewish parents in 1811 on the island of St. Thomas in the British West Indies, Benjamin was brought up in Charleston, South Carolina. He attended Yale Law School, but he was expelled after two years, and although the reason is not clear, most reports indicated it was for thefts from classmates. At any rate, his plea for readmission was denied. He then moved to New Orleans to practice law, quickly becoming a highly successful commercial and constitutional lawyer. He purchased a large plantation outside the city and married an attractive French Creole, Natalie St. Martin. They were later estranged but never divorced, and she moved to Paris and took their daughter with her.

A man of subtle intellect and diplomatic temperament and a renowned orator, Benjamin was once considered by President Franklin Pierce for the U.S. Supreme Court. A linguist (he spoke both French and Spanish), he rose quickly in state politics. He was a U.S. senator from Louisiana at the time of the secession.

But his Senate detractors found other labels for him: "wily," "sphinx-like," "enigmatic." The "Mephistopheles of the rebellion . . . brilliant, sinister," said Republican politico James Blaine. "An Israelite with Egyptian principles," echoed Ohio's Ben Wade. In truth, Benjamin's personal secretiveness *was* sphinx-like. For example, throughout his life he burned any personal papers or letters he received as well as any letters of his own that he could recover. He conceded the obsession but gave no explanation for it. Still, throughout the war, in an often strife-torn cabinet, he remained Davis's closest personal adviser and friend.

And now, shedding his elegant clothes for homespun, he made his way through Florida disguised as an immigrant French farmer looking for farmland on which to settle. He even spoke broken English like a Frenchman. When he reached the outskirts of Tampa, friendly Confederate loyalists guided him south to the Robert Gamble mansion at present-day Ellenton near the Manatee River. There he joined an unsurrendered Rebel, Captain Archibald McNeill. After only several days, they were surprised by a squad of Federal soldiers and just barely escaped by running out the back of the house and hiding in a thicket. After searching the mansion and the surrounding woods and finding nothing, the soldiers retired to their boat on the Manatee River.

Several days later, McNeill took the impatient fugitive to see a veteran Rebel blockade runner, an actual French immigrant named Captain Frederick Tresca. Tresca agreed to try to get his distinguished charge to either Bimini or Nassau, and after locating a sixteen-foot yawl, the pair, along with a hired sailor named H. A. McLeod, sailed out of Sarasota Bay on June 23. The trip was uneventful until they reached the open expanse of Charlotte Harbor and a Federal ship loomed into their path from behind Gasparilla Island. They waited tensely as a launch boat was lowered and headed toward them. Tresca reported later that he and McLeod convinced the "Yankee sailors" of their "harmless" fishing activities. The Federals hardly took note of the squat, swarthy "foreigner" wearing a cook's get-up, his face daubed with grease and soot, poking at the charcoal embers in the "sandbox" stove on the bow.

Further south the three reached the Keys where, at Knights Key, they purchased a larger boat rigged with full sails. Four days later, on July 10, Benjamin entered Bimini Harbor.

The relieved and jubilant Benjamin promptly chartered passage to Nassau, moved on to Havana, and from there made his way to England.

On arriving in London, Benjamin was enthusiastically received, especially by the titled classes who had openly supported the Confederate cause. He immediately entered law practice and, in 1868, won renown with his legal treatise on "Sales of Personal Property"; it is still a standard legal work in England. This launched him on a lucrative career that lasted seventeen years, after which he retired and moved to Paris, where he died in 1884. While in Paris, he visited his still-estranged, now ailing wife and built for her and their daughter a large home there.

At his death, characteristically, he left few if any papers for would-be biographers. Asked once if he had any regrets over his role in the bloody conflict that had torn his former country apart, he cited only two: the loss of his law library in New Orleans and the confiscation of his cellar full of aged Madeira wine. To his death he retained fond remembrances of Florida, the state that provided him a ticket to freedom.

50.
A Seaside Palace for a Merchant Prince

James Deering's sprawling estate of Vizcaya on the shores of Biscayne Bay was a palace to rival Versailles and Windsor.

Back in the early days of this century, when there were no income taxes, inheritance taxes, or Securities and Exchange Commissions, America's titans of industry and commerce, riding the peak of the Industrial Revolution, had amassed such hordes of wealth that, literally, they often did not know what to do with it all.

A dollar really was a dollar then, and Andrew Carnegie took in twenty-three million of them in one year alone. He and the Goulds, Astors, Morgans, and Belmonts built numerous princely residences and often gave generously to charities, hospitals, schools, libraries, and other worthy causes, but still the coin and cash poured in with cornucopian vigor. Many lived like lavish monarchs. But such courtly ways could strike an incongruous note, such as the glimpse of the steel tycoon, Henry Frick, "seated on a Renaissance throne under a baldachin and holding in his little hand a copy of the *Saturday Evening Post.*"

But one of these moguls was a true art lover. He spent many years gathering art treasures from Europe and elsewhere and he dreamed of building a great palace in which to display such treasures.

He was James Deering, the tractor king of International Harvester. He had traveled the world—Egypt, the Riviera, North Africa, southern Italy, and a few American resorts—to find just the right climate and setting for his palatial vision. But, fastidious of taste and something of a perfectionist, he had little success until 1912 when he visited his friend William Jennings Bryan in Miami. Deering discovered a wild tropical setting sprawled over 130 acres and situated right on beautiful Biscayne Bay. (The current address is 3251 South Miami Avenue.) "This is it," he exulted. By December he had paid Mrs. Mary Brickell $25,000 cash for the tract.

The year 1912 was an eventful if peaceful one. In Germany, of course, the Kaiser was slowly building his mighty armament machine; at home, Princeton professor Woodrow Wilson was elected president; the "unsinkable" *Titanic* struck a huge Atlantic iceberg and, indeed, sank; Flagler's railroad extension to Key West was completed; and the federal income tax amendment was ratified by the states, effective January 1, 1913.

But on his newly acquired lush, tropical estate, James Deering was totally absorbed with his grandiose dream. The estate would become America's first bona fide palace (sans royalty, of course), a rival of Versailles, Windsor, the Petit Trianon, or any other European wonder. He would call it Vizcaya, a Basque word meaning elevated place. It would cost an estimated twenty million dollars, but this estimate is thought to be conservative at best.

Clearing the land took months, since the meticulous Deering did not want one tree, shrub, or plant disturbed wherever possible. A large concrete and stucco wall surrounded the property, and the palace itself was constructed of stuccoed concrete and native coral rock. Between 1914 and 1916, more than one thousand persons were employed to build the great seventy-six-room structure, including skilled artisans imported from many European countries: stonecutters, cabinet makers, plasterers, painters, and landscape gardeners. Deering personally supervised construction in his typically perfectionist manner, even leasing special warehouses in which to construct experimental room designs and layouts. He did not hesitate to tear out and rebuild a section of building if it failed to meet his exact specifications. The Mediterranean spirit would predominate in the structure, a blend of the art and architecture of many cultures which was executed in the grand manner and spacious beauty of an Italian palazzo. At the close of 1916, the millionaire bachelor moved into his "great house," along with two French chefs, four butlers, four housemen, six housemaids, and a squad of gardeners to build the magnificent gardens that would surround this palace by the sea. At Deering's direction, architects Paul Chaflin and F. B. Hoffman, Jr., designed almost every room to open onto a garden, a patio, or the sea.

The brilliant gardens would be constructed over the next several years, in French and Italian styles mainly, but with gardens within gardens laid out in profuse and colorful arrays of rare imported tropical plants and palm trees, roses and exotic orchids, jasmine, bougainvillea, water lilies, Australian pines, and clipped native live oaks. The main gardens would be studded with pools, bridges, walkways, statuary, and early European ornamentation. A bevy of rare tropical birds thrived on the palace grounds, their bright plumage and strange sounds lending an exotic jungle aura to the scene.

Deering loved to entertain lavishly, and the guest rooms of the palazzo were often brimming with visitors: industrialists, political figures, artists, engineers, actors and actresses, and a variety of local Miamians as well. At dockside, he kept his large yacht *Nepenthe* always fully stocked and equipped for a cruise. He kept a magnificent table and cellar; guests always dined sumptuously from the gold-plated china and silver service. A large natural artesian well provided water for both drinking and for continuous flowing in the many fountains, while milk, eggs, fowl, and vegetables were produced on the house grounds.

Often linked to various romances during his lifetime, Deering never married. A brilliant engineer (graduate of Massachusetts Institute of Technology), he had been an ingenious mechanical trouble-shooter for the famous farm equipment company. But it was said that his first and only love was his assiduous pursuit of early-period art treasures, wherever he could find them. Just a sample tour of his palace attests to the success of this pursuit.

One enters the main gate and travels a short winding road through natural jungle hammock, catching the aroma of fragrant subtropical plants. Then comes an entrance plaza with fountains at either end, encircled by great stone figures; aqueducts on either side carry flowing water to the forecourt.

The entrance loggia, with large granite vases on either side, features a marble statue of Bacchus poised over a Roman bath pool dating from the second century A.D. Tall carved wooden doors (c. 1800) open to the entrance hall, its walls in neoclassic-designed wallpaper printed in Paris from woodblocks made by Dufour (1814).

The ample library is completely furnished in eighteenth-century English furniture designed by Robert Adam. A Copley print of the Regency period hangs over the walk-through bookcase. The reception room is done in mid-eighteenth-century rococo, with French and Italian furniture and carved and lacquered wall panels taken from a Sicilian palace.

One proceeds down the north hallway, with its walls carved in wormy stone and a groin vaulted ceiling, and enters the great Renaissance hall, spacious and high beamed. On its south wall hangs a lustrous tapestry woven for the duke of Ferrara in 1550. The grand fireplace came from a sixteenth-century French chateau, and the long sweeping hall rug was made for a Spanish admiral in 1473. A rich seventeenth-century baldachin, woven in gold-silk baroque, frames a Welte organ console. Towering, carved Spanish gilt-wood bookcases hover over the Renaissance Florentine furniture and an ancient marble Roman tripod.

The east hallway is lit with sixteenth-century lanterns, setting off a coffered and tiled ceiling. The stone and marble east loggia has at each corner tall cedar doors with bronzed overlays set in carved marble jambs from the Torlonia Palace in Rome. The music room is walled with rococo murals from a Milanese palace, and the ancient instruments include a harpsichord made by Albana in 1645. The tea room contains eighteenth-century murals, marble floors from Naples, and imposing iron gates from the Pisani Palace in Venice.

Massive and severe, the great banquet hall contains a long, sturdy Renaissance stretcher table and chairs from the Combe Abbey in England. Beyond the Italian sideboard (c. 1500) is a marble fountain group that includes an ancient Roman sarcophagus. Wall paintings include an oil by de Miranda (seventeenth century) and portraits of the early (seventeenth century) Deering family. Over the carved Italian fireplace hangs a sixteenth-century tapestry woven in Belgium, along with tapestries once owned by the poet Robert Browning.

Upstairs are the guest rooms, including the Manin, furnished in nineteenth-century German Biedermeier style; the Cathay, of eighteenth-century Chinese decor; and the Espagnolette, of carved wood paneling and mural paintings, Venetian furniture, and a gilded trumeau hanging over the marble chimney place.

Deering's master bedroom has silken walls with a gold-wreathed ceiling, French First Empire furniture, an eighteenth-century marble chimney place from Ireland, and a plush Aubusson carpet. Beneath a linen canopy, the marble-clad master bath walls are studded with Sheffield silver plaques, and two pairs of tub faucets furnish either fresh or salt water. In the sitting room are eighteenth-century wall silks framed with giltwood molding, a ceiling of sculptured seahorses, First Empire furniture, a marble mantle with Sevres vases, and a Savonnerie rug.

Wandering through the numerous gardens, one passes pools, fountains, and every variety of eighteenth-century statuary, both classic and pastoral. The fountain garden contains the baroque fountain, which originally stood in the town square of Bassano di Sutri in Renaissance Italy.

If the tropical heat has by now begun to tax the touring visitor, he or she can plunge into the large swimming pool, built half in sunlight, half in shade, with the sheltered end covered by a ceiling that was sculpted and painted by Chanler.

The retired philanthropist remained at his magnificent palace until his death in 1925. But it was not open to public view until November 1952, when two of his nieces, Marion Deering McCormick and Barbara Deering Danielson, made arrangements with Dade County to make Vizcaya a public art museum. It has been open to the public since then, but its future fate is at least uncertain. Several years ago, a Miami newspaper editorial reported that the grand structure was "sagging at the seams" but that offers by interested private parties to repair the mansion were "stymied by Dade politics." (It is one of the most valuable tracts of property on the Gold Coast.)

With a top listing in the National Register of Historic Places, it is acknowledged that Deering's palace was a grand original and an American first, not a Renaissance copy. Concerned Dade citizens hope that it will stay that way, its fabulous art treasures held in trust for the future.

51.
Florida's Granddaddy of Boondoggles

The cross-state barge canal has been the state's historical phoenix—but a controversial and costly one over the years.

Government boondoggles, those socially toxic offspring of traditional political patronage, are usually born of the times, and more often than not, they arrive as political gratuities rather than economic necessities.

Every state has had its share of them, but perhaps Florida boasts the granddaddy of all boondoggles. It is rooted so far back in her past that it resembles some historic phoenix perennially rising from the ashes, a Lazarus-like corpse interred a dozen times only to be ghoulishly disinterred as often. The irrepressible Cross Florida Barge Canal is the remnant of Florida's past which continues to come back to haunt the present. The canal is a dubious ditch, which would slice a waterway through the north half of the peninsula. Over the years, it has ignited more controversy than any other single public project.

Over four hundred years ago, St. Augustine's founder, Pedro Menendez, dreamed of such a short cut for his ships. So certain was he that the St. Johns River had a west coast tributary that he sailed around the state to take a look. But because of attacks by hostile Indians, he balked at exploring the interior part of the panhandle. Yet, based on his conjecture, both British and Spanish maps of Florida indicated such a passage for almost two centuries.

President Jefferson first viewed such a ship canal as an advantageous thing, especially if it decreased Cuban threats to U.S. merchant ships. But not until 1818 did War Secretary John Calhoun order a study of such a canal (both men were certain of eventual acquisition of Florida by the United States). However, the study was perfunctory at best, and in 1824, the state legislative council asked Congress for an on-site survey of a ship canal which would encourage the development of agriculture, enlarge Atlantic-Gulf commerce, facilitate naval operations in wartime, and help ships avoid the perilous Straits and the Florida Keys where a mounting toll of annual shipwrecks was becoming the scourge of both merchants and insurers. An interested Congress funded $20,000 for the U.S. Corps of Engineers to go down and look the site over, but the Corps' final report branded the project "impracticable." Politically persistent, Floridians secured another study in

1833 but with no estimate attached, so President Jackson let the survey gather dust. It remained shelved until 1852 when War Secretary Jefferson Davis approved another study, this time a plan for a canal with locks, terminating in Tampa Bay and costing an estimated $3.6 million. But Civil War storm clouds were gathering and the report lay dormant again; Davis himself by now had moved south for a change of employment.

After the war, except for some abortive private efforts and an unsuccessful effort by U.S. Congressman Josiah T. Walls, no further official studies were made of the canal until 1909, when President Theodore R. Roosevelt, convinced that waterways were cheaper for transportation than railroads, ordered another study. Again, the U.S. Corps of Engineers returned an unfavorable report; a review of this report in 1924 was similarly negative. The first significant canal boost came in 1927, when President Coolidge approved the Rivers and Harbors Act. This time the Corps of Engineers studied twenty-eight possible canal routes, deciding as most feasible a route from the St. Johns and Oklawaha rivers, then passing overland near Ocala to Dunnellon and into the Withlacoochee River. Nationally, pressure for the project was led by Florida Senators Duncan Fletcher and Park Trammell and Congressman (later Governor) Millard Caldwell. But opposition mounted, too, from port interests in Miami and Tampa and from citrus growers and environmentalists who pointed to geological surveys indicating the dangers to state water supplies and wildlife areas from possible contamination of the canal. Arthur Vandenberg, Michigan's powerful senator, labeled the project "a boondoggle . . . an indefensible extravagance."

In truth, the project had always failed to meet the traditional criteria of cost-benefit ratios. The most favorable reports over the years determined only that the canal might break even at best. Nevertheless, in 1935, President Franklin Roosevelt authorized $5 million for it (mainly as job relief for rising unemployment), and north Florida proponents hailed the victory. "[It will] advance the commercial development of Florida by 100 years," declared financier Ed Ball. "The outstanding achievement of the century," Caldwell echoed. But more funds were needed to build the canal, and a bitter Senate floor fight ensued. Pleading "with tears in his eyes," Senator Fletcher sought $12 million in funding for the project—and he won it on a vote of 35-30, but his untimely death months later (reportedly exhausted from the fight) came on the day the House voted to reject that outlay.

As that decade closed, chances for a $200 million ship canal looked bleak, so new Senator Claude Pepper proffered a new package at a vastly reduced price: a *barge* canal, twelve feet deep with high-level locks to avoid scratching the great water aquifer and costing a mere $44 million. Its potent "justification" tag—national security—seemed also timely. Nazi U-boats by now were ranging far west and, by early 1942, would play havoc with Florida coastal tankers. All of this argued in favor of the canal. On July 23, 1942, both U.S. houses officially "authorized" a barge canal.

Still, however great, the victory remained a paper one. The country could not spare the scarce strategic war materials needed for canal construction. And surprisingly, even after the war the project lay in limbo until the mid 1950s, when canal forces led by Congressman Charles Bennett, the Jacksonville Democrat, and Governor Farris Bryant made a powerful push for the project. They finally won pre-election approval from President-to-be John Kennedy, and in 1960, the latter secured from Congress $195,000 for engineering design work, supplemented with an extra $205,000 when Congressman Bob Sikes, the veteran Crestview Democrat, swapped pet "pork" projects with four other states in a separate canal bill. President Johnson came up with $1 million to get digging under way in Palatka in February 1964, and with this, canal backers had "struck gold." In 1965, Johnson approved $4 million; in 1966, $10 million; 1967, $16 million; 1968, $10.4 million. But soaring inflation associated with the Vietnam War defense budget caused funding to be cut sharply to $4 million in 1969. By 1979, funding ceased. But with close to $50 million spent so far, the canal was only one-third completed, and the two-thirds remaining to be built were the most expensive. Earlier, the state canal authority had so poorly managed funding that it was forced to borrow $1.6 million from the six-county canal district just to keep work going.

In 1971, after extensive review of the project, President Nixon ordered all canal work suspended.

But the canal was still "authorized," and through the 1970s, its proponents still fought for work resumption. In 1977, U.S. engineers estimated completion costs at an additional $256 million, noting that post-1977 inflation could double the figure. Conversely, it would cost only $15 million to restore the canal environment. President Carter asked Congress for "deauthorization" of the project, but since then, two measures for deauthorization pushed by Senator Lawton Chiles, the Lakeland Democrat, have been blocked by Bennett and Congressman William Chappell, the Democrat from Daytona Beach. Former Republican Senator Paula Hawkins also moved to block deauthorization. Canal maintenance alone, meanwhile, totals $900,000 annually, even as forces led by retiring Senator Chiles and Senator Bob Graham exert pressure to do away with the costly ditch permanently.

And thus a Banquo's ghost out of Florida's past continues to haunt its present, while its only certain victim—the boondoggled public taxpayer himself—remains unrelieved.

52.
Tom Edison's Florida Bridal Bower

Conventional history shuns its mention, but the inventor's impact on Fort Myers—and Florida— stemmed from another "electric" power.

Thomas Edison was taken with the climate and beauty of the Fort Myers area. (Florida State Archives)

When Thomas Alva Edison came to the little frontier hamlet of Fort Myers back in the 1880s, folks thought he came for the climate and for a chance to search nearby jungles for a new fiber filament for his incandescent lamp.

Partly true. Edison had visited north Florida a year earlier and found the climate beneficial to his health. On his first visit to Fort Myers a year later, he was enchanted with what he saw as an "exotic paradise": a sun-drenched scene of royal palms and giant tropical flowers. The bamboo stands, some of which were sixty feet tall, especially intrigued him since, in his search for the perfect lamp filament, he had recently sent agents to the Far East and Brazil for bamboo varieties.

But at this time of his life, lamps, bamboo, and scenery were only incidentally on his mind. It seems that the man who lit up the world was aglow himself with another luminescence, one revealing a little-known facet of his character. For, despite the crusty, plain-spoken, homespun image that he fondly cultivated publicly, Edison privately nurtured a streak of the incurable romantic. Put simply, the wizard of Menlo Park was in love—the second time around—and it wasn't fiber filaments but the prospect of an idyllic tropical retreat to which he could bring an attractive young bride that lured him to Fort Myers.

Edison was now pushing middle age, and his propensity to work while others slept gave him periodic bouts of illness and exhaustion. In this balmy climate he felt his strength and youth would return to full vigor, and like the suddenly awakened Faust, he decided "he must now live in the sun and enjoy the love of a young maid."

This was Edison at his most atypical, especially in the age when men— particularly older, more mature men of the practical world—were hardly inclined to express such romantic notions. But the great inventor unexpectedly found himself as smitten as a schoolboy.

In his early years, Edison had married the sweet and simple 16-year-old Mary Stilwell in 1871. They had a daughter and two sons, and then tragedy struck: Mary died suddenly in 1884 after contracting typhoid fever.

By this time Edison was already a millionaire and head of a large industrial enterprise, a result of the scores of inventions he had patented. These included his most significant: the carbon telegraph transmitter that would make the Bell telephone possible, the electric light, and the phonograph. Characteristically, he overcame his grief by plunging into work, but this proved a poor substitute for the lonely void left in his life. He was also finding it difficult to care adequately for three growing children.

Edison became, after his wife's death, one of America's most eligible widowers. Scores of unknown ladies wrote to express their condolences, often proffering more personal consolation. Friends, too, conducted a few sly "chance meetings" with a number of women, but Edison was often annoyed with their rapt wonder or exaggerated compliments toward him.

It was not until a visit to the Boston home of two intimate friends, Mr. and Mrs. Ezra Gilliland, in the winter of 1885, that he met a striking brunette whose charms and virtues "staggered" him. Eighteen-year-old Mina Miller was asked to sing and play the piano that evening. Edison was at once impressed with the young lady's composure and aplomb and her dignified directness of manner. He caught himself staring at her "rich black hair and great dazzling eyes."

Mina was the daughter of Lewis Miller, a wealthy Akron, Ohio, farm tool maker and noted philanthropic churchman. Peers described her as "accomplished and serious, with a liking for charity and Sunday school work," although a "veritable belle with an imposing figure." The former interest derived, no doubt, from her work with the renowned Chautauqua Association of which her father was cofounder.

The inventor, who was more than twice Mina's age, could not explain the electric effect she had produced in him, but he was determined to see more of her. They socialized briefly but warmly before Edison had to leave that same winter for urgent business in Chicago. By now he had dubbed her his "Maid of Chautauqua" and began to woo her "via the post office."

In Chicago Edison became seriously ill from overwork and a severe cold. He was confined to bed, but the illness worsened. He was finally persuaded to go to Florida for his health, accompanied by the Gillilands and his daughter, Marion. This was the trip that would lead them to Fort Myers.

The climate and beauty of the Fort Myers area overwhelmed the inventor. After barely two days of exploring the scene, he took an option on a thirteen-acre site on the Caloosahatchee River and ordered lumber from Maine to construct a home and a laboratory. The town itself was little more than a general store and a dilapidated inn, with exactly 349 inhabitants and quite a few more cows. (At one time, Edison offered to light the town's streets, but the locals declined for fear it would unsettle the cows. Later, disregarding real or imagined bovine sensibilities, they accepted.) To Edison, the outpost was like a remote Shangri-La. Moreover, having felt near death in Chicago, he was wonderfully revived in the salubrious climate.

The area was certainly saturated with many varieties of plant fibers for possible filaments, but the only "light" in Edison's mind then was the image of a girl whom he vowed to bring to this balmy paradise. To his companions, it seemed his every thought and word dwelled on the charms of Miss Miller. So much so that he began to notice the effect on his daughter, Marion, who was only several years younger than the prospective stepmother; she became obviously jealous. "She [Marion] threatens to become an incipient Lucretia Borgia," he amusedly noted in his diary.

Although fairly well read in the literary classics, this master electrician was hardly a poet. Nevertheless, he now found himself waxing into flights of florid prose (punctuated with self-mockery) in his diary, such as: "Studying plans for our Floridian bower . . . with that charmed zone of beauty where wafted from the table lands of the Orinoco and the dark Carib sea, perfumed zephyrs forever kiss the gorgeous florae—RATS!"

Returning to New York, the "awakened Faust" remained in his euphoric state, and hazardously so. His diary notes that, preoccupied with a look-alike Mina on the street one day, "I came near being run over by a streetcar. If Mina interferes much more, I will have to take out an accident policy."

For the first time, Edison threw aside his busy schedule and journeyed to Lake Chautauqua where the Millers were attending the annual Chautauqua Convention that summer; he could not tolerate the separation from his beloved. He had a younger rival suitor—a childhood friend who seemed destined for Mina, at least from their parents' viewpoint. However, the impassioned inventor proved the more ardent suitor.

They were together often—on steamer excursions, boatings, and even an extended mountain tour—but always with a chaperone. The couple found little opportunity for the privacy and intimacy of expression so vital at that stage of a relationship. This was more confounded by Edison's near deafness. But typically, the whiz was equal to the challenge, as he relates: "I taught the lady of my heart the Morse code, and when she could both send and receive we got along much better than we could have with spoken words, by tapping out remarks to one another on our hands."

Finally, as they drove on a carriage trip one day in the New Hampshire mountains, Edison tapped a proposal of marriage in Mina's palm. Her telegraphic response was quick—and affirmative. He then made an eloquent, formal application to her father; her parents approved.

It seemed that all of northern Ohio turned out for the lavish wedding and reception held at the Miller home in Akron on February 24, 1886. Large crowds were also on hand to see them off that night on the train to their Florida home.

Due to supply snags, the Fort Myers home was not complete upon their arrival, and living conditions were initially somewhat rugged. But the newlyweds seemed completely oblivious to everything around them. In fact, both seemed to have vanished from sight under the enchantment of their tropical love bower, according to a secretary who tried in vain to reach Edison with pressing business affairs. "We have written to him; we have telegraphed him. We get no response. He ignores the telegraph and despises the mail."

The idyll was complete and would remain so until Edison's death in 1931. As with his first wife, Mina would bear him a daughter and two sons.

Over the years, the Edison home would attract many notable visitors to Fort Myers, from President Hoover and Henry Ford to John Burroughs and Harvey Firestone. But the local folks would always recall that it was not great worldly works that drew their famous citizen to the town but simply age-old true romance. The crusty wizard had found himself afflicted with love, decided it was an inexplicable invention, and eagerly accepted his fate.

Calamities and
Social Turbulence

53.
An Air Disaster Spawns a National Myth

The disappearance of Flight 19 off the Florida coast gave rise to a popular fantasy, the Bermuda Triangle.

It was a stunning disaster that could not—should not—have happened. But it did.

On December 5, 1945, five U.S. Navy Avenger torpedo bombers, carrying fourteen men on a routine training flight from Fort Lauderdale Naval Air Station, disappeared. A huge Martin Mariner flying boat with thirteen men, sent out to search for them, also disappeared. No trace of men or planes was ever found, despite the most massive air, land, and sea search in Florida's history. "This unprecedented peacetime loss seems to be a total mystery, the strangest ever," a naval board of inquiry member remarked at the time. It was never determined exactly what happened to the five planes on Flight 19, although the board said that flight commander Lieutenant Charles Taylor may have exercised "faulty judgment." (Another naval board later exonerated Taylor.) Thereafter, the tragedy seemed destined to become just another grim naval statistic.

Instead, it was later exhumed as the focus of one of the most sensational theories ever to grip a national imagination, the Bermuda Triangle—a theory proposing that strange, unseen forces off the Florida coast caused the disappearance, plus a similar fate for more than one hundred other ships and planes over three decades. The "triangle," an ocean area extending south from Bermuda to Puerto Rico, then to Florida's coast and back to Bermuda, would become the grist for scores of sensational articles and (mostly fictional) "docu-dramas" about Flight 19, including two runaway best-selling books. For a time, many private pilots and ship owners were prompted to navigate around the so-called Bermuda Triangle.

But what were the *known* facts about Flight 19, according to the naval board's four-hundred-page report? Taylor and four student officers, all recently transferred from Miami, left Fort Lauderdale at 2:10 P.M. in clear weather. The big single-engine bombers, each with pilot, gunner, and radioman (with one radioman left behind), would fly due east 123 miles, then north 73 miles past Grand Bahama Island to Great Sale Cay, then southwest 120 miles back to base. All seemed smooth until about 3:45 P.M. when Lieutenant Robert Cox, flying over the home station, picked up a radio call from Taylor saying Taylor was "lost" and believed his compasses were out. Taylor added, "I'm sure I'm in the Florida Keys but I don't know how far down." Directing Taylor to fly northeast, Cox said he would "fly south and meet you." But as Cox flew south, Taylor's radio contact grew weaker, not stronger. Cox called Fort Lauderdale, checked Flight 19's flight plan, and deduced that Taylor had to be over the Bahamas, not the Florida Keys which they closely resemble. Taylor also was clearly disoriented.

Disorientation, a peculiar psychological condition that can afflict the best of pilots, Cox knew, is only enhanced when a pilot flies over water, especially if the pilot relies on compass readings without identifiable landmarks. The longer the disorientation, the more confused the pilot becomes as he tries to reorient himself without a radio fix. In 1945, there were no instruments to tell pilots *where* they were. Heading northeast with no landing yet in sight, Taylor was convinced he was over the Gulf. The commander, at 28, was a veteran pilot with a distinctive Pacific combat record; he could find a distant moving carrier or make a rescue search with pinpoint accuracy. Now, in peacetime, for the first time in his life, he was totally confused.

Cox hurried back to the station and asked permission to take an emergency "ready" plane, fly northeast, and radio-guide Taylor and his men in. But the flight officer refused the request. Lost planes were routine, he noted; they always returned. If radios faded out, one then followed the standing order: "Fly west." However, Cox knew that if Taylor was certain he was over the Gulf, he was not about to fly west, far out of fuel range.

The Atlantic weather by now had worsened; a cold front was also moving in, bringing stormy conditions. Both Fort Lauderdale and Port Everglades found radio contact with Taylor either weak, static-ridden, or silent. One of the final clear messages from Taylor queried, "One of my students thinks we should fly west." Unaccountably, neither land station confirmed this direction. Nor did they "blind" transmit the message "fly west," in hopes Taylor or a student would pick it up. When, at 6:00 P.M., they got an approximate position fix on Flight 19 from Miami—due east of New Smyrna Beach—they failed to notify the Banana River naval station (Cape Canaveral) and other stations further north, which had been alerted, about Flight 19.

When Banana River finally got the fix and sent out two Martin Mariners at 7:27 P.M., Flight 19 had estimated fuel for only half an hour. One of the Mariners (often called "flying gas tanks" because of their fuel load) exploded twenty minutes later. The crew of a passing freighter, *Gaines Mill,* witnessed the crash, thus explaining the Mariner's "disappearance." By 8:00 P.M. the storm-lashed seas were rolling with waves up to fifty feet high. In normal seas, a "ditched" Avenger had a flotation time of thirty seconds or less; in the high seas of that night, there would have been no flotation time.

At 6:00 A.M. the next day, more than two hundred military airplanes of every kind took off from Fort Lauderdale, Boca Raton, Miami, Sarasota, Tampa, Orlando, Jacksonville, Banana River, and Vero Beach for the greatest peacetime search in history. Naval ships, a carrier, many private vessels, and a Bahamian British air squadron joined them. For five days they scoured an area extending three hundred miles east into the Atlantic and over four hundred miles north and south. The entire state of Florida was searched in case one plane somehow reached land. But not a trace of Flight 19 was ever found.

The tragedy was all but forgotten when, in the early 1950s, sensational and often fictionalized articles began appearing now and then in adventure magazines, retelling the story of Flight 19, tying it into, as one put it, "a sea mystery . . . a watery region off the Florida coast where ships and aircraft mysteriously vanish." Since none of the writers ever read the navy's report on Flight 19, they felt free to create "facts" of their own, such as "vanished on a clear, calm, sunlit day" or the pilots being "seized with unnerving fear" over "strange" appearances in sky and ocean. Later writers reworked and embellished these "facts" with new ones of their own: "magnetic aberrations," "time-warp zones," "a hole in the sky," "UFO space aliens," and other "strange forces." By 1964, one of these writers, Vincent Gaddis, had coined a new term, "the Bermuda Triangle," in a story on the flight in *Argosy.* The label caught on. By 1974, it would produce two runaway best sellers: *The Bermuda Triangle* by Charles Berlitz and *The Devil's Triangle* by Richard Winer. Few of these works reported the real facts of Flight 19. But, it seemed, the more bizarre the theory, the more believable it became.

True, many ships and planes have been lost "without trace" over the years in the vast area of the "triangle." But other areas with more than the usual "disappearances" might also merit "triangle" labels: one in the Mediterranean, another off Australia, and in the "Devil's Sea," south of Japan. Certainly the Florida Straits along the Keys, where over the centuries hundreds of ships have "vanished without a trace," would rate "rectangle" if not "triangle" status.

But finally, in 1975, Larry Kusche wrote *The Bermuda Triangle Mystery—Solved,* in which he painstakingly examined all the facts relating to ships or planes "vanishing without a trace" in or near the triangle, going back to the nineteenth century. In nearly every case, he found a specific, or even obvious, explanation for the disappearance—hurricanes, storms, collisions, mechanical or structural failures, as well as faulty navigation. The book was widely publicized and was no doubt a factor in the dampening, and gradual dwindling thereafter, of popular media exposure on the subject.

Today the public has all but forgotten the triangle. Like the hyped-up subject matter that spawned it, the Bermuda Triangle may also have just "vanished without a trace."

54.
Nothing Could Stop the Jacksonville Fire

With freakish fury, the great conflagration turned the city into a scorched wasteland within eight hours.

At noon on Friday, May 3, 1901, the thriving resort-port city of Jacksonville had just settled into its daily chores and affairs of commerce. The hot, cloudless sky reflected only another dry, warm, lazy spring day, for there had been no rain in over a month.

But by evening, less than eight hours later, this proud, bustling Florida city of thirty thousand inhabitants lay in rubble and ashes, all but obliterated from the earth's face by a great conflagration that swept over its streets with freakish fury in one of the greatest calamities ever to befall a Southern city. Stately homes, shanties, grand hotels, churches, public buildings, businesses, and banks—over 466 acres of them—disappeared into a scorched and desolate wasteland.

Miraculously, only seven persons perished, but thousands were left homeless. Damages soared into the millions, and a dazed and stricken citizenry picked over the blackened earth next day, uncertain even about which lot, street, or block they had lived on.

The great Jacksonville fire began casually enough. There was no wind that day as workers at the Cleveland Company fiber factory at Beaver and Davis streets gathered for lunch. The watchmen, usually on duty to see that sparks from nearby shanty chimneys did not fly over and ignite the large spreads of moss laid out to dry in the sun, felt it safe to leave and join the workers. Then one worker noticed a glow in a moss patch. He took a water bucket to put it out, only to spot a few other burning patches. He called for help. But then a sudden, swift breeze rose out of the calm, caught up the burning fiber, and swirled it into the moss-packed warehouse shed. Within minutes the pine building was aflame, and a rising wind carried blazing moss swatches over the area, setting fire to the numerous shanties in that section of Hansontown and soon engulfing the entire area.

Fire Chief T. W. Hanley put out a general alarm as he watched great billows of smoke, pushed by strong winds, roll eastward in a flaming swath. Like a fiery scythe, the blaze moved down Adams, Monroe, Duval, and

213

Church streets, crackling swiftly through stores, homes, factories, and shops and turning great oaks into giant torches.

Firemen fought furiously but had to fall back repeatedly when the smoke became so thick they could not even see the buildings. Meanwhile, families had rushed to the streets and then as quickly rushed indoors to load household goods into wagons. Still not sensing the dimensions of the holocaust, they moved their belongings a few blocks away, unloaded them, and then ran back to help their neighbors. But the wind-swept flames often leaped three or four buildings ahead, cutting off street routes in front and rear. Families quickly deserted their belongings as wagons and cargoes caught fire, while horses galloped in frenzied panic with their fiery loads.

People soon began dumping their trunks or bundles and fleeing for their lives in every direction as the fast-moving flames literally licked at their heels. Moving over Main, then Market streets, the inferno leaped blocks at a time as it moved toward the watery boundary of Hogan's Creek.

For over a square mile, the city was now an oven. Concrete and brick glowed brightly while cypress-block pavements roared and buckled. The streets were packed with shrieking swarms of humanity seeking any kind of shelter. They thronged inside the brick-structured Windsor Hotel, only to pour out again as the heat became unbearable. They packed into the courthouse and armory buildings and soon were fleeing those sturdy structures, peering back through the smoke only minutes later to see the tall, massive armory walls cracking like eggshells.

Crowds pushed north on Market Street toward the Hogan's Creek Bridge, hoping to cross it to safety. But when they reached the bridge, near-panic resulted when a report came that the city gas plant, a block away, was about to explode. The report proved false, but many fainted or were overcome by shock and terror, and the crowd suddenly paused in motion as others moved to aid and assist these victims.

Others had pushed south on Market to the St. Johns River edge where they clamored for boats. At this moment, the mammoth wall of flames was pushed by winds into a deadly arc southward, and horror engulfed the waterfront scene. Many leaped into the river or tried to swim to boats farther out which could not reach the flaming shoreline.

The scene intensified when the great heat mass formed with strong air currents to form a huge waterspout. The steamboat *Irene*, moving in to attempt rescue, was caught up by the spout and capsized like a cork. Several of the known fatalities occurred near this scene, such as that of young Will Clark who was busy helping others escape. Last seen carrying a Mrs. Follett to safety, his burned body was discovered floating at wharfside.

Such acts of selfless concern and sacrifice were often the norm. Families threw out their sole possessions to make room in their conveyances for babies, children, and other families. Typical was a man carrying a load of his important papers and valuables who spotted an aged couple trying to drag along a heavy sewing machine. On learning that the machine was their only means of livelihood, he tossed aside his own load, shouldered the machine, and escorted the old couple to safety.

More than a few lives were saved when men forcibly restrained people from re-entering their blazing homes to recover some treasured article. Families in far areas of safety opened their homes and cupboards to both friend and stranger, packing all floor space to shelter them. And, at the city's east boundary of Hogan's Creek, in one heroic effort, scores of men and boys hauled water in a massive bucket brigade until they fell out from exhaustion. But they successfully stopped the entire eastward trek of the fire, saving mills, railroads, and homes east of the creek.

Meanwhile, near the heart of the blaze, young women working at Bell Telephone and Western Union moved coolly and calmly as they relayed hundreds of calls and messages over the country, not leaving until the flames were directly across the street and most wires had been felled.

Valuable county, state, and federal records were destroyed, but a thoughtful city comptroller decided against the risk of his iron safe and carted all office records a mile away to safety. Several major bank buildings were destroyed, but most cash and securities stored in giant thick vaults were intact. The daily *Times-Union and Citizen,* with power shut off to its typesetters, hauled out dusty old handcases of type and, by candlelight, was able to put out a full issue on the fire the next day.

In Savannah, Georgia, 160 miles north, people flooded the weather office with calls when they mistook the huge pillars of black clouds far southward for a great storm brewing.

Meanwhile, fire companies from St. Augustine, Fernandina, Savannah, Brunswick, and Waycross sped to the stricken city on railroad flatcars to aid the exhausted local units, whose fire department had long since burned down. The thick smoke overcame many firemen, while hoses burned up in the hands of nozzlemen even as the water ran through them. Explosives and ammo stored in the flaming Hubbard Building scattered the firefighters as bullets flew in every direction. An Atlanta fire official observed that the combined departments of New York and Chicago "could not have stayed this fire."

Finally, by nightfall, the wind died away, and by 8:30 P.M., the last flames were brought under control. National and state guard troops moved in quickly to secure the area, but no looting or pillaging was ever observed. In fact, the unusually low death toll was attributed to the calm sense, orderliness, and cool heads of the majority of citizens. That night the U.S. government rushed twelve thousand tents to the area, and a tent city mushroomed in Hemming Park.

But the sun rose over a gruesome spectacle that Saturday morning. Over some 148 blocks, one saw only a charred chimney stack here and there, rising up like an occasional grave marker in a bleak cemetery. New York insurance circles, startled by the fire news, learned that only about one-third of the estimated fifteen million dollars in property damage was insured; many individual fortunes had also gone up in smoke. More than ten thousand people were homeless, many possessing no more than the clothes they wore. Some 2,368 buildings were destroyed, including magnificent churches, grand resort hotels, and other unique or historic edifices.

A city was gone—but not forgotten. From all parts of America, heartfelt sympathy and relief poured in. Boxcar loads of food, clothing, beds, sewing machines, tools, medicine, and other supplies inundated the scene—over $200,000 worth within hours. Cash came, too. Within less than a week, $224,913.72 (from $2 to $2,000 individually) was contributed. A Citizens Relief Association had been quickly formed and every homeless person was provided immediate temporary food and shelter. Community kitchens were established at strategic points in the area, and individual aid was provided in the spirit of "no questions asked where need is present."

But a dazed and hapless people quickly recovered, and the dominant mood became not defeat but challenge. The dream of a new city crowded out the nightmare of Black Friday as eager hands and tools plunged into the clean-up task. The first building permit was issued that first Monday morning, and construction shacks soon dotted the barren landscape. The sawmills in the surrounding county soon found they could not turn out lumber fast enough. Citizens seemed determined not just to replace their city but to build a greater one.

And, sure enough, the "Golden Phoenix of the St. Johns" gradually rose from the ashes in those long, arduous months, destined to become what it is today, one of the great cities of the South.

But the memories of the aged are not too dimmed to recall the great holocaust that marked a city's grim and terrible baptism into the twentieth century.

55.
The Horrendous Keys
Hurricane of 1935

*It was small, but it struck with such incredible wind velocity and
destructive force that few would survive it.*

It was a very small hurricane, its eye only ten miles wide, and it had moved
in from the open sea almost by stealth, undetected until it reached a point
280 miles east of Havana.

So when Cuban weather officials notified Miami, the *Miami Herald* of
Sunday, September 1, 1935, merely reported a routine weather update about
a "tropical disturbance" somewhere in the Florida Straits. Even so, a wary
U.S. Coast Guard began herding ships and smaller craft into port, and hur-
ricane-wise residents of the Florida Keys started boarding up.

But for some forty-eight hours, the storm moved about in an odd and
erratic pattern, eluding all attempts by the U.S. Weather Bureau to track it.
As it did, its tightly packed winds intensified in force. When it suddenly
bolted from overcast obscurity and smashed dead center into a section of the
Florida Keys, it struck with the most incredible wind velocity and destructive force of any hurricane ever recorded in the Western Hemisphere.
Revolving cups on wind gauges whirled so fast their bearings burned out and
the gauges broke apart, long before peak winds were reached. Even more
telling of the storm's violence was the macabre manner by which hundreds
were killed or injured in its wake: Victims were decapitated, impaled, and
even sandblasted to death. Heavy steel railroad cars were heaved one
hundred feet off their tracks, iron rails twisted, and solid homes splintered
like matchboxes as, in a grim finale, the shattered Keys were hit with a massive eighteen-foot tidal wave.

It was Labor Day, September 2, and 684 laborers were encamped in
flimsy temporary huts on Lower and Upper Matecumbe Keys. These were
World War I veterans who were among the thousands of jobless "Bonus
Marchers" gathering in Washington three summers earlier to petition for
emergency payment of "adjusted compensation" bonuses already voted to
them. Instead, a panicky President Hoover ordered General Douglas
MacArthur to "disperse" them from makeshift camps near the Capitol, with
fixed bayonets and tear gas. Partially to atone for that shameful episode,
President Franklin Roosevelt provided them emergency relief jobs building

the new overseas highway to Key West. These men were the first contingent. Nearly three hundred of them—the fortunate ones—had gone to Miami for the weekend holiday.

By late that morning, when the winds began to rise, federal officials at the camps ordered evacuation and quickly contacted the Florida East Coast Railway's Miami office for the emergency train it had agreed earlier to provide in the event of a hurricane. Some of the civilian residents on the Matecumbes and Windley and Indian Keys had already left, but many others chose to wait it out. In the end, red tape and poor scheduling delayed the rescue train even as the winds and rain intensified. It did not leave Miami until 4:25 P.M., while veterans and some Conch residents waited anxiously along the tracks.

Already the first full fury of the winds and blinding rain had accelerated, and by the time the train reached Islamorada on Upper Matecumbe at 8:30 P.M., the engineer could not even see the station and went past it. An hour later, every car on the train except the locomotive was swept off the tracks.

Wind gauges had already broken apart as the trapped victims frantically, and unsuccessfully, scurried blindly for refuge. Still the winds screamed in ever-faster velocity. Suddenly the pitch darkness was given an eerie illumination as wind-blasted sand granules generated static electricity and flashed through the air "like millions of fireflies," one survivor later recalled. Objects careened through the air with deadly speed. Sheet-metal roofs became "flying guillotines," decapitating several victims and amputating the limbs of others. Whirling lumber became lethal javelins, impaling victims or knocking them loose from precarious grips on poles and trees. Like exploding atoms, pounding sheets of sand sheared clothes and even the skin off victims, leaving them clad only in belts and shoes, often with their faces literally sandblasted beyond identification. And then came the rushing force of tons of water in an eighteen-foot tidal wave that smashed homes to splinters, crushing or drowning occupants and sweeping bodies pell-mell into tangled mangrove thickets or out to sea.

As dawn broke the next day, survivors stared trance-like at the scene of horror surrounding them. Bodies lay half out of smashed windows, or hanging from uprooted trees, or partly protruding from sand mounds, while parts of bodies grotesquely speckled the barren landscape. Some crumpled forms still clung to rail crossties or splintered poles. Bodies were later discovered in distant mangrove thickets while many more were swept out to sea, lost forever.

Elsewhere, thirty-five miles of railroad tracks and embankments had been washed out and many rails were twisted as if by some gigantic grip, thus ending Henry Flagler's "seagoing railroad." Already bankrupt and in receivership, Florida East Coast abandoned the railroad altogether, but most of its intact trestles and bridgework would later be used in structuring the new overseas highway that would open in 1938.

As rescue teams moved into the stricken islands the next day, removing the survivors and injured and collecting the bodies, President Roosevelt ordered that the dead be identified and sent either home or to Miami for burial. But many bodies were beyond identification, and the search for others in the massive debris and mangrove thickets would continue for weeks. Moreover, work crews could not keep ahead of the sun's fierce heat, and state and health authorities, fearing an epidemic, ordered the mounting pile of bodies cremated at the site.

The first report to Washington listed 252 veterans either dead or missing and presumed dead; another 106 were injured. Of the 500 civilians known to be on the three islands struck by the disaster, 164 were listed as dead or missing. But with official rosters of veterans destroyed in the storm and so many veterans missing or mutilated, many later estimates placed the final death toll much higher—at 500 or more. Accurate estimates were further confounded by the fact that veterans who had left the camps for the holiday, on learning there were no camps to return to, simply moved on.

The 1935 Keys hurricane is one that Keys residents today would just as soon forget; much popular Keys historical literature gives it hasty mention if any at all. Although narrow in path, it still holds the record for the most powerful storm ever recorded in the Western Hemisphere. The barometer fell to the lowest mark ever recorded in the state: 26.35. And the wind velocity was phenomenal. Expert engineers examining varied types of structural damage calculated that winds must have been between 200 and 250 miles per hour at peak force. Survivors, especially those partially sandblasted, readily concurred.

In more recent times, viewing the destruction inflicted by hurricanes Donna and Alicia, where winds were not much more than 100 miles per hour, we can only speculate on how ready Florida would be if its shore were again visited by such a killer hurricane.

56.
Miami Squares off with a Power Goliath

The city was plunged into turmoil in a duel with Florida Power & Light until a "country slicker" oiled the waters.

Private utility companies have never been exactly love objects in the eyes of their customers; you don't see too many bumper stickers proclaiming the driver's "heart" for Gotham Gas and Power Corporation.

But rarely have a community and a power utility engaged in such extended and bitter warfare as did the city of Miami and Florida Power & Light Company some fifty years ago. The six-year conflict would be acridly fueled with court suits, criminal charges, indictments, and general social turmoil, and the outcome would have a long-range economic impact on the entire state, at least in setting the rate costs of public power service. But there were no public service commissions in those days, and utility companies often indulged the doctrine of laissez faire with cavalier abandon.

Such was the case in the heady land-boom days of 1925 when FP&L was created by its parents, Electric Bond & Share and American Power & Light Company, to serve 115,000 customers on most of the east coast of Florida, in some central sections, and on the west coast from Bradenton south. In the euphoric boom climate, FP&L had little trouble securing a rate base from its prime customer, Miami, that charged citizens a whopping 12 cents top per kilowatt hour (compared to a relatively modest 3.2 cents in 1950). FP&L also owned Miami's water system and operated the city-owned streetcars and buses with a city guarantee against operating deficits.

But boom, bust, and depression had induced some sobering doubts, and by 1932, Mayor E. G. Sewell was sharply inquiring why Miami citizens were paying "about three times the [electric] rate" that other U.S. cities paid. The query went unanswered, so in 1933 the city enacted Ordinance 1066, cutting electric rates by one-third. The utility refused to submit and the war was on. Miami suspended payments to FP&L for streetlights and hydrants. The utility stopped paying its taxes and then went to court, successfully, to enjoin the ordinance's enforcement. The city appealed, and in 1935 a U.S. district court dissolved the injunction and ruled the ordinance valid. FP&L appealed and the suit dragged on for nearly three years.

By 1937, the hostile mood from both press and public spurred an anxious FP&L president, Bryan C. Hanks, to go into lengthy sessions with city officials to reach some settlement on rates and other tangled issues. He also agreed to sell the city the water system it had long sought, if the price were right.

But in January 1938, the city abruptly ended the negotiations and pressed on with the rate fight in court. A few days later, Hanks stunned the public with a boldfaced three-column ad in local newspapers entitled: "I Won't Pay A Bribe." He charged that an unnamed "city representative" informed him that a settlement "would only be effective on the secret payment of $250,000" to be divided among certain city figures. This, he asserted, was the cause of the cancelled talks. Mayor-Commissioner Robert L. Williams angrily retorted that Hanks much earlier had informed the mayor of a bribe solicitation and that Hanks sought to use the story "to compel me [Williams] to agree to the settlement of the rate case on his terms."

In a glare of publicity, a crossfire of virulent charges filled the air until late that month when a grand jury probe ended with indictments of the city's rate consultant, Thomas E. Grady, Mayor Williams, and city commissioners John W. DuBose and Ralph E. Ferguson on bribery and conspiracy charges. (Ferguson's case was later nol-prossed.)

Miamians may have long been suspicious about "city hall dealings," and indeed, a recall election petition was circulated against the three defendants, but their preponderant sentiment was hostility toward and distrust of FP&L. When the city finally won its rate fight in court that year, citizens were cynically certain that FP&L would find some way to wriggle out of refunding customers $3.6 million. This hostile attitude was vividly punctuated on November 18, 1938, when a jury took exactly eight minutes to acquit the defendants; the latter, in turn, promptly sued FP&L for libel, asking sums totaling $2.5 million. The beleaguered utility's image was in dire need of a facelift, and fast.

McGregor "Mac" Smith was reluctant to leave the presidency of Louisiana Power and Light Company where the only big problem he ever had, he said, was "getting along with [Governor] Huey Long and trying to stay honest at the same time." But his New York bosses needed him there and so he went in early 1939. In this same period, a stormy recall election replaced the erstwhile defendants with three new commission faces. Smith's task was formidable. He knew nothing of the city, the issues, or the parties involved. A touchy strain was also added when his bosses insisted he deal directly with New York and ignore his nominal boss, Hanks. But he plunged in.

Smith's first impression on Miamians was that he did not look or act "like a utility man." Indeed, the folksy, slow-drawling Tennessean disdained the corporate sheen. He seldom even wore a tie as he walked about

Miami's streets, cheerfully greeting ordinary passers-by, pausing to chat or relate an anecdote or even whipping out the cheap harmonica he always carried in his back pocket to play some lively country tune. He injected himself into civic affairs with the same sanguine air and would openly solicit the friendship of even a bitter antagonist. But this was his code. He once related: "The crook gets what he wants from a man by paying him money; that's the short way. The honest man has to make friends. That's the long way—and it's my way."

Smith's public relations style was vintage corn, but it worked. He knew, for example, that citizens would expect delays or even sharp practice in refunding the $3.6 million in back rates. And so he promptly rented a building to hold thousands of old bills and publicized through the newspapers exactly how and when a customer could get his money. He then hired two hundred clerks, instructing them to pass out every check with a smile. Skeptical Miamians were pleasantly amazed.

But Smith had astutely grasped the remaining issues, and city negotiators found him to be a tough trader, slow to retreat but fair. Miamians would long remember the "red bandanna" incident. Smith had held out for a quarter-million dollars more than the city felt it could pay for the water system. He also held out for his price on two smaller items. Finally, when it seemed the talks were hopelessly deadlocked, Smith rose and plunked down on the table a small bundle knotted in a red bandanna. "Gentlemen," he said, "you have already talked me out of my coat and pants and shirt." Untying the handkerchief, he took out and held up a ragged pair of shorts marked "$250,000" and tossed it across the table. "I guess you might just as well have my drawers." Before the laughter could begin, he quickly held up two homely cloth objects (symbol of the two smaller items) and asked, "How about letting me keep my socks?" The long tension, released in a burst of laughter, enabled Smith to get his price on the two smaller items. Elsewhere he negotiated a withdrawal of the libel suits; the settlement totaled less than $7,500. The following September, Smith was elected president of FP&L.

At about the same time, after some years of scrutiny of Electric Bond, American Power, and its Miami subsidiary, the Securities and Exchange Commission decided the parent companies were unfit and took custody of FP&L. It then performed some deft but painful surgery on the orphan for a bad case of "dropsy" ($34 million in watered assets). But under SEC guidance, the patient recovered and was on its way to becoming the fastest-growing independent utility company in the country.

But it might have been a much rougher road for a city and a power firm if an affable "country slicker" had not ministered some healing balm over a troubled Gilead.

57.
The Anatomy of a "Florida Fix"

Florida is usually blamed for tampering with—and tipping—the 1876 Tilden-Hayes election, but the real "fix" had other origins.

Was the state of Florida the lone culprit in "fixing" the most controversial presidential race in American history, the Tilden-Hayes election of 1876?

Florida has always been the traditional villain in any discussion of that epochal event, and historians generally agree that Democrat Samuel J. Tilden legally won both Florida's and the nation's popular and electoral vote; that Florida's four electoral votes were the pivotal "scale tipper"; and that the state's canvassing board, which later admitted it, certified a fraudulent vote return.

Yet all evidence today suggests that there was a colossal national fix behind the state fix, without which the latter would have been nullified. That broader scheme involved an unlikely alliance of powerful Northern newspaper publishers, a zealous railroad magnate, and a solid bloc of not radical Republicans but conservative Southern Democrats! It also witnessed the "Party of Lincoln" abandoning its idealistic aims for peace, scuttling the hard-won fruits of the Civil War, and halting the Reconstruction era virtually overnight.

It was a crucial and volatile election in which the nation once more almost verged on the brink of civil conflict. At one point, fifteen states were ready to organize military veterans to take action in the event of a fraudulent election.

The initial facts were simple enough. Tilden received over 250,000 more popular votes than Hayes, plus 184 uncontested electoral votes, just one short of the number required to elect. Hayes trailed with 166 electoral votes. He had strong Republican control over the electoral votes in two disputed states—South Carolina and Louisiana—but the Florida vote was a tossup.

In that turbulent era, Florida elections were often marked by intimidation, fraud, ballot-stuffing, and violence. Both parties engaged in such practices, but the greater culprits were often Democrat-inspired Ku Klux Klan terrorists and "regulators." Blacks often had to arm themselves when going to the polls. Therefore each county's returns were in dispute, with a host of charges and countercharges, even before the Board of State Canvassers met in Tallahassee. The board was composed of two Republicans, Secretary of State Samuel B. McLin and State Comptroller C. A. Cowgill, and a Democrat, Attorney General William A. Cocke.

In the interim, however, "eminent statesmen" from both parties rushed into the crucial state, laden with bribes, promises, and every manner of pressure, to influence the board and lesser county officials. Powerful New York Republican W. E. Chandler assured locals that "funds [payoffs] will be on hand to meet every requirement," and local Democrats urged the raising of $100,000—later cut to $50,000—to offer one board member. McLin, who was rewarded with the post of justice of New Mexico, later admitted that Tilden had legally won Florida's electoral votes and, with some understatement, lamented: "I feel that there was a combination of influences that must have operated most powerfully in blinding my judgments and swaying my actions." Needless to say, the board certified the electoral returns for Hayes, and the Democrats promptly forwarded a separate return to Washington for Tilden. Congress was forced to set up a fifteen-man Electoral Commission,

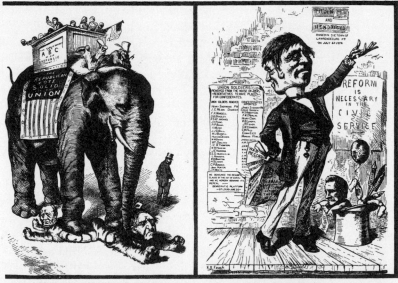

THE REPUBLICAN ELEPHANT tramples over the two-headed Democratic tiger — Tilden and Hendricks.

"MR. FACING-BOTH-WAYS." Samuel Tilden, the Democratic candidate, stands on the Reform platform.

The popular press viewed the Republicans as winning the 1876 presidential election by crushing the Democrats—with Florida's help.

composed of five representatives, five senators, and five Supreme Court justices, to canvass Florida and decide the presidency as a tense and suspenseful nation looked on.

Meanwhile, the Republican party had slowly been changing its policies from radical-reformist to favoring vested interests and big business. Hayes now felt threatened by the defection from his camp of old-line Republican faithfuls, along with the rise of rank-and-file populist farmer and labor movements in the west and east, not to mention insurrectionary rumbles from angry Democrats ready to contest forcefully any fraudulent election.

He even reflected to friend and adviser William H. Smith that it was time the South "put business above politics."

At this time, a group of national publishers, led by Joseph Medill of the powerful Chicago *Tribune,* was urgently advising Hayes to dump Reconstruction, which Medill termed "a failure," and make an all-out attempt to win over the Southern Democratic bloc. They were joined by a singularly influential figure, Colonel Thomas A. Scott, president of the world's largest freight carrier, the Pennsylvania Railroad, who was also attempting to bust the Union and the Central Pacific rail monopoly by building a cross-country Southern route, the Texas and Pacific, a prospect that greatly enticed the leaders of a destitute South. Scott mobilized a whirlwind task force to fan out over key Southern states. Armed with promises of "very liberal" economic treatment and the end of Reconstruction, directly from Hayes, Scott was able to win a solid Southern bloc in support of Hayes (the beginning of the so-called Solid South). He even won over the bellicose publisher of the Louisville *Courier-Journal,* Henry Watterson, who only weeks before was calling on one hundred thousand Democrats to march on Washington to ensure Tilden's inauguration.

Scott's greatest coup, however, came with the Electoral Commission which, on February 8, 1877, voted 8 to 7 to give Florida's electoral vote to Hayes. The deciding vote was cast by Supreme Court Justice Joseph P. Bradley. Bradley had been leaning to the Democrats, but after a long visit by Scott the night before the vote, he changed his mind.

A Washington hotel meeting between Southern Democrats and Northern Republican leaders where more binding economic concessions were purportedly wrung out of the Hayes administration has been debated by historians ever since the election. Dubbed the "Wormley House Bargain," it was, according to historian C. Vann Woodward, called mainly to pacify any Southern Democrats concerned over their leaders' "apostasy." It was also much easier to explain than complicated arrangements regarding patronage, postmasters general, speakerships, railroad subsidies, branch banks, and internal improvements, which were Hayes's payment in return for Southern support. Learning of the promises, enraged Northern Democrats threatened a filibuster, but without the Southern Democrats who had defected en masse to Hayes, the threat was futile. Hayes was now president.

The euphemistically labeled "Compromise of 1877" had in fact been clearly the most momentous election fix in history. Metaphorically and literally, the war-torn and destitute Southern maiden, hungry for Northern capital and federal aid, had simply bartered her Southern charms for a marriage of convenience, and she was not disappointed by her Yankee Republican groom. Almost within days, federal troops were pulled out of every Southern state, home rule was established, and the era of Reconstruction ended.

And so, even though Florida's radical Republican government did in fact fix the state's election for Hayes, the Democrats of Florida—and the South—hardly minded. With their deal to support Hayes, they simply usurped the other party to make the grandest fix of all.

58.
The Great Marine Disaster of 1715

A hurricane-smashed Spanish fleet yields its sunken treasures to a weekend beachcomber 250 years later.

General Don Antonio de Echeverz had a foreboding as he scanned the odd milky haze of the horizon and the lead-colored seas. The foreboding sharpened when he noted later in his cabin that the usually clear vial of shark oil he used for weather forecasting was now turning cloudy.

He had been fuming with impatience until July 24, 1715. Then, after three years' delay, the Spanish treasure fleet he commanded sailed from Havana for Spain carrying twenty-two hundred passengers and a crew and laden with fourteen million pesos in gold, silver, and jewels (in 1715, a silver peso, one "piece of eight," was equal to roughly twelve dollars). De Echeverz was anxious to clear the treacherous Florida Straits between the great Bahama Bank and the Florida reefs before the tropical storm season set in. And now the twelve-ship flota he commanded laid on full canvas to run the narrow passage.

But the fleet would never make it, as nature primed her elements for the greatest maritime disaster in Florida history off Cape Canaveral. It claimed more than seven hundred lives and most of a fantastic fortune. The treasure, moreover, would lay forgotten in its watery stronghold for almost 250 years until a weekend beachcomber with a fifteen-dollar army-surplus metal detector made a discovery that launched a fabulous modern-day treasure hunt.

By Sunday, July 28, the winds in the Straits became erratic, and at this point a French frigate, the *Grifon*, which was making the crossing as escort to the Spanish fleet, pulled away from it and tacked a different, faster course. Her captain, Antonio Darie, was impatient with the flota's slow progress under her Spanish commander. It would prove to be a providential move for the friendly French vessel—the only surviving ship.

By Tuesday, July 30, the easterly winds rapidly increased, the rolling swells grew larger, the scudding grayish clouds turned blue-black, and almost before General de Echeverz and his second in command, Juan Esteban de Ubilla, could reduce sail, a shrieking forty-knot wind brought lashing, torrential rains. By 2:00 A.M. Wednesday, the full fury of an eighty-

227

mile-per-hour hurricane bore down on the helpless flota. Frantic efforts to chop masts and overthrow cargo were futile. De Echeverz's 471-ton flagship was the first to strike the shoals south of Canaveral, smashing the bottom with such force that the entire lower hull sheared away, taking 120 tons of silver coins in boxes to the bottom. Ubilla and 220 others drowned at once. The other ships soon followed and were smashed to pieces in the raging surf, strewing wreckage and bodies up and down some thirty miles of the bleak, uninhabited coast. Most of the women and children drowned. Survivors, including General de Echeverz, hugged palmetto scrub for shelter.

The grisly scene was made even more ghoulish the next day by seamen and some passengers who were seen looting bodies for valuables. Outnumbered, the ships' officers were unable to stop most of the looting. (There was retribution, however. The looters set off on foot for the nearest settlement, St. Augustine, but they were arrested when their deeds were discovered.) By the time all survivors had gathered at a campsite just above Sebastian Inlet, a head count put the death toll at more than seven hundred. Fortunately, some food along with two longboats and a launch were salvaged. The longboats, carrying women, children, and the injured, were sent to St. Augustine and the launch to Havana; all arrived safely. Havana authorities sent seven ships to the campsite to rescue survivors and salvage as much of the treasure as possible. Captain Darie, meanwhile, waiting for the fleet at the Carolina capes, decided they were caught in "a prolonged calm" and did not learn of the disaster until arriving back in Europe. A good portion of the treasure was salvaged, and a portion more was looted by British privateers over the next three years. But when the Spanish finally abandoned the site in 1719, the greater part of the fortune still lay in its briny, undersea crypt.

Forgotten, it remained there until after World War II when an Ohio building contractor, Kip Wagner, came to the little town of Wabasso in south Brevard County to build a motel. An inveterate weekend beachcomber, Wagner began to find silver coins and even a few gold coins as he walked the six-mile stretch between Wabasso and Sebastian Inlet. His inquiries revealed that others had also found coins in the area, but no one knew of any shipwrecks in that section of the state. Some artifacts, mostly cannons and ship-fittings, had been discovered and gathered by amateur divers near the inlet, but no one associated those with a major wreck. A clue came when the coins were cleaned. Working with a friend, Dr. Kip Kelso, Wagner found that none of the coins was dated later than 1715. Perusing a dusty, buried record in the Library of Congress, they learned that there had indeed been a great shipwreck off that part of the Florida coast in 1715. Further details regarding probable wreck sites, campsite, and recovered treasure came off microfilm sent from documents held in the General Archives of the Indies in Seville, Spain.

Certain now that he was on to what might be "the biggest jackpot" of his life, Wagner acted fast. With Dr. Kelso, he organized the Real Eight Corporation, secured from the state exclusive salvage rights on specific wrecks over a fifty-mile area as far south as Stuart, and borrowed an army metal detector to locate the original campsite. The detector soon revealed the site, and Wagner bulldozed the thick scrub out and began digging. He soon uncovered Mexican ceramics, delicate Chinese porcelain still intact in its packing, cutlasses, plus chunks of silver, coins, and a two-and-a-half carat diamond and gold ring set with six smaller diamonds. But, for the first two wreck sites—one at Fort Pierce, another south of the Sebastian Inlet—Wagner needed help.

He first recruited Colonel Dan Thompson, an expert diver and engineer, and Lieutenant Colonel Harry Cannon, who owned a boat, both of Patrick Air Force Base at Cape Canaveral. Then four other area men joined the venture. Their search began in earnest in the early 1960s. Working strenuously in the tricky sea currents, they gradually moved the heavy rock ballast formations which pinpointed the wreck sites and soon began to uncover a massive pile of silver and gold coins; silver wedges, plates, and ingots; long, delicately designed gold chains, emeralds, and other jewels; more porcelain; plus other valuable artifacts like cannon, anchors, swords, daggers, and dinnerware. Sometimes the men would run across blackish-green "rocks" weighing up to seventy-five pounds; the "rocks" turned out to be solid clusters of up to fifteen hundred silver coins. Despite long interruptions because of bad weather, the excited team worked exhaustively over both wreck sites, and by 1966 their treasure strike had exhumed over $3.5 million in valuables (one fourth, of course, going to the state). Many of the items brought even greater returns when they went to auction in exclusive houses like New York's Parke-Bernet Galleries.

With only two wrecks covered, what was reported to be the greatest treasure find of its kind in history continued. Wagner himself was not able to fully enjoy his newfound wealth; he died in 1972. But the Real Eight team is still digging today, still retrieving chunks of the great scattered treasure, and slowly unfolding both history and the wealth from a 250-year-old watery shroud of sand and coral.

59.
A Golden Odyssey Ends in Tragedy

Mediterranean refugees came to Florida with New World dreams but ended up in a New Smyrna "gulag."

Following an inquiry into the treatment of the early colonists, Governor Patrick Tonyn ordered that they be given their freedom. (Florida State Archives)

They were fleeing oppression, poverty, and war as they packed themselves by the hundreds into ships bound for the New World, a golden odyssey spurred by the promise of land and freedom.

It would be the largest importation of white inhabitants ever into America at one time: 1,403 men, women, and children—a colorful Mediterranean mix of Greeks, Italians, and Spanish Minorcans.

But the shimmering expectations of these eager colonists would be brutally shattered soon after their arrival in Florida in June 1768. The wilderness colony of New Smyrna would become for them little more than an early-day "gulag"—a hellish scene of hardship, starvation, cruelty, revolt, and death. And it would last for a decade.

The tragedy of New Smyrna unfolds shortly after England acquired Florida from Spain in 1763 and began to search for ways to cut its gold drain, especially for Mediterranean products like indigo, cotton, silk, and wine. And so when a London physician, Dr. Andrew Turnbull, proposed a scheme to colonize Florida with native Greeks, he met with an enthusiastic response. Governor James Grant, of British East Florida, provided land grants totaling 101,500 acres, and prominent Britons Sir William Duncan, Sir Richard Temple, and Lord George Grenville offered, as partners, to put up expenses for the project. Turnbull would develop it.

The colonists would agree to various terms of indentured service, from five to seven years. They would clear and farm the land, share in its produce, and, at the end of their terms, receive their freedom plus a substantial land grant. Unfortunately, the contracts with each colonist were ambiguously verbal, not written. And, portending trouble from the start, whether from excessive ambition or simple avarice, Turnbull recruited almost three times the five hundred colonists that the partnership terms called for.

From the Mediterranean base at Mahon, on the Spanish island of Minorca, Turnbull went port-hopping from the Greek mainland and islands to Italy and Corsica, regaling natives with bright New World promises. But little hard-selling was needed for Greek farmers, then under the oppressive rule of the Ottoman Empire, or in political strife-torn Italy or drought-ridden Minorca. With a number already far in excess of provisions, Turnbull even kept on board two hundred Minorcan stowaways. Thus, during the three-month voyage to Florida, 148 men, women, and children would die of scurvy and other illnesses for lack of food.

Arriving at Mosquito Inlet, the colonists were put to work at once to clear swamp, hammock, and forest. The promised housing was nonexistent, and the settlers were forced to build small, dirt-floor palmetto huts. Food shortages soon became critical, and a disturbed Governor Grant called the over-recruitment "an impetuous act that [would have] frightened a wiser man." Grant assisted the colony with emergency corn shipments but advised London authorities: "I doubt much of it's [the colony] turning out to good account."

When they ate sufficiently at all, most colonists' main diet over the next ten years would be hominy grits. And other problems plagued them: the unfamiliar humid heat, torrential rains, snakes, insects, and swarms of mosquitos which brought malaria to many. They were also subjected to back-breaking labor from sunup to sundown seven days a week under harsh overseers, most of whom were renegade ex-British noncommissioned officers who spared neither lash nor chain. Many who collapsed in the fields from illness or hunger were beaten as "shirkers." More than a few of these died. So obsessed was Turnbull with getting the first crops in that he forbade colonists from taking time to fish, although nearby rivers and inlets teemed with a variety of seafood.

The powder keg of oppression exploded on August 22, 1768, while Turnbull visited St. Augustine. Some three hundred angry, desperate settlers overcame their overseers, ransacked supplies, seized one of Turnbull's ships, and made ready to sail to Havana. But St. Augustine authorities quickly learned of the revolt and dispatched a frigate to overtake and capture the vessel. Some thirty-five men eluded these captors by taking a smaller boat southward, but they were captured later at Key West. In January 1769, two of the five "ring-leaders," Carlo Forni and Guiseppe Massiadoli, were executed. A third, Elia Medici, was spared on condition that he execute the first two. He refused at first, relenting only after the doomed pair pleaded with him to do so.

After the revolt, settler Tony Stephanopoli wrote: "The rest of the people being starved, they began to die, 10 or 11 a day and some days 15." By just over two years later, a total of 627 settlers had perished from overwork, starvation, disease, and abuse.

Meanwhile, Turnbull was lushly prospering from this de facto slave labor. Aside from large production of sugar, corn, and turpentine, the biggest colony crop—the valuable indigo—poured into English markets, 42,283 pounds of it from 1771 to 1777. But this prosperity did not relax Turnbull's brutal iron grip on his colonists; in fact, when their indenture terms expired he would confine and beat them until they signed an extension of their service.

But both times and circumstances were changing fast. Turnbull's lavish personal expenditures had put him in default with his partners and he left for England to try to resolve it; he also hoped to scheme for the removal of the new Florida governor, Patrick Tonyn, who had sharply warned the doctor about his financial liabilities. More significantly, the heady winds of the American Revolution, begun a year earlier, were wafting even into the hapless colony at New Smyrna. In great secrecy the colonists would gather at night to discuss the revolution, especially the issues of "freedom" and "inalienable rights." So intense were their feelings that three of them were emboldened one day to slip away and journey to St. Augustine, where they met with Governor Tonyn. After hearing their stories, Tonyn promised them a full investigation. On learning of this, the colonists suddenly ceased their labors one day in April 1777, gathered en masse, and, "armed with wooden spears," marched off to St. Augustine. The full hearing took place in May.

In simple but moving language, as recorded in the British Public Record Office, the shocking stories were related: Anthony Musqetto was beaten to death when he was too ill to work; Louis Margan and Petros Cosifachis were flogged, chained, and starved until they agreed to extend their indenture; young and pregnant Paola Lurance, after refusing to have sex with the overseer Simon, was beaten so badly that her baby was born dead three days later; Rafael Simenis, Clegora Calamaras, and Michael Grasias were severely whipped by Turnbull himself for going fishing in the inlet. On and on the horror stories poured forth, similar and countless.

On July 17, 1777, Governor Tonyn ordered full freedom for the colonists, with permission granted them to settle in St. Augustine.

Turnbull, having failed to resolve his financial problems, returned to his colony only to find "a deserted village." Tonyn had also ordered the doctor's arrest on matters that included Turnbull's financial dealings. Somehow the doctor managed to elude the warrant and fled to Charleston, South Carolina, where he remained until his death in March 1792. But the shame of his infamy remains on record. Of the original 1,403 colonists, only 291, plus 128 colony-born offspring, were alive in January 1778.

Nevertheless, through the years they managed to thrive and prosper, becoming farmers, fishermen, artisans, even doctors and teachers. Today evidence of the original colonists is found throughout the nation's oldest city, in buildings, churches, and street names. They were remembered by one of their more noted Minorcan descendants, writer Stephen Vincent Benét, who used the colony's setting for his 1926 novel, *Spanish Bayonet*. But then, perhaps none of their progeny could ever forget that ancestral golden odyssey that would so suddenly come more to resemble a Greek tragedy.

60.
The Rise and Fall of a Mystery City

St. Joseph was once the queen of Florida cities, but virtually overnight, she vanished.

It was truly the state's "mystery" city, mushrooming overnight—booming, flamboyant, and wicked—and for several years it remained the metropolis queen of Florida.

But almost as suddenly, the thriving seaport town of St. Joseph disappeared from the face of the earth, obliterated by yellow fever, fire, and a hurricane, save for a scattering of moss-covered bricks and a few rusty rail irons. And folks in Apalachicola, twenty-eight miles away, would nod solemnly and assure one and all that God destroyed the city for its iniquitous ways—one of its chief iniquities being, of course, that it almost ruined the bustling seaport town of Apalachicola.

One could possibly debate historian Frederick Dau's label of St. Joseph as "the wickedest city in America," but many would agree with another historian, James Knauss, that no city in Florida before or since has equaled St. Joseph "in human interest and historical importance."

The former stems from its flourishing existence and sudden doom; the latter by its selection as the site of the territory's first constitutional convention (prior to Florida's statehood) and its serious consideration as the state's capital. Situated on the perfectly landlocked harbor of St. Joseph's Bay, slightly north of the present Port St. Joe, it was settled by the French who built a fort on the bay's north shore in 1717, christening it—somewhat portentously—Crevecoeur, or "Broken Heart." The fort was later destroyed.

Then, in 1835, the U.S. Supreme Court decided in a title dispute that 1.25 million acres of middle Florida, including Apalachicola, belonged to the then despised Apalachicola Land Company. Not long after, a group of citizens of Apalachicola decided to build its own town on St. Joseph's Bay, outside the land firm's jurisdiction.

With the help of a powerful coalition of south Georgia and Tallahassee cotton merchants and bankers, the town began with the organization of The Lake Wimico & St. Joseph Canal Company. Settlers hoped to divert the lush and lucrative cotton traffic from three states carried by steamer down the Apalachicola River, which joined three other rivers (the Flint, Chattahoochee, and Chipola). They also hoped to ruin the company-owned town of Apalachicola through which most export business was then funneled.

Wealthy Tallahasseeans like planter-bankers Major Benjamin Chaires and Colonel George Grattan Gamble sank fortunes into the bold plan. A city of three-quarters of a square mile was soon laid out. Steamer traffic was diverted from the Apalachicola River in Lake Wimico and then by rail overland eight miles to the great three-quarter-mile wharf with its sixty-foot double-docking pier extending eight hundred feet into the bay. A newspaper, the St. Joseph *Times,* under the brilliant editorship of a colorful and influential political figure, Peter W. Gautier, Jr., brought such publicity to the new town that it began to boom overnight. As Knauss reports: "Everywhere there was a wild orgy of real estate development, aided by cheap paper money issued by banks with enormous capital." Another railroad was later built twenty-eight miles northward to Iola Landing, directly on the river, thus facilitating transport of the tremendous cotton exports.

Apalachicola, by now literally teetering on the edge of economic ruin, railed bitterly at the new town, charging that its backers were "a small band of speculators who would . . . dupe the people by their arts and untiring zeal." But the boom continued unabated, and by 1838, with a reported population of six thousand, St. Joseph was the largest city in the state. After failing to wrest the county seat from Apalachicola, it simply formed a new county, Calhoun, with St. Joseph, naturally, its seat.

The city was striking, with beautiful homes and brick buildings lining its wide tree-shaded streets while its shimmering crystal-clear harbor, bounded by towering forest-clad hills, was packed with ships from every nation. It seethed with the activity of speculators, tradesmen, laborers, and new settlers.

But with its flush flow of wealth and speculative cash, the town developed some less pristine characteristics, including gambling at the Calhoun horse track, casino gambling in every hotel, plain and fancy brothels on every other street, saloons, floating con games and prizefights, fist fights and homicides, and motley crowds of every nationality, a mix of every type of renegade and shady character from Canada to Key West.

Perhaps the peak measure of St. Joseph's renown came when it was picked to host the territory's first constitutional convention. Gala celebrations welcomed Florida's most prominent leaders in the specially built Constitution Hall on December 3, 1838. After long, arduous sessions, the historic document was completed and signed on January 11, 1839. (Statehood was still six years away.) At this time, legislative leaders seriously considered the selection of the city as the state capital. In the ensuing months, however, St. Joseph's economy felt a severe pinch as a spin-off from the land panic of 1837; banks that had speculated recklessly in the flush years found capital stocks exhausted.

But the darkest specter hovering over St. Joseph was barely noticed in September 1840 in two small items in the *Times*. One noted that Captain L. L. Kupfer of the schooner *Herald* out of Havana had died aboard ship of yellow fever. The other mentioned that the *Herald* had sailed for Boston, leaving several fever victims behind. The disease lay dormant that winter and spring and then struck with fury in the summer. Panic and horror gripped the city as victims fell to yellow fever by the scores daily. Soon the only activity was the rumble of death wagons in the city streets gathering bodies. The epidemic struck equally the high and low, slave and free. By July 1841, nearly seventy-five percent of the population was dead; they filled three cemeteries, while many more had to be buried in trenches. By August 25, there were only five hundred survivors, and many of those quickly disposed of their property and fled.

This great tragedy was followed barely a month later by a huge forest fire that swept into town and destroyed dozens of homes and businesses. By now, most of the fever survivors had fled, and by the summer of 1843, it was with some grim irony that Apalachicola residents came over to dismantle the deserted houses, shipping them back to their own town for re-erection.

Then, on September 8, 1844, as if to add a final devastating postscript to the town's demise, a mammoth hurricane pouring forth giant tidal waves smashed over the city with unrelenting fury, crumbling the empty brick buildings and houses and literally burying the town under great mounds of sea sand. The once-proud queen of Florida cities had now been literally removed from the earth's face, its barren desolation complete.

If any memory of St. Joseph remained, it would not be noticed until almost one hundred years later when someone noticed how remarkably preserved a few of its old iron rails were. After so long an exposure to salt and erosion, they were still in good condition. The rails were sent off to a steel-rail maker in an effort to find out why rails made so long ago were more durable than those made in the 1930s. An answer was never received. As if by some curse in perpetuity, the town really was forgotten.

61.
When Anti-Semitism Plagued Miami Beach

The scurrilous seeds of anti-Semitism unleashed a toxic virus
that once threatened the Beach's future.

It is a curious irony of history that sometimes some of its ugliest chapters can become the catalyst for improbable success stories. Miami Beach is just such a story.

To understand the Beach's transformation after World War II into one of the most opulent and popular tourist resorts in the world, one must recall its darker genesis, an ignominious time when anti-Semitism threatened to scar permanently that town's people and future.

Florida, with its polyglot mix of peoples, has historically been notably free of anti-Semitism. Generations of Jewish settlers have mingled and married freely with Gentiles, and many Jews have risen to prominence in the state. Florida's first U.S. senator was David Levy Yulee; David Sholtz was a popular governor.

In America generally, anti-Semitism was absent until the post-Civil War period, when a booming industrial expansion spawned a host of millionaires and the Gilded Age. In this same period, many of the German-Jewish emigrants of the 1840s also rose to prominence in commerce and finance, a fact that began to chafe native-born tycoons. As one historian noted, what the native parvenus could not forgive their Jewish counterparts "was not their religion or national origin . . . but their success." And so they decided simply to close the gilded circle.

Anti-Semitism took root in 1877 when New York banker Joseph Seligman, a man just recently honored by President Ulysses S. Grant for outstanding services in the Civil War, was turned away from a famous Saratoga Springs resort hotel because he was a Jew. Despite outrage and protests from figures as diverse as Mark Twain and Oliver Wendell Holmes, the scurrilous seed had been planted; it spread quickly. By 1900 the infamous restricted covenant deed, barring property ownership to all but white Anglo-Saxon Protestants, was born.

And thus the prejudice that hit Miami Beach was basically a transplant. Even so, it had an oddly schizoid character. Carl Fisher and John Collins, who began developing much of the Beach in 1913 and placed restricted

237

No Jews

WASP covenants into all their property deeds, were Northerners. The Lummus brothers, John and James, whose large tracts on the Beach's south end were open to Jew and Gentile, were early Florida pioneers. This was fortuitous for the first Jewish settlers like the Weiss families, first Joe and Jennie, then Rose. (The two families were unrelated. Joe opened the first Beach restaurant, Joe's Stone Crab, which still flourishes today.)

Even though by 1920 the Jewish population on the Beach was relatively small (of some two hundred families, only twenty were Jewish), anti-Semitism took quick root. Nearly all of the posh and flamboyant hotels and apartments developed by Fisher and others bore the small signs on their portals: "Gentiles Only." Even during the euphoric, lotus-eating days of the 1920s land boom, when both Miami and Miami Beach were scenes of gaudy revelry and entertainment, historian Harry Simonhoff recalls when the bemasked Ku Klux Klan paraded openly with signs bearing anti-Jewish slurs. The popular slogan, "It is always June in Miami," appeared in perversely twisted signs on the back of many cars as "It is always Jew'n in Miami" until the police chief ordered their removal.

But Miami Beach's Jews would soon turn this scourge into a blessing. When the Great Depression quickly followed Florida's boom and the high-rolling subdividers like Fisher were wiped out, the Beach lay in a wasteland of unwanted vacant buildings, empty blocks, and unpaved streets. In this same period, retired or semiretired Northern Jewish business or professional men, barred from most resorts near home, began going to South Beach in increasing numbers. They looked around and saw in this sunny island clime a perfect place to visit or live. Instead of a snobby exclusive resort, why couldn't it be a tourist mecca open to all? They also saw newspaper columns packed with tax delinquent property lists and heard the cries of frantic debt-ridden sellers.

Suddenly, it seemed, restricted deeds became unrestricted as fast as unwanted real estate could change hands. New development slowly accelerated through the 1930s, and the Beach became the first Southern town to recover from the Depression. Tourism nearly doubled in the decade, and by 1940, more than three hundred new hotels and nearly one thousand apartment buildings had gone up.

Still, as a growing Jewish population began to spill over into areas between Lincoln Road and Surfside, so grew the hostility of die-hard Gentiles who warned of Jews "taking over the Beach." The "Gentiles Only" signs grew larger and sometimes more brutally blatant ("No Jews, No Dogs" or "Every room with a view and without a Jew"). Nazism seeped into Dade County, too. Swastikas began appearing on synagogue walls; hate groups like the Silver Shirt Legion openly solicited members; notorious anti-Jewish, pro-Fascist speakers like W. G. Blanchard, Jr., and Gerald Winrod screeched hate propaganda in open public meetings; would-be storm troopers, the "White Front," garbed in boots and khaki, passed out hate sheets supplied by German merchant ships in Miami's port.

Able Jewish leaders like Abe Aronovitz, Rabbi Irving Lehrman, Isidor Cohen, and Burnett Roth, of B'nai B'rith and the Anti-Defamation League, stayed busy night and day curtailing much of this harassment.

All of this seemed like grim scene-setting for an offshore drama that occurred in the summer of 1939 and stirred the national conscience. The Hamburg America Line ship, *St. Louis,* carrying 930 Jewish refugees from Germany, anchored off Miami Beach and urgently sought a special nonquota entry into Miami. Despite nationwide pleas, the Miami entry was denied. As the vessel slowly steamed back to Germany, the refugees were saved when the Jewish Defense League raised the huge sums needed to debark them in Britain, Holland, Belgium, and France.

With tourism virtually suspended during World War II and the Army Air Corps temporarily taking over eighty-five percent of the Beach hotels for training facilities, anti-Semitism became at best a peripheral concern.

Still, it lingered on the Beach until 1945, when Anti-Defamation League official Roth and sixteen other ex-servicemen made a quiet but persuasive assault on scores of "restricted" hotels. It was effective; two-thirds of the offending signs came down. The rest were outlawed in 1949 when an aggressive Beach citizen, Dr. Lee Powell, a Presbyterian, fought all the way to the legislature to legalize a local ordinance banning Beach discrimination against race, color, or creed. In the meantime, the dynamic enterprise of the 1930s had turned the Beach into one of the world's most glamorous and popular tourist resorts.

A sidelight is noteworthy. Before the war, no Jew could be elected to the city commission. By the late 1940s, Dr. Powell—with Jewish support—was the only Gentile on the commission. Quipped historian Polly Redford: "So, on Miami Beach, American democracy finally reached full circle. Where else could you find a token Presbyterian?"

62.
Jacksonville Fights a Fever-Fed Frenzy

The yellow fever epidemic of 1888 reduced the city to a no man's land of death and terror and altered its destiny.

On the morning of July 28, 1888, a stranger stepped off the train in the bustling city of Jacksonville and checked into a hotel.

He would prove to be no ordinary stranger. As he entered his hotel room, he was suddenly seized with chills, then severe body pains. He summoned a doctor. The physician examined the man at length, finally turning away somewhat pale and shaken. The stranger, unwittingly, had brought an unseen guest.

Thus began Florida's last great yellow fever epidemic. Within days it would reduce the state's greatest city to a no man's land of death and terror, in a siege that would tragically alter the city's destiny for years to come.

In 1888 Jacksonville was in its heyday, its twenty-five thousand citizens waxing prosperous in a city that was the thriving center of sea and riverboat commerce. Its twenty major hotels and boarding houses hosted a seasonal peak of 100,000 tourists in 1887. Times were good and such flush economic growth seemed to assure the town a bright future. Or so it seemed, until the stranger came.

The man was rushed to a hospital. Citizens calmly accepted a small *Times-Union* report of the case. But they were less than calm a day later when Governor Edward Perry announced a quarantine in the city. Then, several days later, on August 8, four more cases developed. To avoid panic, the victims were hospitalized under cover of night, but somehow the news leaked out, and by the next day, widespread hysteria had turned into a frantic exodus. On August 10, the *Times-Union* reported "every train and steamer going out [of the city] was loaded to the utmost capacity," while roads were choked with carts and wagons packed with people and belongings. Such news moved like lightning, traveling as far north as Charleston and as far west as Mobile. Most of the hapless refugees would face rejection, often violent, as they sought safety from the disease.

Communities around the state quickly set up "shotgun" quarantines aimed at keeping out the Jacksonville refugees and their illness. Armed patrols met strangers at every road and train station, turning them away. At

240

St. Augustine, heavily armed guards patrolled roads and seashore, ready to shoot if any of the migrating throng tried to stop there. Armed citizens in Waycross, Georgia, threatened to blow up the railroad if trains carrying refugees attempted to pass through their town even at a high speed with windows and doors locked. As far away as Montgomery, Alabama, the mayor offered a one-hundred-dollar reward for information of quarantine violators who tried to come to his town. Such behavior prompted the *Times-Union* to urge Jacksonville's citizens to stay home where it was "much safer to fight the fever than to fight the fear of it."

The panic lessened somewhat but the fever accelerated after August 21. By then, forty-five cases were identified and eight proved fatal. The U.S. Surgeon General ordered a nationwide quarantine of Jacksonville. But the city was already cut off from the outside world. Commercial shipping was suspended, and outgoing mail had to be fumigated piece by piece. Schools, offices, businesses, and banks closed. The 13,757 citizens who had been unable or unwilling to leave town faced unemployment and critical food shortages in addition to the dreaded killer. Food thefts increased, suspected

Fires crackled along Bay Street as residents tried to fight the yellow fever epidemic by "burning out" the germs that caused it. (Florida State Archives)

"fever" houses were burned, and even the three hospitals, where most patients were taken, were threatened.

Finally, a citizens committee, under the able direction of Colonel J. J. Daniel, restored a semblance of order. Public kitchens were opened and food distributed and two camps were set up just outside the city for refugee shelters. Over five hundred men were employed to clean sixty miles of ditches and to fumigate the streets and all premises with sulphur and lime. Pitchpine fires and tar cauldrons burned night and day on every block, but the number of yellow and black flags flying from infected houses only increased. And the deaths mounted: 156 out of 1,203 cases by September. A coffin shortage would soon force burials to take place in common graves outside the city. As one writer observed: "Theirs was a city lime-coated and smelling of fumigating gas, a city of fear-stricken people listening hypnotically to the rattle of death carts in the night."

The fever's symptoms alone could evoke terror. Chills first, then delirious fever, followed by headaches and intense pain in limbs and back, the skin turning light yellow, often red-splotched. Finally, the agonizing retching. After death, the body turned bright yellow, then black.

Remedies abounded. The medical profession then generally held gaseous vapours as the cause, thus the sanitation projects. Smoke from pine and tar was thought effective, too. The city fired heavy cannons on the theory that the concussion killed "microbes"; the cannon firing shattered windows instead. A few rationalized that alcohol killed "inhaled germs" of the fever, so they proceeded to consume it in large draughts. (No one had heeded the "mosquito" theory of Cuban physician Carlos Finlay in 1880; Tampa doctor J. P. Wall was mocked by colleagues for a similar theory.)

As the death toll mounted and food and other supplies were nearly exhausted, a desperate Colonel Daniel appealed to the nation for help, and the response was generous. From groups, individuals, and even children, donations poured in for a cash total of $331,972. President Grover Cleveland sent a personal check for $200 and promised another $175,564 in federal aid. Volunteer doctors and nurses arrived, but some immediately succumbed to fever; in all, five doctors died. The indefatigable Colonel Daniel himself took fever and died on September 22, but an able citizen, Patrick McQuaid, quickly took over his duties. In September, when the fever peaked, there were 229 deaths.

Finally, on October 8, after the death of a young mother (victim 304), the fever began to abate. With near-freezing temperatures in November, the number of new cases dropped sharply. With only five deaths in early December—and no more after that—the quarantine was lifted, both statewide and nationally on December 15. Refugees began pouring back into the city by road, rail, and water. But barely a family had been left untouched. Of the total 4,704 cases, there were 430 deaths. Other victims were left with long-term disabilities.

But that was not the end of it. The terrible visitation also had severe long-range consequences. Both seaport and St. Johns River traffic sharply decreased; commerce diverted to other cities during the epidemic remained diverted; railroads rapidly replaced much water traffic. The tourist trade steadily declined as visitors traveled further south to newer resorts. By 1890, the population of Jacksonville fell by thirty-two percent. Together these factors induced a sharp economic recession of several years' duration. And the situation would be aggravated periodically by intense political factionalism and even racial strife.

Still another grim specter loomed unseen: There would be little enough time for recovery before the great fire of 1901 which literally reduced Jacksonville to ashes.

Ironically, the original fever-carrying stranger on the train, an R. D. McCormick, who had arrived from Tampa for a visit, survived the fever and was released from the hospital. Promptly, and gratefully, he made his way home.

63.
Florida Foils a Presidential Bid

Lincoln cabinet member Salmon P. Chase hoped to unseat his boss in 1864, but his grand plans went haywire in Florida.

On a September day in 1862, despite his busy schedule in the midst of the Civil War, U.S. Treasury Secretary Salmon P. Chase let his thoughts wander far away, as far away as the seditious little state of Florida.

Florida might not remain seditious for long, Chase reflected. Union forces now occupied key coastal sections of the state amid reports of growing Union sentiment among a disaffected populace. Such sentiments might easily be turned into political capital, the kind that could aid Chase's bid for the 1864 Republican presidential nomination.

Such reflections were about to make Florida an unusual prize in an even more unusual political tug of war between the powerful secretary and his boss, President Abraham Lincoln.

Chase had long aspired to the highest office, pursuing it unsuccessfully in 1856 and 1860. But now serious divisions plagued the Republican party over Lincoln's "plodding" conduct of the war. An embryonic "Chase movement" had taken shape, and the job seemed within grasp.

The president himself, while not exactly overjoyed with his haughty secretary's ambitions, viewed them generally with a benign tolerance. He had diagnosed the case as "White House fever." No cure, he prognosed; just let it run its course. He assured alarmed friends that Chase's fever over the next presidency was his "horsefly," one whose bite stimulated and energized the secretary's vital work in the Treasury Department. Therefore, he reasoned, "Let the horsefly alone."

But the president also had been shrewdly eyeing Florida's political potential. In fact, he had the state in mind when, in 1863, he issued his "ten percent" Amnesty Plan, whereby if ten percent of the legal voters in a Rebel state took an oath of allegiance to the United States, the president would recognize a state government of their own creation. Such a government, just by the way, could send delegates to the Republican convention.

Chase's Florida strategy evolved from the Direct Tax Law of 1862, which enabled him to appoint three tax commissioners to assess real property in occupied Rebel districts, advertise the taxes due on same, and sell at auction the property of delinquent owners. Chase named John Sammis, a businessman; Harrison Reed, a former Wisconsin editor (later to become Florida's Reconstruction governor); and Lyman D. Stickney, a somewhat opportunistic Vermont lawyer. Their "unofficial" duties were to search out and organize loyal Unionists in Florida, and particularly loyal Chase Unionists.

Stickney, a man of forceful personality but disarming demeanor, quickly won Chase's favor. Generally speaking, Chase was often regarded as a man with a monumental ego and prima donna temperament. A more trenchant assessment came from Lincoln biographer Carl Sandburg: "Under the portentous exterior of the handsomest man in the Cabinet was an over-sized marionette borne down by delusions of grandeur." Stickney, at any rate, sensed such traits and fed them with the flattery of a courtier. Chase, in turn, made Stickney his "political" man in Florida.

Such favor led the confident Stickney to ignore the mundane duties for which he was appointed while he set about to make Florida a "Chase state." Reed clashed with Stickney often, especially when the latter refused to help with assessments at Fernandina. Instead, Stickney set up a newspaper in that town, *The Peninsula,* and named his brother, John Stickney, as editor. The paper's content was mainly devoted to Chase's speeches and writings and was circulated widely. From Fernandina to St. Augustine there were many Union loyalists—but not half so many as Stickney's glowing, inflated reports would indicate. But such reports greatly pleased the secretary, especially since a "Chase boom," led by Senator Samuel Pomeroy of Kansas, was now rumbling through Congress.

Stickney's strategy was to bypass the ten percent amnesty plan, forego elections, and "hand-pick" Chase men to draw up a revised Florida constitution from which would issue a "Free State" government. To this end, he rounded up a large group of loyalists for a "Union meeting" in St. Augustine late in 1863, and they set a constitutional convention date for March 1, 1864.

Chase had by now secured the appointment of his secretary, Homer G. Plantz, to a district attorneyship in Key West, where Plantz would organize Chase Unionists in the Key West–Fort Myers area.

Both Chase and Stickney agreed that before Florida could have a "reconstructed" state, a military operation into the interior to "clear out" remaining enemy forces would be vital. They found General Quincy Gillmore, Southern Department commander at Hilton Head, South Carolina, receptive to such an operation. Later, in December 1863, Gillmore won permission from U.S. General-in-Chief Henry Halleck to conduct any Florida operation he deemed necessary. Gillmore made plans for an expedition in early 1864.

During this period, Lincoln and his private secretary, John Hay, had been keeping abreast of Stickney's activities as well as the numerous reports (often embellished) of growing Union sentiment in Florida. Stickney had earlier corresponded with Hay. As a result, the commissioner exultantly reported to Chase that he had Hay "completely fooled" about the Florida convention plans, just in case Lincoln sent Hay down to thwart such plans.

But Stickney had fooled neither Hay nor Lincoln. In fact, the pair agreed now that the time was ripe to try the amnesty plan in Florida. Hay was commissioned as an army major, and on January 13, 1864, he set off for Florida with oath blanks and certificates.

The young secretary was at first encouraged. Early on, he obtained oaths from several hundred Rebel war prisoners, many of them Floridians, who were now free to return home. In Jacksonville, where General Gillmore had sent over five thousand troops under General Truman Seymour, the secretary signed up sixty area citizens. But gradually he began to see that earlier reports of a flourishing Unionism in the state had been greatly exaggerated.

The bloody battle of Olustee all but ended Salmon P. Chase's hopes of a presidency.
(Florida State Archives)

Meanwhile, as the time for rounding up delegates drew closer, Chase wrote Stickney on February 1, impatiently noting that "federal military movements [in Florida] are by no means so energetic as they should be. We cannot afford [prolongation]." But Gillmore's orders to Seymour had been simply to occupy the west bank of the St. Johns River, set up depots, and wait for further orders.

There is no record that Chase, Stickney, or any other Chase man contacted Seymour during this period. However, whatever his motives, against orders and without knowledge of either the size or the exact location of enemy forces, Seymour suddenly marched five thousand men into the interior.

On February 20, reaching Olustee near Lake City, he blundered into an entrenched force of five thousand Confederates under General Joseph Finegan. The ensuing battle was a bloody one. The Federals were routed into withdrawal after suffering 1,355 casualties.

This shocking reversal dampened, where it did not suspend, all Unionist organizing plans. A dismayed Hay reluctantly left the state. Nor was Hay much consoled, while sailing home, as he read the sensational—and exaggerated—Northern newspaper headlines screaming "Murder for Politics" and "The Price of a Set of Florida Delegates—1,000 Lives." This anti-Lincoln clamor would cease only after the written instructions of Lincoln to Gillmore and Gillmore to Seymour were soon made public.

Thus was ended an unusual tug of war for Florida's "reconstructed" political favor. Both sides were sent sprawling when the political rope was snapped at Olustee; it would not be joined again. And so in early March 1864, a disheartened Chase, whose "horsefly" had fatally bitten him in Florida, formally withdrew from the presidential nomination canvass.

BIBLIOGRAPHY

Numbers below refer to chapter numbers.

1. Brown, Warren J. *Florida's Aviation History*. Largo, Florida Aero-Medical Consultants, 1980.
   Lazarus, William C. *Wings in the Sun*. Orlando, Tyn Cobb's Florida Press, 1951.
2. Proctor, Samuel. *Napoleon Bonaparte Broward: Florida's Fighting Democrat*. Gainesville, University of Florida Press, 1950.
   Broward, N. B. *Autobiography* . . . Miami, n.p., 1938.
3. Davis, Elmer. "New World Symphony." *Harper's*, May 1935.
   Langley, Joan and Wright. *Key West, Images of the Past*. Key West, Belland & Swift, 1982.
4. Murray, Marian. *Plant Wizard, The Life of Lue Gim Gong*. New York, Crowell-Collier Press, 1970.
5. Fritz, Florence. *Unknown Florida*. Coral Gables, University of Miami Press, 1963.
   Hanna, Kathryn A. and Alfred J. *Lake Okeechobee*. New York, Bobbs-Merrill Co., 1948.
6. Laudonnière, René. *Three Voyages*. Gainesville, University of Florida Press (translation), 1975.
   Bennett, Charles E. *Laudonnière & Fort Caroline*. Gainesville, University of Florida Press, 1964.
7. Caughey, J. W. *McGillivray of the Creeks*. Norman, Okla., University of Oklahoma Press, 1959.
8. Johnston, Alva. *The Legendary Mizners*. New York, Farrar, Straus and Young, 1953.
   Pratt, Theodore. *The Story of Boca Raton*. St. Petersburg, Great Outdoors Publishing, 1963.
9. Erickson, Ruth. *Frederick deBary, The Man and His Mansion*. Celery City Printing Co., 1964.
   Brooks, Edith G. *Saga of Frederick deBary*. Convention Press, 1968.
10. Kendrick, Banyard. *Florida Trails to Turnpikes, 1914–64*. Gainesville, University of Florida Press, 1964.
    Tebeau, Charlton W. *Florida's Last Frontier*. Coral Gables, University of Miami Press, 1957.
11. Klingman, Peter D. *Josiah Walls: Florida's Black Congressman of Reconstruction*. Gainesville, University Presses of Florida, 1976.
12. Matthews, Janet Snyder. *Edge of Wilderness*. Sarasota, Coastal Press, 1983.
    Grismer, Karl. *The Story of Sarasota*. Sarasota, M. E. Russel, 1946.
13. Brooks, Abbie [Silvia Sunshine, pseud.]. *Petals Plucked From Sunny Climes*. Nashville, Methodist Publishing House, 1880.

14. Pierce, Charles W. *Pioneer Life in Southeast Florida*. Coral Gables, University of Miami Press, 1970.

    Frisbie, Louise. *Peace River Pioneers*. Miami, E. A. Seemann Publishing, 1974.

15. Pratt, Theodore. *The Story of Boca Raton*. St. Petersburg, Great Outdoors Publishing, 1963.

16. Bishop, Jim. *The Murder Trial of Judge Peel*. New York, Simon and Schuster, 1962.

17. Will, Laurence. *Cracker History of Okeechobee*. St. Petersburg, Great Outdoors Publishing, 1964.

    Hanna, Kathryn A. and Alfred J. *Lake Okeechobee*. New York, Bobbs-Merrill Co., 1948.

18. Davis, T. Frederick. *MacGregor's Invasion of Florida, 1817*. Florida Historical Society, 1928.

    Library Service Project. *Occupation of Amelia Island*. Tallahassee, Works Progress Administration, 1938.

19. Prior, Leon O. "German Espionage in Florida During World War II." *Florida Historical Quarterly* 39(1961):374–77.

    Aswell, Edward C. "The Case of the Ten Nazi Spies." *Harper's,* June 1942.

20. Flynt, Wayne. *Cracker Messiah*. Baton Rouge, Louisiana State University Press, 1977.

21. Asbury, Herbert. *The Great Illusion*. Garden City, N.Y., Doubleday, 1950.

    Carter, James Asbury. "Florida and Rumrunning During National Prohibition." *Florida Historical Quarterly* 48(1969):47–56.

22. Davis, Jess G. *History of Alachua County*. Florida Historical Society, 1959.

    ———. *History of Gainesville, Florida*. Florida Historical Society, 1966.

23. McIver, Stuart B. *Fort Lauderdale and Broward County*. Woodland Hills, Calif., Windsor Publications, 1983.

    Kefauver, Estes. *Crime in America*. Garden City, N.Y., Doubleday, 1951.

24. McKay, D. B. *Pioneer Florida Vol. II*. Tampa, The Southern Publishing Co., 1959.

25. Williamson, Edward C. *Florida Politics in the Gilded Age, 1877–1893*. Gainesville, The University Presses of Florida, 1976.

    ———. "William D. Chipley, West Florida's Mr. Railroad." *Florida Historical Quarterly* 25(1947).

26. Cochran, T. E. *History of Public School Education in Florida*. Lancaster, Pa., New Era Printing Co., 1921.

    Lovell, Broward. *Gone With the Hickory Stick*. Ocala, Bicentennial Publication, 1975.

27. Stallman, R. W. *Stephen Crane, A Biography*. New York, George Braziller, Inc., 1968.

28. Mahon, John K. *History of the Second Seminole War, 1835–1842*. Gainesville, University of Florida Press, 1967.

Sprague, John T. *The Origin, Progress and Conclusion of the Florida War.* Gainesville, University of Florida Press, 1964.

29. Thrift, Charles T., Jr. *The Trail of the Florida Circuit Riders.* Lakeland, Florida Southern College Press, 1944.

    Smith, George G., Jr. *The History of Methodism in Georgia and Florida From 1785 to 1865.* Macon, Ga., Burke, 1877.

30. Williams, Ames W. "Stronghold of the Straits." *Tequesta* 14(1954):3–24.

    Camp, Vaughan, Jr. "Capt. Brannan's Dilemma: Key West 1861." *Tequesta* 20(1960):31–43.

31. Davis, William W. *The Civil War and Reconstruction in Florida.* New York, Columbia University, 1913.

    Durrent, Richard N. *Three Carpetbag Governors.* Baton Rouge, Louisiana State University Press, 1967.

32. Adams, Charles Francis, ed. *Memoirs of John Quincy Adams.* New York, Books for Libraries Press, 1969.

    Adams, William R. "Florida Live Oak Farm of John Quincy Adams." *Florida Historical Quarterly* 51(1972).

33. Graff, M. B. *Mandarin on the St. Johns.* Gainesville, University of Florida Press, 1953.

    Stowe, Harriet Beecher. *Palmetto Leaves.* Boston, J. R. Osgood and Co., 1873.

34. Archer, Jules. *Indian Friend, Indian Foe.* New York, Macmillan, 1969.

    Griswold, Oliver. "William Harney." *Tequesta* 9(1949):73–80.

35. Jahoda, Gloria. *River of the Golden Ibis.* New York, Holt, Rinehart and Winston, 1973.

    Bothwell, Dick. *Sunrise 200.* St. Petersburg, Times Publishing Co., 1975.

36. Peters, Thelma. *Lemon City.* Miami, Banyan Books, 1976.

    Straight, William M. "The Lady Doctor of Coconut Grove." *Journal of the Florida Medical Association* 52(1965):479–85.

37. Schellings, William J. "The Advent of the Spanish American War in Florida." *Florida Historical Quarterly,* 39(1961).

38. Matschat, Cecile. *Suwannee River, Strange Green Land.* New York, Literary Guild of America, 1938.

    Mueller, Edward A. "Suwannee River Steamboating." *Florida Historical Quarterly* 45(1967).

39. Allen, Frederick Lewis. *Only Yesterday.* New York and London, Harper & Brothers, 1931.

    Sessa, Frank B. "Anti-Florida Propaganda and Counter Measures During the 1920s." *Tequesta* 21(1961).

40. Silver, James W. *Edmund Pendleton Gaines, Frontier General.* Baton Rouge, Louisiana State University Press, 1949.

    Mahon, John K. *History of the Second Seminole War, 1835–1842.* Gainesville, University of Florida Press, 1967.

41. Porter, Kenneth W. "Negroes on the Southern Frontier." *The Journal of Negro History* 33(1948).

Anderson, Robert L. "The End of an Idyll." *Florida Historical Quarterly* 42(1963).

42. Arnade, Charles W. "Who Was Ponce de León?" *Tequesta* 27(1967).

Davis, T. Frederick. "History of Juan Ponce de León's Voyages to Florida." *Florida Historical Quarterly* 14(1935).

43. Tebeau, Charlton. *A History of Florida*. Coral Gables, University of Miami Press, 1971.

Jahoda, Glorida. *Florida, A Bicentennial History*. New York, W. W. Norton & Co., 1976.

44. Grismer, Karl. *The Story of Sarasota*. Sarasota, M. E. Russel, 1946.

45. Dibble, Dr. Ernest F. *Ante Bellum Pensacola and the Military Presence*. Pensacola, Mayes Printing Co., 1974.

Parks, Virginia. *Pensacola: Spaniards to Space Age*. Pensacola Historical Society, 1986.

46. Dimock, A. W. *Florida Enchantments*. New York, Frederick A. Stokes Co., 1908.

47. Burghard, August. *Half a Century in Florida*. Fort Lauderdale, Manatee Books, 1982.

Sherwood, Robert E. *Roosevelt and Hopkins*. New York, Harper & Brothers, 1948.

48. Plowden, Gene. *Those Amazing Ringlings and Their Circus*. Caldwell, Idaho, Carton Printers, 1967.

North, Henry Ringling, and Alden Hatch. *The Circus Kings—Our Ringling Family Story*. New York, Doubleday & Co., 1960.

49. Hanna, A. J. *Flight Into Oblivion*. Bloomington, Ind., Indiana University Press, 1938.

50. Adams, Adam G. "Vizcaya (James Deering)." *Tequesta* 15(1955).

51. Bennett, Charles E. "Early History of the Cross-Florida Barge Canal." *Florida Historical Quarterly* 45(1966).

Ryan, Lanue B. "The Cross-Florida Barge Canal, Fact or Folly." *Apalachee* 7(1968–70).

52. Josephson, Matthew. *Edison*. London, Eyre & Spottiswoode Publishers, 1961.

Conot, Robert. *A Streak of Luck*. New York, Seaview Books, 1979.

53. Kusche, Lawrence D. *The Bermuda Triangle Mystery—Solved*. New York, Harper & Row, 1975.

Berlitz, Charles F. *The Bermuda Triangle*. New York, Doubleday, 1974.

54. Harrison, Benjamin. *Acres of Ashes; The Story of the Great (Jacksonville) Fire*. Jacksonville, J. A. Holloman, 1901.

Davis, T. Frederick. *History of Jacksonville, Florida*. St. Augustine, The Record Company, 1925.

55. Griswold, Oliver. *The Florida Keys and the Coral Reef*. Miami, The Graywood Press, 1965.

56. Author unnamed. "Florida Power & Light, How a utility made itself popular." *Fortune*, April 1950.

57. Shofner, Jerrell H. "Fraud and Intimidation in the Florida Election of 1876." *Florida Historical Quarterly* 42(1964).
    Woodward, C. Vann. *Reunion and Reaction*. Boston, Little, Brown and Company, 1951.

58. Marx, Robert F. *The Lure of Sunken Treasure*. New York, McKay, 1973.
    ————. *Spanish Treasure in Florida Waters*. Boston, The Mariners Press, 1979.

59. Panagopoulos, E. P. *New Smyrna, An Eighteenth Century Greek Odyssey*. Gainesville, University of Florida Press, 1966.
    Corse, Carita Doggett. *Dr. Andrew Turnbull and the New Smyrna Colony of Florida*. St. Petersburg, Great Outdoors Publishing Co., 1919.

60. Knauss, James O. "St. Joseph." *Florida Historical Quarterly* 5,6(1927), 18(1938).
    Porter, Louise M. *The Lives of St. Joseph*. Chattanooga, Tenn., Great American Publishing Co., 1975.

61. Simonhoff, Harry. *Under Strange Skies*. New York, Philosophical Library, 1953.
    Redford, Polly. *Billion Dollar Sandbar*. New York, E. P. Dutton & Co., 1970.

62. Davis, T. Frederick. *History of Jacksonville, Florida*. St. Augustine, The Record Company, 1925.
    Martin, Richard A. *The City Makers*. Jacksonville, The Convention Press, 1972.

63. Futch, Ovid L. "Salmon P. Chase and Civil War Politics in Florida." *Florida Historical Quarterly* 32(1954).
    Sandburg, Carl. *Abraham Lincoln: The War Years, Vol. III*. New York, Harcourt, Brace & Company, 1939.

INDEX

257

If you enjoyed reading this book, here are some other Pineapple Press titles you might enjoy as well. To request our complete catalog or to place an order, write to Pineapple Press, P.O. Box 3889, Sarasota, Florida 34230, or call 1-800-PINEAPL (746-3275). Or visit our website at www.pineapplepress.com.

Florida's Past by Gene Burnett. Collected essays from Burnett's "Florida's Past" columns in *Florida Trend* magazine, plus some original writings not found elsewhere. Burnett's easygoing style and his sometimes surprising choice of topics make history good reading. **Volume 1** ISBN 1-56164-115-4 (pb); **Volume 3** ISBN 1-56164-117-0 (pb)

The Florida Keys Volume 1: *A History of the Pioneers* by John Viele. As recently as 80 years ago, fewer than 300 inhabitants tried to eke out a living without electricity, running water, radios, or telephones in the subtropical heat of the Florida Keys. As vividly portrayed as if they were characters in a novel, the true-life inhabitants of the Keys will capture your admiration as you share in the dreams and realities of their daily lives. ISBN 1-56164-101-4 (hb)

The Florida Keys Volume 2: *True Stories of the Perilous Straits* by John Viele. Thousands of people have died in shipwrecks, attacks by natives, sea battles, and pirate boardings along the treacherous Straits of Florida. Excerpted from ships' logs, captains' diaries, court-martial transcripts, and newspaper accounts, here's a selection of gripping stories during the age of sail from the time Spanish navigators discovered the straits to the end of the Second Seminole War in 1842. ISBN 1-56164-179-0 (hb)

The Florida Keys Volume 3: *The Wreckers* by John Viele. Culled from various sources, these true stories capture the drama of the lives and times of the Florida Keys wreckers, those daring seamen who sailed out in weather fair or foul to save lives and property from ships cast up on the unforgiving Florida Reef. ISBN 1-56164-219-3 (hb)

The Florida Chronicles by Stuart B. McIver. A series offering true-life sagas of the notable and notorious characters throughout history who have given Florida its distinctive flavor. **Volume 1** *Dreamers, Schemers and Scalawags* ISBN 1-56164-155-3 (pb); **Volume 2** *Murder in the Tropics* ISBN 1-56164-079-4 (hb); **Volume 3** *Touched by the Sun* ISBN 1-56164-206-1 (hb)

A Yankee in a Confederate Town by Calvin L. Robinson. Edited by Anne Robinson Clancy, the author's great-granddaughter, this personal journal follows a loyal Unionist who loses his business and home, his money, and nearly his life in Civil War–era Jacksonville, Florida, when he refuses to join the Secessionist movement. A fascinating, true account of a pivotal time in U.S. history. ISBN 1-56164-267-3 (hb)

Discovering the Civil War in Florida by Paul Taylor. The Civil War in Florida may not have been the scene for decisive battles everyone remembers, but Florida played her part. From Marianna and Tallahassee in northwest Florida to Fort Myers and Key West in the south, this book covers the land and sea skirmishes that made Florida a bloody battleground for four sad years. ISBN 1-56164- 234-7 (hb); ISBN 1-56164-235-5 (pb)

200 Quick Looks at Florida History by James Clark. Florida has a long and complex history, but few of us have time to read it in depth. So here are 200 quick looks at Florida's 10,000 years of history from the arrival of the first natives to the present, packed with unusual and little-known facts and stories. ISBN 1-56164- 200-2 (pb)

Florida Portrait: A Pictorial History of Florida by Jerrell Shofner. An in-depth reference—packed with hundreds of rare photographs—that chronicles Florida's history from the earliest Spanish explorers and Native American cultures to the space-age and rampant population growth in the late twentieth century. ISBN 1-56164-121-9 (pb)

The Florida Reader: Visions of Paradise edited by Maurice O'Sullivan and Jack Lane. Selections in this collection of stories and essays about Florida range from tales of adventures among Native Americans by the Spanish Gentleman of Elvas to the short stories of Marjorie Kinnan Rawlings, from the romantic reflections of William Bartram and Silvia Sunshine to the carefully crafted prose of Zora Neale Hurston and John Muir. ISBN 1-56164-062-X (pb)

Southeast Florida Pioneers by William McGoun. Meet the pioneers of the Palm Beach area, the Treasure Coast, and Lake Okeechobee in this collection of well-told, fact-filled stories from the 1690s to the 1990s. ISBN 1-56164-157-X (hb)

The Gulf of Mexico by Robert H. Gore. A synopsis of the history, geology, geography, oceanography, biology, ecology, and economics of this great body of water. The only book of its kind. ISBN 1-56164-010-7 (hb)

Key Biscayne: A History of Miami's Tropical Island and the Cape Florida Lighthouse by Joan Gill Blank. This is the engaging history of the southernmost barrier island in the United States and the Cape Florida Lighthouse, which has stood at Key Biscayne's southern tip for 170 years. ISBN 1-56164-096-4 (hb); 1-56164-103-0 (pb)

Legendary Islands of the Ocean Sea by Robert H. Fuson. From the diaries and charts of early explorers comes the intriguing story of the real and imagined islands of what we now know as the Atlantic and Pacific Oceans. ISBN 1-56164-078-6 (hb)

African Americans in Florida by Maxine Jones and Kevin McCarthy. This book examines the lives and contributions of more than 50 notable African Americans during four centuries of Florida history. ISBN 1-56164-030-1 (hb); 1-56164-031-X (pb); 1-56164-045-X (teacher's manual)

Native Americans in Florida by Kevin M. McCarthy. A chronicle of Florida's Native Americans, from the first Paleo-Indians to modern-day Seminoles. A clearly written narrative that covers a broad range of topics, from archaeology, middens, and languages to the Seminole Wars and reservations. ISBN 1-56164-181-2 (hb); 1-56164-182-0 (pb); 1-56164-188-X (teacher's manual)

Florida's First People by Robin C. Brown. Filled with photos of replicas of technologies used by early peoples in their daily lives, this book brings to life the first humans who entered Florida about 12,000 years ago. Great for a budding archaeologist or historian! ISBN 1-56164-032-8 (hb)

Legends of the Seminoles by Betty Mae Jumper. This collection of rich spoken tales—written down for the first time—impart valuable lessons about living in harmony with nature and about why the world is the way it is. Each story is illustrated with an original painting by Guy LaBree. ISBN 1-56164-033-6 (hb); 1-56164-040-9 (pb)

The Everglades: River of Grass, 50th Anniversary Edition by Marjory Stoneman Douglas. This is the treasured classic of nature writing that captured attention all over the world and launched the fight to save the Everglades. This Anniversary Edition offers an update by Cyril Zaneski, environmental writer for the *Miami Herald*, on the events affecting the Glades since 1987. ISBN 1-56164-135-9 (hb)

Marjory Stoneman Douglas: Voice of the River by Marjory Stoneman Douglas with John Rothchild. Nationally known as the First Lady of Conservation and the woman who "saved" the Everglades, Marjory Stoneman Douglas (1890–1998) founded the Friends of the Everglades. This story of her influential life is told in a unique and spirited voice. ISBN 0-910923-33-7 (hb); ISBN 0-910923-94-9 (pb)